# 50 MOUNTAIN BIKE RIDES

## Great Offroad Routes in England, Scotland and Wales

# Jeremy Evans

**The Crowood Press**

First published in 1993 by
The Crowood Press Ltd
Ramsbury, Marlborough
Wiltshire SN8 2HR

**British Library Cataloguing-in-Publication Data**
A catalogue record for this book is available from the British
Library.

ISBN 1 85223 743 0

**Acknowledgements**
Many of these rides have been published in various issues of the
*Mountain Biker Ride Guide* magazine. The six rides for the Far
North section (39–44) and the Glen Shieldaig ride (46) were
supplied by Ralph Henderson; all other rides and photographs
are by Jeremy Evans. Thanks to Lester Noble of Orange Mountain
Bikes who supplied the necessary hardware.
Maps drawn by Sharon Perks.

Typeset in Melior by Avonset, Midsomer Norton, Bath.
Printed and bound in Great Britain by
BPCC Hazell Books Ltd
Member of BPCC Ltd

# Contents

# Introduction

Here are fifty more mountain bike rides, to add to those already published in the first book of this series – *Offroad Adventure Cycling*. The new rides encompass England (north and south), Wales and Scotland, divided into seven accessible areas, with a wide enough selection to last the most enthusiastic rider for up to a week or longer in each area.

Since writing *Offroad Adventure Cycling* the main change has been in the number of bikes going offroad. Otherwise things have stayed much the same. In some areas this growth of the sport has caused friction, and it is becoming increasingly important for all mountain bikers to create a good impression in the countryside. Stick to the Code of Conduct given in this book, take it easy when you ride, and be sensible. If you want to race, go to a properly organized competition. Please don't use these ride routes as race tracks, don't ride in a huge bunch of bikes, and never fail to respect walkers, horseriders or the countryside.

Jeremy Evans

# Offroad Cycling Code

1. Stay on the trails, either public bridleways or byways. Going off the trails can damage plant and animal environments. Learn how to prevent skids and ride with control to prevent erosion. Footpaths are out of bounds.
2. Be courteous and considerate to others. Always give way to walkers and horse riders, even if it means dismounting and lifting your bike out of the way. Give warning of your approach when coming up from behind.
3. Plan your route using OS maps. Make sure the bike is safe to ride. Learn basic maintenance and take essential spares. A helmet should be worn.
4. On offroad rights of way the Highway Code applies. Moderate your speed – you can be prosecuted for riding dangerously. Any form of racing is illegal, even in practice.
5. Cycling on private tracks or open ground is not allowed without permission from the landowner.
6. Some offroad routes such as byways are shared with vehicles; they should give way to cyclists, but may not expect you.
7. Follow the Country Code. Shut gates behind you and keep dogs under control.
8. In cases of difficulty contact the British Mountain Bike Federation Access Directors on 0531 633500/0602 732674.

# Good Riding

Walkers don't take kindly to being mown down by a pack of bikers, whooping through the countryside at 40mph (64kmph). Always slow down, be polite, and try to leave a good impression. People use the country to get away from the hassles of town; don't disappoint them. Remember that the Rambler's Association is an extremely powerful organization – bikers need the RA as an ally fighting for rights of access, not an enemy infuriated by bikers' lack of consideration for walkers.

If you have ridden a horse you will know that, like a mountain bike, it can be very exciting to ride, but the difference is that it is much, much more difficult to control. In simple terms, the more racy the horse the more nervous it is likely to be, prone to react wildly for no very obvious reason. Always slow down when you see horses, give them a wide berth, and overtake cautiously. Most horse riders are amiable; a few are not and may do things like refusing to let you get past on a narrow trail. They must be educated to accept that mountain bikers should be treated with equal courtesy; the BMBF and British Horse Society are currently working well together on behalf of both sets of riders.

## TRAVEL BY CAR

There are three ways to get to the start of a ride – by bike (the pure way), by car (the impure way), and by train (the middle way). When carrying bikes on a car there are three methods:
1. Roof Systems. These require a roofrack. The main disadvantage is that they increase fuel consumption.
2. Boot Systems. These hang off the back of your boot, by means of straps and gravity. They can be difficult to attach securely, make it tricky to get into the boot, and may obscure the rear lights and numberplate, which is illegal.
3. Tow-bar Systems. These keep the bike/s away from the car, saving on scratched paint, and often allow access to the boot. They may also obscure the rear lights and numberplate, though the best systems, such as the English-made Hobo, come complete with trailer lighting board.

Make sure your bike is securely attached with straps. Your insurance against theft will almost certainly be invalid unless the bike is locked to the car, though faced with the modern bike thief all locking systems are vulnerable.

## TRAVEL BY TRAIN

At best, the train is a brilliant way to travel with a bike. Ride to the station, buy a ticket (the bike goes free), push your bike along the platform, stick it in the guard's van, and travel in comfort, then repeat the procedure at the end of the ride. At worst, it is a real hassle – you're not allowed to take the bike on certain trains, it costs money, and finding out exactly when and where these restrictions are enforced can be a problem. Sadly, the latter situation seems to be on the increase as rail travel switches from being a public service to a profit-driven operation. The concept of encouraging biking as a quiet, environmentally friendly means of travel is steadily being eroded. It now seems too much to hope that BR will in future have a blanket policy which favours the use of bikes.

## BLOCKED TRAILS

Cyclists are now used to being on the defensive on Britain's roads; offroad they should stand up for their rights. The relevant landowner and local authority have the responsibility to maintain bridleways and byways and ensure that they are passable, with gates that work. It is illegal for a landowner to block a right of way, close or divert it (only the local authority or central government can do this), or to put up a misleading notice to deter you from using it. It is also illegal to plough up or disturb the surface of a right of way, unless it is a footpath or bridleway running across a field. In that case the farmer must make good the surface within twenty-four hours, or two weeks if it's the first disturbance for a particular crop. A bridleway so restored must have a minimum width of 2 metres (6.5ft), and its line must be clearly apparent on the ground. A farmer also has a duty to prevent any crops other than grass making a right of way difficult to follow. A bridleway across crops should have a 2-metre (6.5ft) clear width; a field edge bridleway should have a clear width of 3 metres (9.5ft).

If you run into difficulty on any of the above, you can file a complaint with the Footpaths Officer at the local council, giving full details of the offence and a precise map reference. The wheels of bureaucracy move slowly, but with right on your side the matter should be pursued to a satisfactory conclusion.

## WHEN IS A BRIDLEWAY NOT A BRIDLEWAY?

OS maps, which are based on the definitive maps of public rights of way, are an almost failsafe guide to bridleways and byways but even they can sometimes disagree. For instance, the 1:50000 Landranger may show a footpath where the 1:25000 Pathfinder shows a bridleway. Quite often a route marked as a bridleway on the OS map is signposted as a footpath on the ground. This is frequently because the local council did not have any Bridleway signs! However, sometimes the route in question is clearly not used by horses and is only really suitable for walkers, so if in doubt dismount.

# OFFROAD RIGHTS OF WAY

**Bridleways** – Open to walkers and horseriders, and also to cyclists, since 1968. This right is not sacrosanct and there are some local politicians working actively to ban bikes. Hopefully this will not happen.

**Byways** – Usually unsurfaced tracks open to cyclists. As well as walkers and horseriders, you may meet occasional vehicles which also have right of access.

**Public Footpaths** – No rights to cycle. If forced to go along a footpath you probably have the right to push a bike and certainly can carry one.

**Open Land** – Usually no right of access without landowner's permission.

**Canal Towpaths** – British Waterways Cycling Permit required.

**Forestry Commission** – Access on designated cycle paths, or by permission from local Forest Manager. At present there is a general presumption in favour of bikes using Forestry land gratis; with increased privatization this may change.

**Designated Cycle Paths** – Urban areas, Forestry Commission land, disused railway lines, etc.

**Pavements** – Cycling is not legal, though with the state of our roads it is frequently much safer!

# Expedition Planning

The first rule of offroad touring is to allow enough time. Getting caught by nightfall is foolhardy and potentially dangerous, particularly if the ride ends in an onroad section and you have no lights. So before you leave, work out how much time to allow, and be pessimistic. Your speed will depend on your skill, level of fitness, and the riding conditions. Tackling a route after heavy rain in mid-winter may take three times as long as the same route in dry summer weather. Riding along a disused railway line will be fast and easy; riding up and down Lakeland fells can be exceptionally demanding, and the difference in speed between a good and not so good rider will be much greater.

## BACK UP

I don't like groups which are much bigger than three. They put an unacceptable load on other people's enjoyment of the environment – walkers and horseriders were there first, and while they can cope with small groups of bike riders, it's no fun for them when a dozen or so Tour de France lookalikes tear through their favourite countryside. In fact I prefer to ride alone; you cause minimum upset to others, and also don't have to worry about keeping up with the fastest member of the group, while the slowest rider doesn't have to worry about keeping up with you.

The golden rule is **tell someone**:
– When you're going.
– When you expect to be back.
– Give them some idea of your route.

It doesn't happen often, but riders do occasionally fall off and knock themselves out or break a few bones in the middle of nowhere – if that happened to you, it would be nice to know that someone would come looking for you, and that they'd be able to locate you before too long.

## DRESS SENSIBLY

Offroad touring poses the same dangers as fell and hill walking. A beautiful warm day can soon turn to mist, rain and a biting wind. Your big advantage over the walker is that you can get down to low ground and civilization faster; but it won't help if you get lost, and the added windchill of being on a bike is an additional problem. Once you're wet and cold, you can only get colder.

The obvious solution is to wear layers to regulate thermal insulation, stripping off for the uphills and putting it back on for the downhills so that all your sweat doesn't turn you into a frostbitten jelly. Riding in the summer you can get away with minimal clothing, but remember that if you come off on a hard surface any naked flesh is vulnerable. In colder weather it pays to carry extra clothing in a pack – thermal tights to replace the shorts; a thermal sweater; a windproof top; and a waterproof – the latter should ideally be some fluorescent colour for easy visibility, and made of a non-sweat fabric such as GoreTex which is expensive but worth it.

The answer to the question, 'Should I wear a helmet?' has to be that you should. There's no law about it, and in my opinion there certainly shouldn't be, but the plain fact is that if you come off you may hit your head on something hard, and if that happens you'll be better off wearing a helmet. Having neglected to wear one in the early days, I've now got used to the idea, and feel uncomfortable without one. However, on a hot day I'll reserve the right to take it off and sling it over the handlebars for a long uphill. Make sure the helmet is a good fit and satisfies the minimum safety standards; it should also be lightweight, and properly ventilated to prevent cerebral overheating, and in this respect I have found the 'Etto Classic' to be a reasonable compromise.

At the other end of your body, the kind of footwear you choose will to some extent depend on how much time you spend in the saddle, and how much time you spend pushing. For the person who can ride 99 per cent of the time, a dedicated pair of high-performance cycling shoes are the answer, but many of these don't cope well when you resort to walking and carrying the bike over slippery rocks and through bogs. For all-round use the compromise style of lightweight hiking/riding boots is still a good bet, not least for much better walkability and positive ankle support and protection.

Finally, what about your fingers? In winter they can get painfully numb and cold, but a pair of neoprene nylon-lined road cycling gloves are the perfect answer. They give adequate protection and much better 'feel' than mittens, are light enough to be worn in warmer weather, and can easily be carried in your pockets.

## BREAKDOWN – PHYSICAL

A First Aid kit is only of value if someone knows how to use it, and even then the constrictions of space and weight on a bike will make its application limited – some bandages and plasters will be enough to deal with minor cuts and abrasions, or possibly support a fracture. In most cases injuries from falls are fairly minor, and you can keep on riding; in more serious cases it will probably be a matter of getting help a.s.a.p., while caring for the injured rider as well as you can.

## BREAKDOWN – MECHANICAL

Never go offroad without a pump! The quickest way to deal with a puncture is to swop the flat tube with a spare tube; you will also need two tyre levers, plus tyre patches and glue in case of further punctures.

If your bike is well maintained there is no need to carry a massive tool kit, which is undesirably heavy and bulky. The only other likely breakdown is a broken chain, which requires a chainbreaker; beyond that it's handy to carry a screwdriver, allen keys, and a shifting spanner, all of which can be combined in a lightweight, compact multi-tool.

# The West Country

*The Quantock Hills and Exmoor both provide memorable riding in the north of Somerset, while south Devon and Dorset offer the opportunity for a connected offroad tour of the area, plus a look at the extraordinary White Giant.*

## Ride 1   THE QUANTOCK HILLS

**Area:** Somerset. A tour of the Quantocks.
**OS Map:** Landranger 181.
**Start & Finish:** The Library/Information Centre car park in Nether Stowey, on the A39, at grid ref 191398.
**Nearest BR station:** Bridgwater.
**Approx length:** 25 miles(40km). Allow around 4 hours, plus time for pub stops.
**Ride rating:** Moderate.
**Conditions:** Plenty of ups and downs, but nothing too taxing. Generally good tracks.
**R & R:** Pub and shops in Nether Stowey; pubs at West Quantoxhead and Holford.

The Quantocks are an exceptionally attractive small range of hills, not far from Exmoor and within sight of the sea. The ride starts from Nether Stowey, the village where Samuel Taylor Coleridge lived in a small cottage and composed such classics as the 'Rhyme of the Ancient Mariner'. You can visit his cottage (National Trust) in the summer season, though it is not as he would have remembered it. Coleridge was much given to tramping over the nearby Quantocks with his friend Wordsworth; the hills haven't changed much, and if those two had had mountain bikes I am sure they would have used them! Wordsworth himself lived at nearby Alfoxton Park, a much grander house which is now a hotel and would no doubt be a nice place to stay in the area; if you're looking for something cheaper, the Holford Youth Hostel is almost next door.

You can park conveniently in Nether Stowey in the Library/Information Centre car park on Castle Street. From here turn right up the hill, and then take the first left turn for Marsh Mills and Aisholt. Keep on along this pleasant country road for just under 3 miles (4.8km), passing through Marsh Mills and Plainsfield, keeping a careful look out for the sign for Aisholt which bears left a short way on.

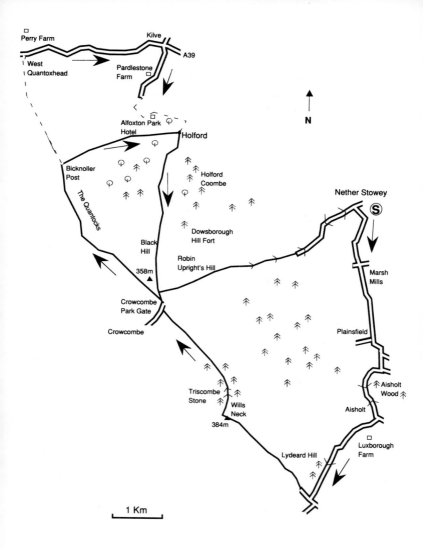

Careful navigation is needed on these narrow country lanes; I overshot the Aisholt turning, and spent about 30 perplexing minutes retracing my tracks! Ride down the steep, steep hill into Aisholt, which is no more than a hamlet with a few houses, passing a striking white house at the bottom of the hill and then heading up the other side past the interesting church on the left. At the top of the hill turn right, down a lane marked by a dead-end sign, just by an old well on the corner.

Ride on past Luxborough Farm, and then keep on along the track as it becomes rougher and rougher, and starts to head uphill through trees. The riding is steady though the going can be muddy, as you head up towards the top of the Quantocks. Where the track appears to fork right and left either side of beech woods, take the left track on a slight downhill, keeping alongside the woods until you eventually come to a quiet road.

Turn right here, passing over a cattle grid and coming to the Lydeard Hill car park. From here on it's a great ride along the backbone of the Quantocks, heading more or less straight on all the way towards West Quantoxhead. Go through the gate and follow the main left-hand track along the side of a wire fence, heading through an area which is frequently muddy as it is churned up by forestry vehicles. The track soon improves, and you follow it on to the Trig Point at Wills Neck where there is a clear view across to Hinckley Point and the Bristol Channel, with Wales beyond. Coleridge and Wordsworth would have enjoyed the same view, though without the gloomy presence of the atomic power station.

At the Trig Point, take the track which bears right downhill, with a rocky but fast descent towards the car park at Triscombe Stone, where the track is overhung with trees on either side. When I rode this section it was raining and visibility was down to about 20 yards (18m) – navigation is straightforward, but these hills do seem to attract cloud and rain, so take care. Past Triscombe Stone the track continues to follow the tree line, coming out on to a very minor road at Crowcombe Park Gate where you follow the track straight across to the other side.

Keep on along the main track which is pretty level all the way along the top, ignoring gates and signs off to the left as you pass a Trig Point at 1,175ft (358m) above Dowsborough Hill Fort and Holford. Follow the track across an invariably beautifully coloured moorland landscape, with the deep combes filled with trees which are very fine in autumn. As you head downhill, there are glimpses over the coast from Watchet as far as Minehead, and then you soon come to the lonely sign at Bicknoller Post. This points directions to West Quantoxhead, Perry Farm and Holford, so which way do you go?

The easiest way is straight downhill to Holford. However, I felt inclined to finish the ridge ride to the end of the Quantocks, hoping for a complete bridleway circuit, avoiding the A39 main coast road. To go this way, carry straight on along the middle track bound for West Quantoxhead, heading on a slight uphill and then commencing a long and very fast descent between Stowborrow and West Hill. The going is good on a very wide, grassy track, as you come downhill with fine views ahead over the sea as far as Wales. The track keeps close to the woods of West Quantoxhead on the left, heading steeply down under overhead powerlines. About 200 yards (180m) past them, look for an unmarked track bearing off to the right which leads down steeply to the A39; if you miss it, carry on straight down the steep hillside, and then turn right at the bottom by a wire fence close by a stile.

I had intended riding on a bridleway which is shown on the OS map, following the contours a short way up the hillside all the way to Holford. In practice this is very difficult to find; I compromised by giving up and turning right along the main road, though I never willingly surrender when it comes to lost rights of way. You can follow the A39 for 2 miles (3.2km) into Kilve. For a main road it's relatively pleasant riding, and the pub at Kilve is reputed to be a good place to stop.

Opposite the pub, turn right off the A39 onto a dead-end road, signposted to the YHA. Keep on past Pardlestone Farm and the riding stables, ignoring the left turn to the YHA unless you want to check in there. Then follow the road as it bears left through the grounds of the Alfoxton Park Hotel, where from this direction the drive is an unmarked bridleway. On my visit the hotel wasn't open to non-residents, and is probably a bit too smart for passing mountain bikers. Follow the drive out through the main entrance, where the road goes straight ahead through woods, bearing right to pass the old Dog Pound – a weird monument – where you turn left into Holford.

This turn is where the bridleway comes straight down from the Bicknoller Post, if you prefer a shorter circuit. From the Post it's a fast downhill ride over the moor across Longstone Hill, coming to another bridleway crossroads at the top of Pardlestone Hill where you go straight ahead for a more invigorating downhill on a tree-lined track into Holford.

Holford is a pretty place with a fine village green, though sadly the pub is down by the main road – even so it's a good place for muddy bikers, with plenty of outside seating. From Holford there are a number of routes back to Nether Stowey, as this side of the Quantocks is laced with bridleways and other usable tracks. I opted to take the high route, following the bridleway track to Crowcombe and Park Gate. The bridleway sign is hidden away on the far side of the village green – ride on past it, and then take the track which bears left uphill, turning right at the top.

From here on it's a steady climb up to the top of the Quantocks, passing the conspicuous pink hotel – an old water mill – in Holford Combe below. If you're presentable, they serve snacks and teas to non-residents in a very pleasant setting. The direction is due south; when in doubt take the track that bears left. It's a hard climb, but on a good surface all the way with fine views over the woodlands of the Quantocks below. The track eventually brings you up Black Hill to the Trig Point at 1,175ft (358m), joining the road at Crowcombe. Turn left along this road, ready for a long and very fast downhill all the way to Nether Stowey, which is a classic way to finish the ride. Past the car park at Robin Upright's Hill you take the right fork as indicated, heading downhill at record speed towards the start/finish point. When the road levels out, take the right turn with a width limit, and this will bring you back to the centre of the village.

# Ride 2   CROYDON HILL

**Area:** Brendon Hills, Somerset. Monksilver to Croydon Hill.
**OS Map:** Landranger 181.
**Start & Finish:** Monksilver, due south of Williton and Watchet on the B3188, at grid ref 073375. Parking space is very limited. Alternatively start from Washford on the A39 at grid ref 045412, where parking is much more plentiful.
**Nearest BR station:** Washford.
**Approx length:** 26/28 miles (42/45km). Allow 4–5 hours.
**Ride rating:** Moderate.
**Conditions:** Mainly good tracks, but in wet weather some of the tracks get pretty muddy. Some good climbs.
**R & R:** Pubs at Washford, Torre, Monksilver, Roadwater, Kingsbridge, Timberscombe.

This ride takes you through the pleasant countryside of the Brendon Hills on the edge of Exmoor, and along the top of Croydon Hill which is the backbone of the route. Much of the going is on very quiet country roads with a fair amount of up and down riding; there are also plenty of bridleway tracks, but in many cases signposting is poor and in wet weather the going can be very muddy – like so many rides, this is one that's at its best in dry weather.

The ride starts from Monksilver, which is a very pretty little place with a nice looking pub, but parking is tricky. If you need to leave a car, I would recommend starting the ride from Washford. This adds 2 miles (3.2km) but reduces the overall time as it cuts out the return section to Monksilver, which is time consuming whether on or offroad.

Coming into Monksilver from the north on the B3188, take the first right turning after the church and you will find the bridleway track clearly signposted off to the left, a short way uphill. Ride up this track which is signposted to Colton – it's a long, steady haul uphill, mainly ridable when dry but hard going when wet. The track takes you up along the side of Bird Hill, eventually levelling out through fine woodland. Just past the next signpost, follow the track on ahead and ignore the left-hand fork. This brings you out to the road on the top of the hill by a dead-end sign.

Go straight over here, passing a sign on the right to a viewpoint. The next track on the right is the bridleway, though unmarked when I rode it except for a faded blue stripe on one of the trees. This leads straight into more woodland, taking you downhill towards Sticklepath. Ignore turns off to the left as you head down, and enjoy this good descent in fine offroad surroundings. At the next road turn right downhill, and then

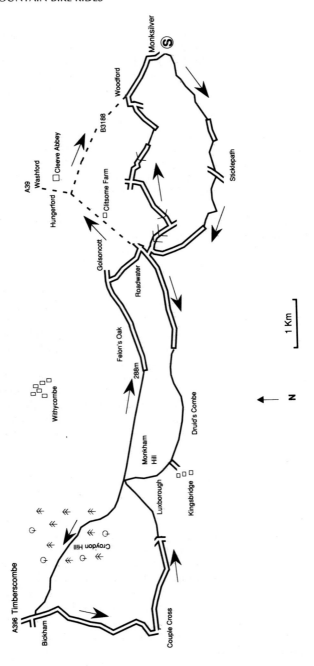

almost immediately left down a lane with a dead-end sign. Just past some buildings take the first turn to the right. This is a tarmac byway, following a narrow lane that leads you downhill under an old road bridge.

Just past here, fork right downhill onto a rougher track, riding round to the right between a couple of houses and coming out to a bridleway crossroads where you turn left, following the sign for Roadwater. A long, straight, narrow lane takes you to this quaint village; a bridleway is shown on the OS map running alongside this lane, but its location is not obvious and there seems little point in bothering to find it.

When you come to Roadwater, turn left past a terrace of thatched cottages, and left again past the pub. Continue on the road towards Luxborough, just over 3 miles (4.8km) distant, forking right on the quiet road which follows the river valley along Druid's Combe. When you come to the end of the woods, take the right turning signposted to Withycombe; or alternatively ride on for a further ¼ mile (0.4km) to get to the pub at Kingsbridge. A short way up the road, take the first track to the left, marked by a bridleway sign. This takes you up the side of Monkham Hill to the top of Croydon Hill, albeit steeply.

At the top, turn left onto a wide forestry track, following the sign for Timberscombe. From here it is a good fast ride through the woods, with downhill riding most of the way and clear views to Dunster and Dunkery Beacon ahead. The track comes to a road where you go straight over, keeping on to the edge of the forestry where the track divides. Go straight ahead through a gate here (unmarked), following the tractor track across a rough grass field as it bears left down to a gateway. Go through and turn right through the adjacent gate signposted to Timberscombe, following a narrow track through gorse along the hillside which drops slowly downhill. From here it bears left to zig-zag down to a gate, where you turn right onto a lane that leads down into Timberscombe on a rough made-up surface.

Ride round the village until you come to the 'square' where all the essentials are situated – pub, church, well, and village shop/Post Office. From here follow the road left up past the church, signposted to Luxborough. This is a long, long uphill that takes you up for 2 miles (3km) before starting to drop downhill. Turn left at the crossroads at Couple Cross by a strange semi-fortified house, following the sign for Luxborough on a long fast downhill. At the next junction the road swings left to Dunster or turns right to Luxborough – you go straight ahead up an inviting unmarked track, which takes you back up to the top of Croydon Hill with a good steady climb into the forestry. Keep right and ignore the fork to the left, arriving once again at the bridleway crossroads above Monkham Hill.

Turn right here, bound for Roadwater, cruising through the forestry on a fast track which soon brings you to the edge of the woods by another bridleway sign. Go straight ahead here through the gate – on a clear day you'll get fine views out over the coast – and on across the next grass field, keeping to the line of trees on the right. Go through the next gate, following a narrow track with high hedges. This can be ultra muddy, and with deep ruts either side may require some pushing.

Reaching the road at a height of 945ft (288m), go straight over onto another track which heads downhill, though once again mud and the churning effect of horses' hooves can make riding tricky in wet weather. This track heads on down to the road junction by the entrance gate to Croydon Hall School where you ignore the turning to Rodhuish and take the second turn to carry on downhill onroad. After about ⅔ mile (1km), take the right turning to Golsoncott (signed as being unsuitable for heavy vehicles), bearing right past here for Roadwater with a long fast downhill into the village.

From here you can retrace your wheeltracks to Monksilver along the outward offroad route, or try an onroad route with big up and downhills as it zig-zags its way eastwards, joining a short bridleway track to reach Nettlecombe Court Field Study Centre on the way to Woodford. Alternatively, if returning to Washford, take the road which goes north along the side of the Washford River. This is pleasant enough riding, and it's worth stopping to investigate the ruins of Cleeve Abbey (English Heritage) which you pass on the way.

# Ride 3  TWO COMMONS CIRCUIT

**Area:** South Devon. Colaton Raleigh and Bicton Commons.
**OS Map:** Landranger 192.
**Start & Finish:** Car park on the south side of the A3052, just over 1 mile (1.6km) west of Newton Poppleford between Exeter and Sidmouth, at grid ref 057897.
**Nearest BR station:** Lympstone.
**Approx length:** 10 miles (16km). Allow around 2 hours. Both time and distance can easily be stretched, or reduced.
**Ride rating:** Easy.
**Conditions:** Good tracks, small hills, and fairly straightforward navigation.
**R & R:** Nothing in the immediate ride area, but pubs can be found nearby at Newton Poppleford, East Budleigh, and Woodbury.

This ride and the rides which follow – a total of three in south Devon and one just over the border in south-west Dorset – give some good offroad cruising in an area which has fine up and down countryside, but on the Devon side is poorly served by bridleways and tracks usable by bikers. The rides can be tackled separately or linked together two at a time – someone really energetic could even consider riding the whole lot in a single day!

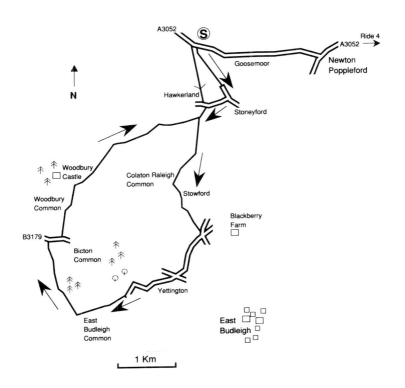

Sadly there is virtually no biking along the South Devon Coast Path, which despite some excellent tracks is footpath almost all the way. I met someone who said he'd had a great time biking along the cliff tops, but 'Pity about all those steps . . . '. This is the way to get biking a bad name, and indeed on my visit there were anti-mountain bike rumblings in the local paper.

The combined area of Colaton Raleigh Common and Bicton Common is an exception, a kind of mini Dartmoor a few miles inland with lots of tracks and bridleways that offer excellent potential for biking, though you'll also have to share them with dog walkers and horseriders, so take care. As with so many places, biking is better when no one else is about, so try to avoid peak times such as warm summer weekends.

You can really make your own route up here; the tracks and trails lead all over the place and become quite confusing, with many not shown on the OS map. They offer a lot of very pleasant riding – mostly easy with a few mildly technical sections, and in my experience little trouble with mud, despite a week of heavy spring rain. You could amuse yourself for most of the day on these commons, but the ride which follows gives a good tour of the area by keeping near to its boundaries, and has the advantage of sticking to the main tracks and bridleways.

To find the start point car park, turn south off the A3052 at the top of the hill (always a good place to start from), taking the turning marked to Hawkerland. From here there is a view southwards over the whole area of common land, with the English Channel glittering in the sunlight beyond, it is hoped. There are no bridleway signposts in the car park; in the bottom left corner a track heads off to the south-west, taking you onto a fast downhill on a good surface. This leads down through quiet moorland to the road at Stoneyford, where you turn right and then take a short track heading up onto the main area of moorland. Once again there is a lack of signposting, and plenty of confusing tracks. If you take the first track going downhill on the left, you will follow a narrow and quite tortuous track through trees going southwards along the edge of the common, with farmland on the other side. This is good riding, bringing you down to a main crossing track where you turn left to join the road near Stowford – you can follow an alternative winding track through the side of the woods by a stream here, which provides more interesting riding.

Follow the road to Yettington – this is quiet country with few folk about – and then bear left uphill towards Lympstone. After 1 mile (1.6km) or so a track turns right downhill onto Bicton Common, opposite a driveway with a small hut on the edge of neighbouring East Budleigh Common. The turn is not signposted, but it is the bridleway. You may also get a surprise here. When I rode by men were throwing themselves out of the bushes waving machine guns – it's a popular training area for the army, and when the red flags are flying certain parts of the commons are out of bounds.

From here there's a great track leading northwards with a few ups and downs, passing a sand quarry which is the only bad view on the ride. The main bridleway bears left by some trees to the road, but I chose to follow an unmarked track which goes straight ahead across Bicton Common, crossing a lane and continuing over Woodbury Common towards Woodbury Castle, which stands on the hilltop. This is a fine prehistoric hill fort, dated at around 500–300 BC. In its day it would have been cleared of trees, acting as a permanent fortified settlement for the local chief, with a palisade wall round the ramparts, entrances on the north and south sides, and round wooden houses within. It is still an impressive monument, with its ramparts preserved in a fine setting ringed by trees. On the west side there's a car park (very popular with dog walkers) and an information board.

Head round to the east side of the castle, turning right onto a main track (bridleway) which heads south-west. A short way on a track goes steeply left downhill, crossing a marshy area by a bridge and heading on across Colaton Raleigh Common. There are great views from here, and it's fine riding as it brings you back down to the road at Hawkerland from where it's a short climb back to the car park start point. You then have three choices: pack up and go home; ride back onto the commons for some more; or follow the A3052 on to the next ride.

# Ride 4   HARCOMBE HILL

**Area:** South Devon. A tour of the Harcombe Hill area.
**OS Map:** Landranger 192.
**Start & Finish:** Steven's Cross on the A3052, ½ mile (0.8km) west of Sidford, at grid ref 140898. Roadside parking nearby.
**Nearest BR station:** Honiton.
**Approx length:** 15 miles (24km). Allow from 2–4 hours depending on the conditions.
**Ride rating:** Moderate/Hard.
**Conditions:** This is a hilly area, and there are some short but severe climbs. Much of the route suffers from bad mud in wet weather.
**R & R:** Pub at Steven's Cross; nearby Sidmouth is a pleasant seaside town with all manner of pubs and cafés.

If you want to connect this ride with the Two Commons Circuit (Ride 3), the quickest, most direct route is to follow the A3052

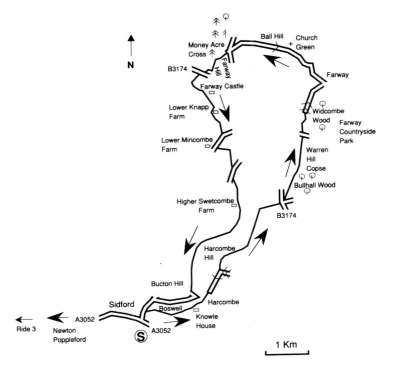

through Newton Poppleford and on to Sidford, a distance of some 6 miles (10km), much of which is downhill going eastwards.

The start of the ride is at Steven's Cross, a crossroads on the eastern outskirts of Sidford just as the road starts to go steeply uphill – there's a Texaco garage and a pub on facing corners here, so you can't miss it. Turn left by the garage, and then take the first right up a tarmac lane with a dead-end sign. The big hills to the left are where you're heading!

Ride on through the fancy entrance gates to Knowle House. It looks private, but is in fact unmarked bridleway. Just past here you bear left, joining a narrow track for the first real offroad session. This is pretty easy, bringing you across a field to a lane by a farmhouse. A bridleway sign points right here, but that's the wrong way for the ride. Head straight up the hill ahead which gets steep, and then very steep. Even on tarmac it's a serious climb, but at least you're unlikely to meet any cars on the way.

Near the top of the hill the road bends round to the right by some magnificent beech trees. You turn left offroad here, going up a rough track to the top of the hill and bearing right through forestry land by the side of Harcombe Hill. This is the start of a well-defined track which leads on by the side of the woods, heading north across level ground through very pretty woodland. In dry weather it must be great riding; in wet weather it's pretty gruesome and you'll be reduced to a lot of pushing. When you reach a crossing track, turn right and follow this hard track to the road.

Turn left and almost immediately right, joining a narrow track that runs diagonally up the side of a field. The OS Landranger shows this as footpath; the Pathfinder shows it as bridleway – with no signpost I was interested to find out which was right. The track is initially pretty narrow, and you have to hop off at a few places – do stop and make way if there are walkers. Just past a large farmhouse over to the left, the track bears right to join a much wider one where there are plenty of hoofprints, a sure sign that this route is used by the local horseriders. It leads on by the side of Bullhall Woods, coming to a lane where you go straight ahead by some farm buildings. The farmer actually held the gate open for me here, and in reply to my question said, 'Yep, it's a bridleway!'

After a week of rain he might have wondered what I was doing here on a bike. There was some serious knee-deep mud at the next gate, and the track which followed on across Broad Down varied between being marginal and horrific, though there's no doubt it would be a fine ride when the going was dry. Negotiating a bunch of curious cows I reached the next lane where I misread the map, shooting eastwards past the Farway Countryside Park towards Southleigh on a great downhill – as it got steeper and steeper, I realized I was going the wrong way! The right way goes on straight ahead through a bridle gate, and from here the going was much better, crossing grass and then heading on a good downhill track by the side of Widcombe Wood to come out on the road above Farway.

It's a really steep downhill to Farway, which is no more than a small collection of quaint houses and some incredibly ancient petrol pumps by the roadside. Take the turning signposted for the church here, and follow the road on through Church Green and up the side of Ball Hill. This is peaceful countryside riding at its best, though be prepared for an uphill which is pretty long and steep. From the top of Farway Hill there are great views out over the sheltered valley below, with Boycombe Farm looking like an agreeable place to live. Go straight over the road here at Monkey Acre Cross, and follow the forestry track ahead along the route of a local LDP. At first this looks pretty hopeful – a good forestry fast ride – but the going soon deteriorates and in wet weather becomes sludge riding. Nor is the bridleway easy to follow. The OS map shows it heading due south from the corner of the woods, but a more obvious track follows the edge of the woods and comes to a locked gate by the roadside of the B3174.

The next section of bridleway goes south along a tarmac driveway towards Higher Knapp Farm, with an incorrect footpath sign showing the way. A little way on a quaint bluebell bridleway sign confirms you have a right to ride here; however, it shows you the way straight on while you want the bridleway that turns left towards Lower Knapp Farm. Despite the lack of a signpost, turn left downhill here by some shabby farm buildings on the corner. This is the beginning of a great track. It heads steeply downhill on an old tarmac road, which deteriorates into a narrow track at the bottom of the valley, where it winds its way through a glen beside a stream – rough but ridable – before coming out of the trees at Lower Knapp Farm. This is not like other farms in the area. It's been converted into holiday homes and is very smart, so watch out for holidaymakers with their kids and dogs in summer. Bear left between the buildings, and out onto the main concrete driveway which leads onto a mild but fast downhill to the road.

Turn right here, and then left again by the next farmstead – Lower Mincombe Farm. A bridleway track heads up the hillside, bending left and right and then going dead straight uphill on grass – this is really challenging to ride and would be great for a competition. If you fail, you can content yourself with the views over the valley behind which are marvellous. At the top of this steep section, go through the gate by a line of trees, and then follow the track which continues uphill, bearing right across the hillside to join another road at the top. A bridleway goes straight ahead, but is not the way to go unless you want to rejoin the outward route. Turn right and then left at the next bridleway signpost, following a tarmac drive towards Higher Swetcombe Farm. This leads to a small farmhouse in a magical setting on the hillside – the right of way is not obvious as the drive ends here, but you just follow the grass track straight ahead past the back of the house, and look out for the big cage with the peacocks and various exotic hens.

This is the start of a long and quite tricky offroad section which takes you to the end of the ride. The grass track leads to a narrow woodland track, and then a short way on, just before Higher Swetcombe Farm, the route turns left through a bridle gate, heading down the hillside into the valley. Navigation is a little confusing here; at the next T-junction you take a left and a right, following a narrow path southwards through dense woods, which is good riding even when it's wet. Coming out of the woods the track passes the back of Lower Swetcombe Farm, which was having major alterations when I rode by. The track looks promising but soon peters out, coming to a gate which I found was securely tied up, with a footpath sign resolutely pointing the way up an overgrown and severely muddy track. I didn't believe this was the right way; it is, and despite the sign it is a bridleway.

The route follows the hillside through more trees, eventually joining a track heading due south along Buckton Hill. Go straight ahead at the road here; a right and a left will bring you back to Steven's Cross at the end of a short but sharp ride, with some great views and plenty of variety. Now try to ride it in under two hours!

# Ride 5   SEATON

**Area:** South Devon. A coastal tour out of Seaton.
**OS Map:** Landranger 193.
**Start & Finish:** Car park in the centre of Seaton by the start of the Seaton Electric Tramway, at grid ref 251900.
**Nearest BR station:** Axminster.
**Approx length:** 17 miles (27km). Allow 2-3 hours, plus time for stops.
**Ride Rating:** Easy.
**Conditions:** A lot of the route is onroad, but it's mostly quiet country lanes and the offroad connections are good riding.
**R & R:** Pubs and cafés at Seaton; pubs at Uplyme and Raymond's Hill; hotel at Rousdon.

From Steven's Cross (Ride 4) it's a pleasant mainly onroad connection to Seaton of around 8 miles (13km). Ride eastwards uphill on the A3052, and then at the top turn off to follow the minor road down past Steep, passing the Fountain Inn and

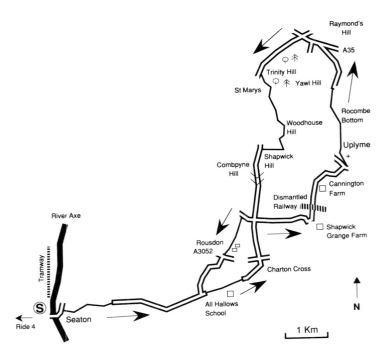

carrying on downhill along the side of the valley through Branscombe, said to be the longest village in Britain. It's a very pretty place – the Mason's Arms pub is so picturesque that it has thatched sunshades. The unspoilt beach at Branscombe Mouth is also worth a visit.

Past Branscombe the road heads steeply uphill on the east side of the valley. At the top, follow the signs to Beer; just past the turning to the Bovey House Hotel a rough track, named Fairfax Lane, leads due east downhill – this is an excellent 1 mile (1.6km) offroad section which brings you down into Beer, from where it's an easy pedal to Seaton.

From Seaton head east across the River Axe by the yacht harbour, and then take the right turn uphill, signposted as the coastal LDP. A steep tarmac lane takes you up to the golf club, and from there it's an on-grass ride up past the bunkers and out onto a rough track the other side. This soon leads to a country road heading eastwards with good views inland. After 1 mile (1.6km) or so you come to some impressive buildings. Bear right to carry straight on past the dead-end sign here, riding through the palatial grounds of All Hallows School and out through the gatehouse on the other side – it's all bridleway. This brings you to the roughest little track of the ride; seriously muddy in wet weather, but not far to the next road at Charton.

Turn left here and cross the main A3052 at Charton Cross. The next right turn leads down past Shapwick Grange Farm. I attempted to ride along the old railway line here, with no clear idea of its legality. Parts were easy, other parts were severely overgrown, but the highlight was finding myself on the top of the incredible viaduct bridge that crosses the road. The top of the bridge has turned into a mellow grass track, but sadly it's not for riding. I found that the bridge is a no-go area, and that only a part of the railway is a footpath. So ride this section on the road! A section of track like this makes you think Beeching not only butchered the railway system but, worst of all, he and his colleagues had no thought for the future of the redundant tracks. A few railway lines have been saved and turned into wonderful biking/walking/horseriding trails, such as the Tissington, High Peak and Downs Link, but most of these old railways have been irretrievably lost, grabbed by farmers, builders, road makers, or simply left to become completely blocked by nature. Britain had the makings of the most incredible network of safe, enjoyable trails throughout the whole country, and allowed 95 per cent of them to be destroyed.

Follow the road under the bridge and on to Uplyme, riding up past the church and straight on at the next dead-end sign. This bridleway is a hard track heading up the side of the valley past Carswell Farm, where it continues uphill as a concrete lane. At the top of Yawl Hill an avenue of trees leads to the road, from where it's a short pedal to the main A3070/A35 intersection close by Raymond's Hill. There's a pub here, but it's hardly the most peaceful place to stop, and the next left turn soon brings you back to more car-free peace once again.

About a mile (1.6km) on, past Trinity Hill, look out for a track turning left into the forestry at St Mary's. Ride on past the Forestry Commission signpost along a great track which heads through the woods and then follows their western boundary; the trees here are well mixed, with the uninteresting forestry conifers on the inside well hidden by an avenue of fine broad-leaved trees which you ride between. The track comes out to the road by an equestrian centre at Woodhouse Hill, from where it's a short distance onroad to the next bridleway section. This runs past the back of houses to the north of Shapwick Hill, crossing a field and joining a track which can be muddy, before coming back to the road.

Turn south here; it's a quiet road and is good downhill riding. At the crossroads turn right downhill towards Combpyne, taking the first bridleway track on the left which leads to the road at Rousdon – you'll find some mud here in wet weather. There's a handy hotel on the corner which may or may not raise an eyebrow at serving muddy bikers; then cross the A3052 and follow the lane ahead towards the coast to rejoin the outward route. It's a good ride, and it gets even better as you run down across the golf course with some fine views

*The out-and-back route from Seaton crosses a golf course.*
*Take it easy going down!*

ahead over Seaton and the coastline, but take it easy with the golfers who won't take kindly to being run down or having their precious turf ripped open by your fat tyres. Back in Seaton there are plenty of pubs and cafés (the café close to the car park was very friendly to a muddy biker), and for a post-ride diversion the electric tramway is pretty amazing!

# Ride 6   CHARMOUTH

**Area:** South-west Dorset. Along the coast from Charmouth and inland.
**OS Map:** Landranger 193.
**Start & Finish:** Car park in Charmouth on the way to the beach – pay and display – at grid ref 365933.
**Nearest BR station:** Axminster.
**Approx length:** 15 miles (24km). Allow around 3 hours.
**Ride rating:** Moderate.
**Conditions:** Plenty of offroading – parts can be seriously muddy in wet weather. Some good hills.
**R & R:** Pubs and cafés at Charmouth; pubs at Shave Cross and Morcombelake.

This ride can be connected with the Seaton Circuit (Ride 5) to double up the mileage. Using a linking route from Uplyme, it's main road all the way. Follow the road downhill into Lyme Regis, crossing the Devon/Dorset border on the way. Lyme Regis is a tourist attraction and tends to be full of cars, but if you've a mind to stop and get off your bike the Cobb, which

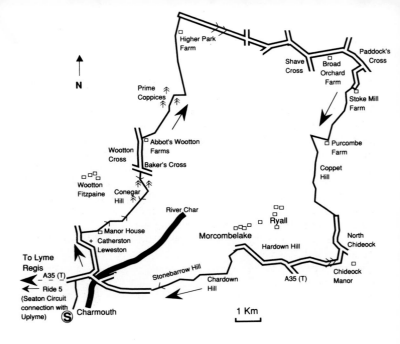

heads out on the seafront, is worth investigating for its fine views. On the other side of the town the road heads steeply uphill and then down to Charmouth, giving about 5 miles (8km) of riding.

The Charmouth car park is likely to act as an overflow for the beach-side car park in the main summer season, but has toilets and all-day parking for a modest 50p. Turn east downhill through Charmouth, and then take the first left turning, signposted to Wootton Fitzpaine, crossing the A35 by-pass. The road heads uphill past the smart entrance to the church at Catherston Leweston with its Manor House, passing a farmhouse where the road levels at the top of the hill. Just as you start to go downhill, take the first track on the right.

This is a bridleway heading uphill, and is the start of an excellent offroad section leading up past a dilapidated building and on through a patch of fine trees. It then follows the tree line out across the open grasslands of Conegar Hill with great views to the north. There's no track as such, but the way is easy to follow, heading downhill to cross a track coming up from the valley and following the side of a field up to an old copse of trees on the hilltop. Go through the gate here and there's a pretty downhill section by the side of the woods on a good track, before a more lumpy downhill leads you to the road at Baker's Cross.

Go straight ahead for about ½ mile (0.8km) to Abbott's Wootton Farms. The bridleway turning here isn't signposted, and there are a number of tracks to choose from. Ride past the farm buildings, and take the track to the right, just before the bungalow on the corner, passing a new farmhouse on the right. The track leads downhill across a field in fine surroundings, and then up towards trees on the hillside ahead, where it goes through a gate onto a track running by the side of the woods. There were some fearsome 'road repairs' with old broken bricks when I rode here, but otherwise it was OK. The bridleway then goes into the woodland of Prime Coppices, following a winding trail. It's all very pretty and would no doubt be delightful to ride in a dry summer, but when it's wet there's a lot of pushing, even when it starts to go downhill! On the far side of the woods a track leads steeply down to some old ramshackle buildings, where a bridleway sign points in an unlikely direction across a stream. Ignore this – it points the wrong way.

Follow the lane to the right, past more shanty buildings. Take the next left which leads up to a farmstead. The bridleway goes straight ahead through the cow pen, via a couple of gates – there is no signpost, but this is the way to go. From there the bridleway carries on due north, keeping mainly to the right side of grassy fields with a wooded valley over to the left. Keep on under the overhead power cables – it's a slight uphill most of the way, but the going is good until you come to the last field where the bridleway meets the road between Baber's and Higher Park Farm. The OS map shows the bridleway going straight across this field, to come to a sagging old metal gate in the hedge which is marked by a bridleway sign. Riding in early spring, I got the impression that the route had been oversown; if you find the way barred by crops, you have every right to press on and/or make a fuss.

Turn east along the road for some quiet countryside pedalling, which is mainly downhill and fast going to the pub at Shave Cross, a decent looking place to stop at about the halfway stage of the ride. Past the pub, ride on eastwards, and after about 1 mile (1.6km) opposite Paddock's Cross take the next lane on the right which has a mountain-bike-friendly dead-end sign. The windy lane heads downhill between high hedges to Stoke Mill Farm, where you pass a wishing well with resident gnome by the roadside, before joining a track that starts as cinders and soon deteriorates to serious mud if it's been wet. This brings you under the powerlines once again, eventually leading on a slight uphill to Purcombe Farm, on a section which when I rode it had some monumental mud.

Turn right through the farmyard – it's still bridleway. Just past the next farm buildings turn left onto a track going up the hill. All I could find to show the way here was a footpath sign lying on its side; further up the hill there are bridleway signs showing that you are indeed on the right and legal trail. It's a good track leading up the side of Coppet Hill, and then running south across grass just below the summit with its Trig Point at 564ft (157m). The route continues as pleasant riding for some distance, but then, just as you're downhilling towards North End Farm, a bridleway sign sends you down to the right on an extremely bike-unfriendly detour. This follows a sunken, overgrown path between the fields – it was a total bog when I rode it, and likely to be pretty miserable whatever the conditions.

Not before time it leads out by the side of North End Farm. Ride straight ahead along the lane here, which is more of the 'best of England' quiet countryside riding that this area is so good for. At the next junction a bridleway turns off right up Hardown Hill; I opted to miss this one, having had enough mud and preferring to do my hillclimbing onroad. Ride on southwards to the next right turning, by some fine old farm buildings near Chideock Manor. From here it's something over ½ mile (0.8km) of steady pedalling up to the main A35; thankfully you can't really see it or hear it as you grind upwards. When you get to the top it's another matter though. This road can be seriously busy, and getting across requires patience and care.

Safely on the other side you pass the Moore's Dorset Knob factory. For anyone who doesn't know, these crumbly delights are well worth investigating and are particularly delicious with cheese, so hop off your bike and see how they make them. From here it's thankfully only a ½ mile (0.8km) pedal along the A35, which is fast riding on a steady downhill, with the best part of the entire route left to last. Just past the pub on the opposite side of the A35, fork left onto a dead-end lane that soon heads uphill. Ignore the left track signposted to Golden Cap, but when you come to the next houses look out for the bridleway signposted steeply uphill to the left. This tells you

*The end of the ride on the Charmouth seafront, with the Golden Cap Estate in the background.*

it's the way for horses and bikes to go to Charmouth, even though it's not shown on the OS map.

The uphill is a bit grim – steep, narrow and likely to be well churned by horses. However, once you're up on top of Chardown Hill it's worth it – fine riding on grass and hard tracks, with fantastic views over the coastline. The National Trust noticeboard further on tells you all about the Golden Cap Estate, and claims that the views from here extend from Start Point off Plymouth to Dartmoor inland. Follow the bridleway route along the top of the down, joining a hard track – be prepared for cars coming up to the car park here – and then there's a fast ride along the top of Stonebarrow Hill and steeply down towards Charmouth, a descent that unfortunately can't be record breaking as it's too steep, too narrow, and there may be cars coming up the other way. Back in Charmouth, which is a nice little place, there are all sorts of cafés, tea houses and pubs, or why not ride on down to the beach (there's a café here too) and cool off with a post-ride swim?

# Ride 7   WHITE GIANT RIDE

**Area:** Mid Dorset. Puddletown via Forston, Ridge Hill, Gore Hill, Up Cerne, Cerne Abbas and Piddletrenthide to Puddletown.
**OS Map:** Landranger 194.
**Start & Finish:** Puddletown on the A35, 4 miles (6.4km) northeast of Dorchester, at grid ref 755944. Roadside parking.
**Nearest BR station:** Dorchester.
**Approx length:** 24 miles (39km). Allow around 4 hours.
**Ride rating:** Moderate.
**Conditions:** Some of the going could be seriously muddy in wet weather.
**R & R:** Pubs and cafés at Puddletown, Cerne Abbas, Piddletrenthide.

This is an excellent ride, not least because it's through very quiet countryside, where you're unlikely to meet more than a handful of walkers or horseriders, let alone any mountain bikers. Despite the fact that there is really no hard climbing there are good views from the top of the ridges, and there's a choice of pleasant pubs and cafés in Cerne Abbas where you'll see the famous 'Giant' on the hillside.

First find the start point. On the west side of Puddletown there are traffic lights at the junction of the A35 and A354 Blandford road. About 100 yards (90m) west of these lights, look out for the start of the Ridge Way track on the north side of the road, signposted by a white building.

This is an ancient road, popular with local dog walkers, so

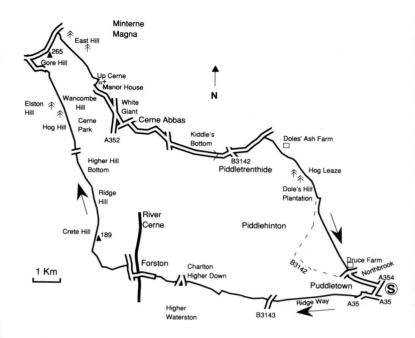

take it easy. The going is mainly good as it heads due west away from the road, though it's steadily and slightly uphill all the way. Like much of this route, it could also be very muddy in wet weather. Follow the course of the Ridge Way straight ahead, crossing the B3143 road. Past a barn the track goes downhill, and then turns left and right round the side of a field – the signposting is good, and finding your way is relatively easy. Keep on across fields towards Charlton Higher Down. When I rode here the corn had just been cut and riding over the stubble was easy, but it looked as if there could be problems at other times of the year.

Cross the next road, going straight ahead down a potholed lane, and then following a track downhill by the side of a large house. At the bottom the track bears left, becomes severely overgrown, and follows the side of more fields from where another track leads downhill to the road at Forston, by the side of the River Cerne. Turn right (north) along the road here for a few hundred yards, looking out for the bridleway on the left just opposite the large farmstead. Go through the gate here, and steeply up the side of a grassy field where you'll most likely encounter inquisitive horses. From here a track continues on up a moderately steep grass hill, passing a convenient seat for walkers and then following the top of the ridge. Take the bridleway right turning, signposted along the side of the woods, going through a gate and following a hard track ahead at the start of the long section that takes you northwards.

From here it's just over 6 miles (10km) to Gore Hill, following the top of the ridge all the way with some great views out to the west. It's mainly easy to follow; at the first bridleway crossroads take the right fork towards the Trig Point on the top of Crete Hill, and then keep on in the same direction past Ridge Hill and Higher Hill Bottom to the next road. The track varies from wide and fast to being fairly narrow, bumpy and lumpy, with parts across plain grass on the top of the hillside. At the next road crossing the track continues northwards. It looks better on the OS map than it really is, and it's quite slow going. Past Hog Hill the big aerial is a useful landmark, and then the route follows the side of woods between Elston and Wancombe Hill, finally joining a hard, fast surface which swings round the side of Eastcombe Bottom – a big bowl of countryside is laid out below to the left – passing a farmstead, and coming to the road at Cross & Hand.

Turn right along the road here until you come to the big car park/recreation area at Gore Hill (GR637038), which would make a useful alternative place to start/finish the ride. The information panel claims you can see from here as far as the Blackdown Hills (26 miles/42km), the Quantocks (32 miles/52km), the Mendips (34 miles/55km) and Glastonbury Tor (23 miles/37km). Follow the road to the north-east. Mostly the signposting on this ride is very good; the next bridleway turning is one exception, being completely unmarked and unobvious. About 1 mile (1.6km) from the Gore Hill car park, look out for a footpath sign on the left. Opposite it on the right, a field slopes downhill towards thick woodland. You can just make out a faint track across the field here, leading to a vague entrance into the woods – go for it! If you reach a sharp right-hand bend in the road, you've overshot.

Once in the woods, the track heads steeply down, and brings you to a great track in a beautiful valley below East Hill. All too soon it turns into tarmac, bringing you in record time to the immaculate hamlet of Up Cerne with its handful of very fine houses and a huge manor house close by the church. It's pleasant to look, and wonder who could possibly afford to live there and find the time to mow that much lawn. From here, follow the road on a quiet, narrow switchback, hitting the A352 where you turn right and almost immediately left for Cerne Abbas. You can't fail to notice the White Giant on the hillside here. He's 180ft (55m) high and thought to be 1,500 years old. He also has a magnificent male member. Locals believe he's all about fertility, and that sleeping on the hillside can cure barrenness. Another legend tells that the outline was cut around a giant who was sleeping off the after effects of a feast of stolen sheep.

Cerne Abbas is an immaculate little place, well tuned in to well-heeled tourists, with a selection of cafés and pubs to choose from, and fine buildings including a terrace of near perfect Tudor houses opposite the 17th-century church. I felt it was all a little too fussy for a muddy biker, and headed on by turning right uphill for the neighbouring village of Piddletrenthide. This follows a switchback road through pleasant countryside with few cars to worry about, and Piddletrenthide itself offers the choice of the Piddle Inn or Kids Café – if it's open, the latter is a cheap, easy and welcoming place for a cup of tea and piece of cake, and all profits go to charity.

For the final section of the ride I followed the road westwards towards Cheslebourne. After a stiff uphill, the road here levels out with some good views to the north, with the bridleway turning just over 1 mile (1.6km) from the B3143 turn-off. It's not marked and is not obvious. Opposite a couple of tracks off to the left, look for the driveway to Doles' Ash Farm on the right. Turn onto it, and then follow the bridleway up the right side of the field ahead, passing some distance from the front of Dole's Ash Farm (which looks a very nice place), and then joining a track which meanders southwards between fields on an easy up and down. The going is good on a hard surface with nothing much around; when the track forks left and right (not very obviously) take the right fork, and continue down by the side of the woodland of Dole's Hill Plantation.

There's a bit of a quandary over the route here. The main track continues straight ahead, and brings you out on the B3142 about 2 miles (3km) outside Puddletown. If the map is to be believed, that's the way to go; I took the more direct easterly route, which posed some problems. First, it's not signposted and it's difficult to find the two turnings. Second, the first part takes you along the side of a field where there's no semblance of a track (the farmer has obliterated it), and then on along a bumpy hillside which is equally hard going. After what seems like a long time but is in fact only a short distance, you reach the main track which is well overgrown with stinging nettles in high summer. This brings you down to Druce Farm; it's a little confusing here, but just keep on straight ahead and you'll hit the road, from where it's a five-minute pedal into Puddletown.

# The Central South

*A big area encompassing two long-distance rides – the Ridgeway and Wayfarers Ride; a tour of Wiltshire and its plains, including visits to Salisbury, Wilton, Amesbury (Stonehenge), and White Sheet Down; and, to finish, three closely connected rides in Surrey and West Sussex that connect the South and North Downs.*

## Ride 8   WHITE SHEET DOWN

**Area:** Wiltshire. White Sheet Down to Kitchen Hill.
**OS Map:** Landranger 183.
**Start & Finish:** The centre of Mere, off the A303, near the Memorial at grid ref 812323. Car park close by.
**Nearest BR station:** Bruton.
**Approx length:** 17 miles (27km). Allow around two-and-a-half hours, plus time to visit Stourhead or find a pub.
**Ride rating:** Moderate.
**Conditions:** The going is mainly good, even in wet weather. Navigation from the top of White Sheet Hill is a little tricky.
**R & R:** Pubs and cafés in Mere; pub at Maiden Bradley and Stourton; NT café at Stourhead in season.

This is a short and highly enjoyable circuit in an area which is not well endowed with bridleways and hills to suit mountain bikers. This is an exception, with two ridges rising up to the north of the small town of Mere, providing an up-down-up-down ride on good chalk tracks with fine views from the tops. There are also plenty of pubs in the vicinity with good quiet country roads for cycling, and the chance to visit Stourhead gardens (National Trust) and the house in season.

If you've driven along the A303 between Andover and Wincanton by daylight, you will have noticed the big hill that suddenly erupts out of some fairly uninspiring country on the north side, with a chalk track cut into its surface which looks as if it's just begging to be ridden by a mountain bike. Thankfully, in an area where footpaths rule and bridleways are the exception, this track is a bridleway and allows you to ride a highly enjoyable circuit which can either be compressed into a fast 2-hour plus sprint, or extended by as long as you like with extra journeying and stops here and there.

Mere is a quaint little place, set well away from the high-

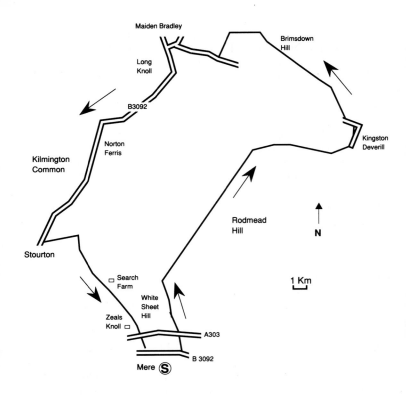

speed hum of the nearby A303, with an imposing clock tower in its centre which is a good place to start the ride. Turn up left past the car park, and then right on a slight uphill through houses on the outskirts of Mere, riding on a lane to cross over the A303, and then bearing left past the entrance to Manor Farm in the countryside beyond. From here you can see that inviting chalk track curving up the side of White Sheet Hill. Turn right through the next gate to join it, and pedal upwards – it's a hard chalk surface, moderately steep, and should be an easy climb for anyone.

As you gain height the view opens out, and you can clearly see the rifle firing range below in Great Bottom which is used by both the army and the RAF. Further on, a number of danger signs warn you to keep on the track and off the hillside which is supposedly full of live ammunition. At the top you're on a perfect ridge, usually with only sheep for company. However, on still days this natural 'bowl' is also much liked by hang-glider and parakite enthusiasts who, despite the warnings, fly imperviously over Great Bottom.

From here on the signposting is not all it might be. Bear right past the tumuli, with the Trig Point of White Sheet Hill over to the left. Ride over the crossing track, which allows the hang gliders to drive up from the road, and then keep on in the same direction across the next field, ignoring the track which bears off to the left and heads downhill into the valley. There's no track across this field, so make your way to the next gate where there is a bridleway sign, taking a left and then bearing right along the hillside at Rodmead Hill, following the fence on your right, with the hill sloping steeply down to the left, and usually full of inquisitive cattle. It's not easy riding along here with just a narrow trail, but it's manageable, and the views over to the other side of the valley are good.

Head for the next clump of trees on the hillside, and then drop down over the next field to join a hard track which is over to the right by Court Hill; again it's none too obvious how you join it. This whizzes you downhill to the village of Kingston Deverill, a pretty little place with the River Wylye running through it, but no pub! There's nothing to stop for, so ride through and out the other side, taking an easy uphill on the road going northwards and then turning left at the top by Whitepits.

Just by the last house on the right, a bridleway track heads up the hillside. This will take you up the side of Cold Kitchen Hill, but the surface is more grass than chalk which makes it a trickier ascent, especially if it's raining. The bridleway bears left up the hillside at a shallow angle, but again is none too easy to follow – just head for the hilltop, and when you're up there join the track which goes through a gate along the ridge.

When I rode this section of the ride the weather had come over very gloomy, but on a fine day it should be a brilliant ridge ride, with fine views over to White Sheet Hill and beyond. The bridleway carries on along the top of Brimsdown Hill, entering hilltop woodland which is nothing like as extensive as is shown on the OS map. Past the woodland, a track goes straight down the hillside to join the road; again the way is none too obvious, but when you come to an isolated mound-shaped clump of trees, head off left and start to ride downhill, and you'll find the track which goes steeply down to a gate. Unfortunately, the going is so rough and bumpy that you can't let your bike go really fast.

Turn right along the quiet lane at the bottom towards Maiden Bradley, passing Bradley House, which looks like a nice place to live in, and if the time is right maybe stopping in the village where there's a pub. From here you've got another 3 miles (4.8km) or so along the B3092 to Stourhead; it's a reasonably quiet road with a few ups and downs, and beyond Norton Ferris you pass an isolated pub by the roadside. Stourhead (National Trust) is about 1 mile (1.6km) further on, and if you have the time and inclination it is well worth a visit. The landscaped gardens are open all the year round and the early eighteenth-century house from April to November. The NT also

own the Spread Eagle Inn by the garden entrance, and if you're
happy to lock and leave your bike it's worth walking through
the grounds to the top of King Alfred's Tower 1-2 miles
(2–3km) to the north-west. This red-brick folly gives extensive
views over Somerset, Dorset and Wiltshire. The land around it
is laced with tracks, but unfortunately none are marked as
bridleways.

On the B3092 opposite Stourhead, a track turns left off the
road, heading past fields towards Search Farm where it goes
southwards towards Mere. The bridleway soon ceases to be
track, and continues by the side of fields on a rough bumpy
surface that is uncomfortable riding and could no doubt be
extremely muddy in winter. Passing the woodland of Zeals
Knoll on the right, it eventually reaches a footbridge which
leads back over the A303, with a track leading down to the road
that goes left back into Mere.

# Ride 9   THE RIDGEWAY

**Area:** Oxfordshire, Berkshire and Wiltshire. The west end of
the Ridgeway and back.
**OS Maps:** Landranger 174 and 173.
**Start & Finish:** The Court Hill Ridgeway Centre (YHA), just off
the A338 to the south of Wantage, at grid ref 393851.
**Nearest BR station:** Didcot.
**Approx length:** 57 miles (92km). Allow around 8 hours; if it's
muddy, the ride could take much longer.
**Ride rating:** Easy, but it's a fair distance.
**Conditions:** The Ridgeway area is best avoided after a long
period of wet weather.
**R & R:** Pub, shops and cafés in Avebury; also in Aldbourne,
Baydon and Lambourn.

The Ridgeway is officially a long-distance footpath, but the
western end is byway and bridleway all the way, and makes for
enjoyable riding, following the top of the ridge through quiet
countryside. This is an excellent ride which improves as you go
south-west along the Ridgeway, but don't try it in extended wet
weather which, we are reliably informed, turns the tracks to
glue. When I rode the route, parts of the track were being
carefully rebuilt to overcome this, with the surface dug out to
lay down a nylon membrane covered with rocks and topsoil.
Avebury, at the end of the Ridgeway, is an interesting place to
look around, and the return ride is as good if not better, with
surprisingly little on the road and plenty of good downhills in
return for a few relatively painless uphills.

This 57-mile (92km) circuit brings you back to your start
point at the handily situated Ridgeway Youth Hostel on the

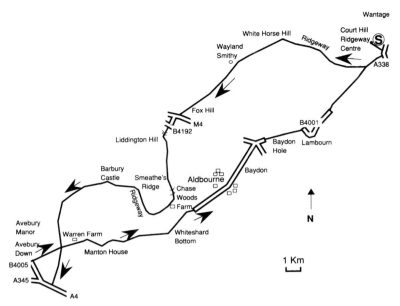

downs above Wantage. This modern, purpose-built hostel is sited on a quiet hilltop within a few feet of the Ridgeway, and would make a comfortable base to explore the tracks of the Ridgeway area over a weekend or a few days. It has bike storage in the stables, attracts both onroad and offroad bikers, and on our visit the food was good by YHA standards. Alternatively, you could start the ride from Streatley further to the east, which has British Rail connections at neighbouring Goring. It's about 15 miles (24km) along the Ridgeway from Court Hill – fast going with good, grassy tracks, so allow around 90 minutes extra each way. Streatley itself is not exciting, but the long downhill towards the town is a good way to finish.

From the Court Hill Centre, turn right (south) along the main A338. After about 500 yards (457m) you'll see the Ridgeway sign pointing right down a track by the side of a house. After a short distance you pass a noticeboard explaining that the Ridgeway is also open to vehicles, and indeed as far as the M4 much of it is like an unmade road and is consequently fast going. Despite its popularity, during a weekday in August I did not meet a single vehicle along its length, encountering a dozen or so walkers and only a couple of horseriders. However, this is serious horse country, and both those I came across looked and behaved like racehorses. I came up on one as slowly and carefully as possible from behind, but it still panicked wildly. (The lady in charge was good enough to blame the horse and not me.) The point is that you will encounter horseriders on the Ridgeway, and they should be treated with adequate respect. As for walkers, most of this section of the Ridgeway is so wide that you should be able to ride without bothering them.

The Ridgeway is mainly extremely easy to follow, being on a clear track which is well signposted all the way to the M4. There are a number of ups and downs, but so long as it is dry the going is comparatively easy. There are also good views from the high ground as you follow the ridge, and several points of interest along the way. Past White Horse Hill the Wayland Smithy burial mound is well worth a look; you have to approach it on foot, though it's only 100 yards (90m) off the main track. If you follow the footpath about ½ mile (0.8km) further on, the fort at Uppingham is also worth a look.

About 3 miles (4.8km) past the Wayland Smithy the track comes down the side of Fox Hill to the road, and here the route is not so obvious. Turn left down the road, and then bear right to go straight over at the crossroads ahead, with a pub on the right. This will lead you over the M4 (ignore the bridleway sign to the right), and on to the next section of Ridgeway which is more interesting, with more variety to the tracks and a wilder feel, though navigation is more difficult.

Past the M4, keep on the road as it bears round to the right. At the T-junction turn left along the B4192, then after 200 hundred yards (180m) uphill turn right onto a track signposted as the Ridgeway. This leads quite steeply up Liddington Hill, bearing left past the Trig Point which is over to the right at the top of the hill, continuing due south on a grassy track along the side of fields. Cross straight over at the first road you come to, following the tarmac lane towards Chase Woods Farm before bearing right onto a track as directed by the Ridgeway sign. This leads you downhill to another lane, where you cross straight over onto a track following the bridleway sign, dropping downhill past an old demolished railway bridge. Ignore the bridleway sign to the left, and keep on to the main A345 road at Southend, having crossed into the area covered by the next map, OS Landranger 173.

Go straight over here and into a dead-end lane, following it round to the right, over a stream and past some houses until you come to a bridleway T-junction with the Ridgeway indicated to the right. Follow the track on a slight uphill through trees until you come to another road, following it straight ahead and then almost immediately turning left offroad as signposted for the Ridgeway. Follow the track ahead through gates, going along a grassy track on a hillside past a water station and straight onto the top of the downs ahead at Smeath's Ridge. Scenically this should have been the best part of the ride – too bad that the weather was grey and grim when I rode by, and that the rain started to chuck it down with a vengeance when I had no cover. Thankfully it didn't rain for long, and the Ridgeway remained relatively solid.

At the end of Smeath's Ridge you go through a gate and turn right along a track by a Ridgeway sign. A short way on, just by

Upper Herdswick Farm on the right, turn left through a gate onto a narrow track which takes you through the car park for Barbury Castle, and then straight on through the castle area itself. This is an impressive ancient hill fort of which nothing but the circular defensive mounds remain; from here on a clear day you can see for miles.

From Barbury Castle the track goes steeply downhill to a tarmac lane. Turn right here, and then almost immediately left, following the track uphill as it swings south along Uffcott Down, passing several old clumps of trees on the right which mark the way along this clear and easily ridden track. Carry on along Hackpen Hill with a few gentle ups and downs leading you past the final clump towards the end of the Ridgeway. Just by a National Trust notice for Overton Down, ignore the bridleway turning right downhill towards Avebury, which is the way you come back up on the return circuit. Keep ahead on a fast chalk track along Avebury Down, riding downhill to the end of the Ridgeway at Overton Hill.

Here you cross the A4 road on a somewhat blind hill, with an ancient site known as The Sanctuary opposite. Turn west along the road, and then when you come downhill to some houses at West Kennett take the first turning on the right. Ignore the official brown tourist signpost here which points straight on along the main road for Avebury. The back road (the B4003) is known as Stone Avenue, leading past a few dozen standing stones by the side of Waden Hill, and finally coming to Avebury itself with its collection of impressive megalithic stone circles.

You've ridden 32 miles (52km) from Court Hill. Avebury is a popular place with the tourists, and there's a pub which is open all day and a café next to the National Trust shop down in the village. You may also like to visit Avebury Manor and the adjoining museum – there's plenty to see and do if you're that way inclined, and a few pleasant hours could be spent here. When it's time to go, a narrow dead-end lane leads eastwards out of the village past the small Methodist chapel. This place doubles as a café, and we found it an unusual and agreeable place for a snack, with a good view of the stones as you drink your tea outside.

## The Return Trip

Ride on along the lane past the chapel, passing the earthworks on the outskirts of Avebury and heading out into open country. You gradually gain height on Avebury Down. Eventually you reach the top on a track at the Ridgeway crossroads, just by the National Trust notice for Overton Down. Go straight ahead through the gate here, following the bridleway along a clear grass track over open ground. Head for the right side of a large

*Some of the Ridgeway is fast, easy riding, and the landscape is typical of the area.*

clump of trees ahead at Grey Wethers, with scattered Sarsen stones over to the right in this area of relatively wild grassland.

Just before the woods you cross what appears to be a race track in the middle of nowhere, one of many race-horse gallops in this area. On the other side of the gallops, go through the gate, and follow the hard track on a fast downhill, bearing left at the bottom and downhill the other side, ignoring a lesser track which goes off to the right. At the top of the next hill go through another gate, and from there on follow the wide, hard track ahead, ignoring all side turnings as it bears south-east round to the right, and swoops downhill towards Manton Down.

After a slight uphill the track levels out past a few trees on the left. Some way on you will see Manton House down a track to the right, and about 150 yards (137m) further on you take the bridleway track off to the left, well before you reach the end of a line of trees on the right. Head downhill on a narrow grassy track between fields – this was the only place where I got held up by a posse of hacking horses, and they were friendly.

At the bottom turn left along a lane, bearing right on a slight uphill and then turning right steeply uphill, ignoring the bridleway/byway sign pointing straight ahead at Old Eagle. Follow this narrow, quiet road past woods and gallops with Maisey Farm on the right, and then steeply downhill into Ogbourne Maizey where the road twists past an imposing mansion close by the A345. Cross straight over the main road here, joining the clear track which bears left and then right up the hillside ahead, taking you up through the treeline with fields on either side.

After a good climb the track carries straight on across open country, passing woods on both sides and then heading on a steep downhill before coming to a five-way crossroads with wooden signposts. Bear left on a tarmac lane here, following the sign for Whiteshard Bottom (not hard left for Ogbourne St George), ignoring the byway turning to the right to Sound Bottom, and carrying on past Warren Farm on the left. Here the lane turns to a byway track, carrying straight on through trees and along an up and down route through open country, passing through more woods and a couple of tracks off to the left at Whiteshard Bottom before leading out onto the road at a sharp bend by Stock Lane.

From here there are about 4 miles (6.4km) or so of onroad work, though it's relatively painless. Ride on to the village of Aldbourne where there is a steep downhill, and then follow the signs for Baydon, going uphill on the other side of Aldbourne. As you approach Baydon ignore bridleway/byway signs off to the right, carrying on through the village until you come to a crossing road by a pub on the left. Turn left and immediately right here – effectively straight over – heading out into open country and soon crossing over the M4.

Just past the motorway, take the first unsignposted road to the right, which at first appears to be a slip road for the motorway. However it soon leads away from the noise and the din, heading downhill to the farmstead at Baydon Hole where you keep left through the farmyard, joining a track (the farmer told me it was 'the old road') marked by a byway sign which leads through trees and onto a sandy surface. Keep straight on, ignoring byways off to the left and right, bearing right where the track appears to fork by the side of a field. This soon leads you down into the village of Lambourn.

Turn right on the road here, slipping down a track on the left side of the church, passing through bollards, and then turning left onto the B4001. A short way uphill take the first lane forking off to the right, climbing past North Farm and keeping left past a second right fork to Eastbury Down. This leads to a long, straight, fast concrete byway, heading across Bockhampton Down and up to a large isolated barn. Bear right here for Warren Farm, keeping straight on where the main track bears off to the left towards Stancombe Farm.

Here you go straight ahead down a wide grassy track which goes up the hill on the other side. Keep on until you come to a crossing track, heading straight over onto another track which soon bears left, going down and up past a couple of disused barns to rejoin the Ridgeway at the top of the hill. From here there are just 2 miles (3.2km) to Court Hill, and going at a reasonable speed this return leg should have taken you some three hours from Avebury.

# Ride 10    THE WAYFARERS RIDE

**Area:** Hampshire. South to north across the county from Hinton Ampner to Inkpen Beacon.
**OS Maps:** Landranger 185 and 174.
**Nearest BR stations:** Winchester and Kintbury.
**Start:** Hinton Ampner, on the A272 between Winchester and Petersfield, at grid ref 598279. Only temporary parking.
**Finish:** Inkpen Beacon, south-west of Newbury at grid ref 365622.
**Approx length:** 42 miles (68km). Allow 6+ hours.
**Ride rating:** Moderate/Hard – it's a good distance and you'll know you've done it at the end.
**Conditions:** The route could be very muddy in wet weather.
**R & R:** Pubs at Hinton Ampner, Cheriton, Tichborne, New Alresford, Dummer, Deane, Inkpen, Kintbury.

The Wayfarers Walk is Hampshire's principal long distance footpath, stretching 70 miles (113km) from south to north across the county. The first 25 miles (40km) or so are mainly footpath and of no use to bikers, but after that it's bridleways and byways most of the way, which has allowed us to create the 'Wayfarers Ride', an end-to-end route that gives a great day out exploring lots of good tracks. It's best ridden in summer when the tracks are dry; in wintertime it could be a very sticky and somewhat grim undertaking!

I started this ride from Hinton Ampner which is where bridleways take over on the Wayfarers Walk, having the luxury of someone dropping me off by car. Otherwise it's about 10 miles (16km) along the not so busy A272 to Petersfield, or closer to 7 miles (11km) along the same road westwards to Winchester. Both have main line railway stations, as has Kintbury at the other end.

Hinton Ampner is really no more than one very large house (National Trust) and its collection of associated buildings plus an attractive church which form the hamlet. If you opt to ride this route from north to south, there's a friendly pub a short way to the west along the A272, and Hinton Ampner house and gardens is open to the public on certain summer season afternoons, while the parkland adjacent to it makes a fine place for a picnic.

Opposite Hinton Ampner a Wayfarers Walk signpost points straight ahead up a track, telling you there are 42 miles (68km) to go to Inkpen Beacon. The WW turns left at the next bridleway crossroads to visit the village of Cheriton, with its pub named the HH (Hampshire Hunt) which claims to be the shortest pub name in Britain. A better route for the biker is to follow the bridleway straight on northwards for another mile (1.6km) or so, rejoining the WW along a very pretty track called

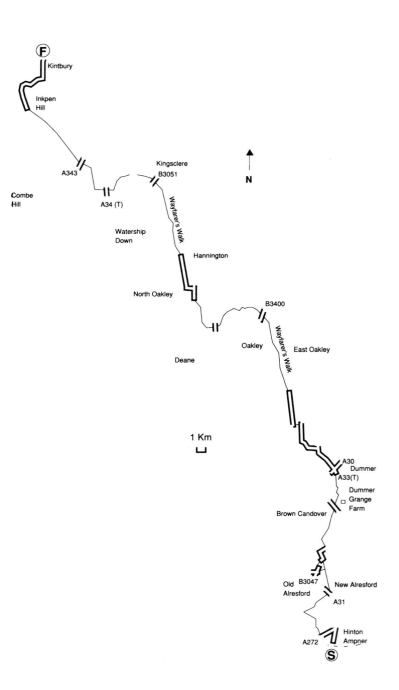

Hinton Lane before coming out onto the road by Crooked Billet. Ride on along the road for 200 yards (180m), with Tichborne Park on the left. Take the track turning right into the trees. (If you want to check out Tichborne, turn left down a narrow lane. This hamlet is known for the 'Tichborne Dole', a custom that originated during the reign of Henry I, when Sir Roger Tichborne promised his bedridden wife flour for the needy from as much land as she could crawl round! She eventually managed 20 acres (8 hectares), an area known as 'The Crawls'.)

The main route follows a track through woodland before dropping downhill to a golf course on the outskirts of New Alresford. Follow the signs across the golf course and onto the footbridge (push here) which crosses the A31, turning right and then left uphill, and following the road along the east side of New Alresford. Past the railway line, you come out onto the B3047 and turn right down the wide and rather grand Broad Street which is lined by trees and an interesting mixture of shops with places to stop for a drink or tea. Despite serious fires in the twelfth, fifteenth, seventeenth and eighteenth centuries, the Georgian architecture here remains very pleasing. At the bottom of Broad Street the route follows a footpath along a track by the side of Alresford's complex waterworks, conceived by the twelfth-century Bishop de Lucy of Winchester. You either have to walk it, or take the B3047 westwards out of town and take the first right turning to cross the River Arle and get back on the trail.

Cross over at a sharp bend in the road, following the wide grassy track ahead. It's known as Drove Lane, as in its day it was a busy route for driving sheep to Alresford's sheep market. The track crosses a road about 1 mile (1.6km) further on, continuing along a leafy way through quiet countryside before turning right at a bridleway crossroads as indicated by a Wayfarers Walk waymark. Here the route passes Abbotstone, a village which once covered 15 acres (6 hectares) and boasted a 100-room mansion built in 1719. Incredibly, nothing survives. It continues along a track through fields, passing a barn by a footpath/bridleway crossroads and coming to the wildlife preserve at Abbotstone Down by a noticeboard next to the car park on the B3046. This 32-acre (13-hectare) area is managed by the County Council as natural downland.

From the Abbotstone Down car park, carry straight on over the road ahead, following the route as it bears left by Oliver's Battery, an Iron Age defensive settlement. The route continues along a wide track known as Spybush Lane going due north, with fast riding and fine views over farmland and woodland to the east. Passing by a belt of trees it joins a hard farm track heading north downhill between fields in open country on the way towards Brown Candover.

As it reaches the farm buildings ahead, the WW route turns

left along a track to divert towards Totford. This track is called the Ox Drove, part of an old route called the Lunway which connected Old Sarum, Stockbridge and Crawley. Past Totford with its Woolpack Inn the WW follows a bridleway which joins a lane on the outskirts of Brown Candover, coming to the B3046 which it follows as far as St Peter's Church, set back from the road on a green. However, from the rider's point of view it makes better sense to follow the bridleway track straight ahead to Brown Candover. Turn right onto the B3046 here, then almost immediately left into a lane, taking the next right turn which reconnects with the WW route.

This brings you to a large modern barn in a clearing which is part of Church Lane Farm. The track appears to bear right, but disappears into nothing; Church Lane which is the WW bridleway continues straight ahead, but is well hidden by a thicket that runs between two fields, and is easily missed. Follow Church Lane down to a gate, going ahead by the side of Lone Barn which has been transformed into rather a smart house. Bear right here as indicated by the right of way sign, following the track by the side of the remains of Micheldever Forest across Becket's Down. This area was once full of chalk pits, a few of which can still be seen.

The Wayfarers Walk waymarks show the way through woodland past Breach House and Breach Farm beyond, going on to the road ahead by Breach Cottages and turning left for a short way uphill. The route then turns right down the long straight driveway that leads past Dummers Grange Farm to Dummers Grange, bearing left to follow a track round the side of the house which remains well hidden. The hard track ahead gives good views over the surrounding countryside, eventually coming to the road on the outskirts of Dummer with just a faint hum to tell you that the M3 is close by. Turn right and then left opposite the twelfth-century All Saints Church. A short way on the Queen's Head Inn is a popular pub which makes a welcome place to stop.

## Second Stage

From the Queen's Head Inn at Dummer, turn left downhill where you will find a 10-foot (3m) wide water wheel, originally built in 1879. Beyond the village the road heads up towards the M3 roundabout. Here the WW takes a long detour down by the side of the motorway, which though easily ridable is marked as footpath. So, ride straight on over the thunderous M3, follow the dual carriageway for a few hundred yards, then turn left onto the equally monstrous A30. A short way on, cross over and turn up the lane going northwards to East Oakley.

The WW goes off on a footpath for 1 mile (1.6km) or so here; you can follow its course on the nearby quiet road which is pleasant countryside riding, rejoining the WW to turn left where the road turns 90 degrees right by the corner of Bull's Bushes Copse. The route joins a track which follows the side of a field, and by the side of trees, to pass under the railway, emerging on the road by Cheesedown Farm. Turn right past Deane Gate Farm, crossing straight over at the B3400 by the Deane Gate Inn, and going up the lane ahead with lovely views of All Saints Church which is set in Deane House's parkland. Once again the WW goes off on a footpath across the fields here; on a bike you have to follow the lane northwards past Deane church, crossing another railway line.

The most obvious route for the biker here is to turn left, and then take a right at the first crossroads to follow the lane for 3 miles (4.8km) or so to North Oakley. This is pleasant enough riding, but if you prefer a considerably longer bridleway diversion you can join the track across Summer Down to get you back onto the WW; it's footpath once again beyond Great Deane Wood, where you'll have to turn off onto the westbound bridleway.

At North Oakley by the Manor Farm you join the WW again; turn left at the bend and go straight ahead on the hard track past Warren Cottages, before turning right down an overgrown track (could be very muddy here) as directed by the Wayfarers Walk waymark. The route climbs up For Down on grass with fine views behind, going through a gate by the side of Walkeridge Farm where you're back on a good track. Cross straight over the lane ahead – this was part of the Portway, a Roman road which connected Salisbury with Silchester to the north of Basingstoke.

Go straight ahead up the side of a field to a gate from where there is a wonderful view of the route ahead looking towards Watership Down. At last you are in hilly country, and the riding gets harder! The track heads downhill, too bumpy to be fast, emerging on the B3051 by the White Hill car park about 1½ miles (2.4km) south of Kingsclere, as you move on to OS map 174. From here on for the last 12 miles (19km) to Inkpen Beacon, the intensive farmland of central Hampshire is left behind, and the chalk downland of the North Hants Ridgeway takes over, with the route following a prehistoric track which stretches from Basingstoke to the Vale of Pewsey in Wiltshire.

From the White Hill car park (GR515565) the route follows the Portway westwards, following a track uphill on chalk and grassland. The chalk drains away any rainwater, so it is never too wet for riding and is equally suitable for the race-horse gallops which are either side of the route on Cannon Horse Down, with warning signs advising you to keep off the track. Watership Down inspired Richard Adams' bestselling book of that name, so look out for friendly rabbits! The downs here are also notable for ancient barrows and hill forts.

*Litchfield Down on the Wayfarers' Ride; once at the top it's a great downhill.*

Passing the Trig Point at 259 yards (237m) on the top of Watership Down, the route follows a narrow track downhill by the side of trees, crossing a lane and following a fine avenue of beech trees, before turning right across open grassland. From here it bears westwards again to reach the great hill fort on top of Ladle Hill, an Iron Age fortification which, with the fort on nearby Beacon Hill, defended the ancient route which is now the A34. The route bears south downhill on a wide grassy track dividing two fields; this is a brilliant downhill section with the A34 in the valley below and fine views of Beacon Hill on the other side. The track twists and turns as it descends Great Litchfield Down, eventually joining a narrow, overgrown tarmac track which heads downhill to the A34, crossing under overhead powerlines.

Go through the old bridge that marks the disused railway by the side of the Wayfarers Walk sign that gives 8 miles (13km) to Inkpen Beacon, and cross the dual carriageway with care. On the west side of the road you can see the memorial to the aircraft builder Geoffrey de Havilland who flew his model planes here as a boy. The track climbs uphill through pretty woodland along Lower Woodcott Down, coming out by the side of a field and passing a copse with good views north to Beacon Hill. From here the route swings north along the grassy hillside of Upper Woodcott Down, heading for a belt of trees and then joining a hard track coming up from the right. All the way along here the views to the north look out over the Highclere Estate which has a 17-mile (27km) circumference, with the rounded top of Sidown Hill in the foreground.

The route joins a woodland track through Grotto Copse,

passing a pretty castellated gatehouse to Highclere Castle before emerging on the A343. This has to be crossed on a blind bend, so take care. The continuing track is about 75 yards (70m) to the left uphill, heavily overgrown, with fields on either side, obscured by trees and ancient hedges – the riding here can be hard going. Over a lane the route continues along another very overgrown and sometimes very muddy track as it follows the North Hants Ridgeway, joining a lane by the side of woodland. Turning right there are fine views of Highclere Castle surrounded by trees in the distance, before the route bears left onto a waymarked track as the road starts to head downhill.

At the top of Pilot Hill the WW passes a Trig Point at 938ft (286m). A little further on the Berkshire border cuts in for the last 3 miles (4.8km) of the route, and from here on the track becomes very fast riding, giving an exhilarating finish to this marathon ride. The track joins a quiet road which continues westwards along the top of the down, coming to the car park at Walbury Hill. A hard chalk track leads on by the side of Walbury Camp, a prehistoric hill fort on top of the highest chalk hill in England marked by a Trig Point at 974ft (297m). This is a massive fortification, covering some 82 acres (33 hectares) with a mile-long ditch and rampart. The track leads on to the car park on the top of Inkpen Beacon, where you are rewarded with brilliant views of the countryside to the north and south, and the sight of a twin signpost marking both the beginning and end of the Wayfarers Walk and the Test Way, which is also bridleway in its northern section.

Combe Gibbet on top of Gallows Down, the official end of the Wayfarers Walk, is ½ mile (0.8km) or so further west on the chalk track that lies ahead. Standing on a neolithic barrow, this is a modern replica of an ancient hanging post. Despite its grim associations, on a clear evening this is the finest possible place to rest and relax after those 42 miles (68km). The nearest BR station from here is at Kintbury, about 4 miles (6.4km) from Inkpen Beacon. Head due north downhill from the nearby car park – it's fast riding on quiet roads, and following signs via Inkpen you can get to Kintbury in no more than 20 minutes. The unmanned station is opposite a pub in a very pleasant canal-side setting, which makes it a nice place to wait for a train on a summer evening.

# Ride 11    SALISBURY

**Area:** Wiltshire. Salisbury via Compton Down, White Sheet Hill, Berwick St John, Ox Drove and Stratford Tony to Salisbury.
**OS Map:** Landranger 184.
**Start & Finish:** Salisbury Cathedral, at grid ref 143295. Extensive car parking in the city.

**Nearest BR station:** Salisbury.

**Approx length:** 37 miles (60km). Allow 4–5 hours, plus time for pub/picnic stops and a look round the Cathedral.

**Ride rating:** Moderate. Navigation is straightforward, but it's a good distance.

**Conditions:** In wet weather be prepared for plenty of mud and some serious puddles.

**R & R:** Pubs, cafés, etc. in Salisbury; pubs at Berwick St John, Alvediston, Ebbesborne Wake, Broad Chalke and Bishopstone.

This ride takes you from the heart of Salisbury along the top of two enormous ridges which stretch westwards, with the valley of the River Ebble in between. Much of the route is byway and navigation is straightforward, but if it's been raining be prepared for some of the biggest puddles you've ever seen! I rode it after some torrential rain in summertime – it was manageable, though fairly wet and sometimes slippery. I've also ridden it in winter when parts can become impossibly muddy.

If you've arrived by car and don't fancy paying to park in Salisbury, you could start from the other end of the ride at the small village of Berwick St John. However, with umpteen tea shops and assorted cafés to choose from, Salisbury is an excellent place to start/finish with its wonderful Cathedral Close. Find your way to St Ann's Gate in the Cathedral Close Wall (east side), and ride south down Exeter Street. At the main roundabout turn right into Harnham Road, following it across the delightful River Avon – good to see this road has bumps and chicanes to slow down motorists – and uphill to the A3094. Turn right and almost immediately left to cross this busy road, going steeply uphill on the Old Blandford Road which is nowadays pretty quiet. After a stiff uphill it levels out and starts to drop down to join the A354 ahead; look out for a bridleway sign on the right, which appears to point down the road but intends to show the way onto a track that goes behind the houses.

This is the start of a long, long bridleway and byway section that leads west as far as the end of the down at White Sheet Hill. You won't need any navigation along here – just keep on pedalling until you hit the A30! It will take the best part of two hours, and an occasional glimpse at the map is reassuring to show how far you've gone. The first part of the track is fairly rough and overgrown. It then joins an old disused road, before going onto a woodland track that runs beside the race course and golf course. On a race day anywhere along here offers free spectating, with fine views over to Salisbury Cathedral in the distance. If it's been wet, you'll already have started to encounter the puddles that this route is infamous for. They are deep and there are a lot of them, so be prepared for a splashy and/or bumpy ride.

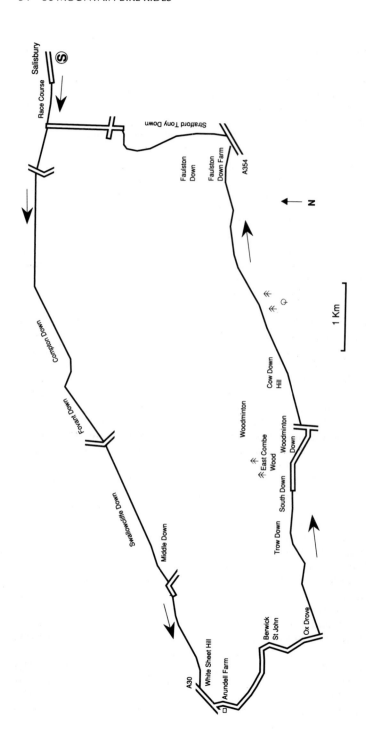

Past the Veuve Clicquot signs on the race course the route joins a tarmac road, passing a camp site on the left. From here on it's byway as far as the end of Fovant Down, so you may find that you have to share the trail with a few motorized vehicles. Thankfully for most of the way it's totally impassable to conventional cars; on a Sunday in August I only met a farmer's Land Rover and a couple of trials bikes, plus three mountain bikes and a handful of walkers, on the whole 37-mile (60km) circuit.

Beyond the race course the route follows a track through the extensive woods at Hare Warren with the potential for more serious puddles – just slalom your way around them – breaking out into the open along the top of Compton Down with fine views across miles of countryside to the north. Passing a Trig Point at 633ft (193m) the track continues on a steady, barely perceptible uphill, passing the old hill fort on the side of the down at Chiselbury and heading along the top of Fovant Down and Sutton Down where another Trig Point at 699ft (213m) shows the way. From here on the track is much improved with a hard chalk surface and good drainage for much of the way, as it heads more steeply up past Gallows Hill to the top of White Sheet Hill at 794ft (242m) – there are great views all round from here, and you can clearly see the Ox Drove ridge which provides the route back to Salisbury running parallel to the south.

At the end of the down, take the chalk track which heads steeply down by the Long Barrow to the bottom of White Sheet Hill – the surface of this track is badly eroded, so you can't go fast. Ride past the farm and turn left for a short way on the A30, taking the first left turning, signposted to Berwick St John. Follow narrow country lanes to this village where you'll find the Talbot Arms pub in the centre – it's a convenient place to stop at about the halfway point of the ride, with plenty of outside seating in agreeable surroundings.

The return to Salisbury is mainly offroad along Ox Drove – once an important route for those driving cattle to the City market – and if it's been wet this can be a very muddy ride. If that doesn't appeal or you're running out of time, the valley bottom road which follows the River Ebble via the villages of Alvediston, Ebbesborne Wake, Broad Chalke and Bishopstone as far as Coombe Bissett can be recommended – it's peaceful riding and there are lots of pubs on the way.

To find Ox Drove, turn up Water Lane opposite the Talbot Arms, passing village houses, with the stream which gives this lane its name running down a culvert by the side. At the top fork left, and then ride uphill to join Ox Drove. This is the steepest climb of the whole ride, and as you gain height there are fine views over Monk's Down to the north-west. Once at the top, turn left onto Ox Drove – and don't stop pedalling until you reach the A354 some 90 minutes or so later! Ox Drove starts as a short section of road, before joining tracks that head along Trow Down and South Down. This is more pleasant riding in a prettier landscape than the first section of the route, with fine views on both sides of the down, but the going can also be seriously muddy. I've tried to get along parts of Ox Drove in winter and been defeated, so it's really best tackled after a spell of dry weather.

Along Woodminton Down the route joins a dead straight section of road going downhill with (hopefully) not a car in sight, joining a track which is byway all the way to the end of Ox Drove. Be prepared for more serious mud in wet weather here, and just before you reach Lodge Farm look out for the world's biggest puddle – when I attempted to ride through it was about 100 yards (90m) long and well over hub deep, and there's no way round it! Past Lodge Farm the route comes to a tarmac crossing lane which at first sight doesn't seem to be marked on the OS map. It appears to be a road, but as far as the public are concerned is only a footpath between Knighton Wood and Knighton Hill Farm. Turn right and left here to rejoin the Ox Drove trail. If you feel in need of a pub, look out for the next unmarked track which turns left down the hill towards Bishopstone, which is an interesting small village.

If you don't want this diversion, head straight on towards the end of Ox Drove. The OS map shows the track coming to an end by Croucheston Down Farm as the byway continues over open ground; in fact, if anything the track improves as it carries on towards Faulston Down Farm, leaving puddles and mud behind. Keep on straight ahead at the farm, passing the farm buildings on the right and joining a narrow grassy track which soon leads out onto the A354. Interestingly, despite this track being marked as byway the farmer has blocked the road-end with a plough – this is no problem for mountain bikers, and good news as it prevents the track from being torn apart by four-wheel-drive vehicles.

The quickest way from here to Salisbury is obviously along the main road – it's also the least pleasant option as cars blast by at 60+mph (100+kph). I opted to rejoin the outward route here, turning left onto a byway track opposite the petrol station some 300 yards (274m) along the A354. This starts as a good track which leads on down Throope Hill to Stratford Tony. The byway continues as the more direct route going over the hilltop through trees, but the unmarked bridleway which forks left over a cattle grid is the better, faster option. This follows a much better track round the hillside before it heads steeply downhill towards Throope Manor. At the bottom turn right on the tarmac crossing track, and then go straight ahead between the farm and the manor house buildings which are in a fine setting. Bear right by a terrace of houses, and join an unmarked narrow track which heads uphill through woods. This bridleway leads past the back of the church at Stratford Tony where you need to ford the River Ebble close by the 'Private Bridge'.

Cross straight over the road ahead, carrying on uphill to rejoin the outward route by the race course. The map shows a bridleway bearing off along the course of a Roman Road a short way up this hill – I found it in a bad state of overgrown disuse, and at this stage of the ride preferred to take it easy; however, like all bridleways it should be opened up for general use. Once on the top, turn right beside the race course with glimpses of the Cathedral coming into view. Despite the apparent distance it's a relatively quick ride back to the delights of Salisbury, at the end of this fairly substantial circuit.

# Ride 12    WILTON

**Area:** Wiltshire. From Wilton via Chilmark Down, Great Ridge, Upton Lovell, Chitterne and Stapleford to Wilton.
**OS Map:** Landranger 184.
**Start & Finish:** Wilton, on the A30 west of Salisbury, at grid ref 093316. Parking in the town.
**Nearest BR station:** Salisbury.
**Approx length:** 31 miles (50km). Allow around 5 hours.
**Ride rating:** Moderate/Hard.
**Conditions:** Surprisingly little mud; easy navigation, apart from the section across Codford Down.
**R & R:** Pubs and cafés in Wilton; pubs at Upton Lovell, Chitterne, Stapleford and Great Wishford.

This is an excellent companion to the nearby Salisbury circuit, starting from the village of Wilton which is famously dominated by Wilton House and Park, and is consequently likely to be busy with tourists in the main season. It's a ride of contrasts which for the first 27 miles (43km) is virtually all offroad, and despite a long period of heavy rain we were delighted that there were few sections that suffered from seriously unridable mud.

On a Sunday in September we were able to park in the middle of Wilton with no problem; at other times and in the high summer season it may not be so easy. Wilton House is very close, one of the few privately owned stately homes of England, and perhaps a good alternative amusement for members of the family or companions who don't want to go on the ride.

From the traffic lights in the centre of Wilton, ride north through the town, passing the enormous and very grand church on the left; opposite there's a place which does teas which may be handy on your return. Where the A30 bends left, turn right onto a minor road signposted to Great Wishford, following under the railway arch. Just past here you'll find a track on the left – the start of the bridleway section. Be warned that this is

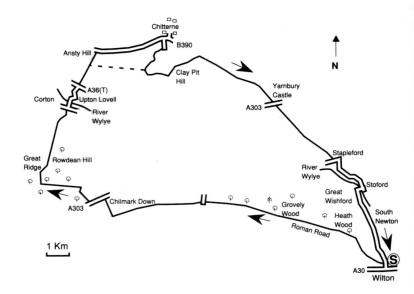

popular horse country, and you'll quite likely meet a posse of riders on the way up or down, so be prepared to pull over and give way.

Head up the track towards the woods on the ridge ahead. It's an easy climb, taking you to the start of the Roman Road that runs straight as a die for around 6 miles (10km) through Grovely Wood. Ignore the first turning to the left and then take the track forking to the right, leaving the woods for a short time before you hit the straight 'road' at Heath Wood.

It really is a road. Much of the surface is tarmac – nicely overgrown and in a moderate state of disrepair – and the sections that are not are all hard riding with few puddles and little mud to contend with. (If you've got young kids who are just on to bikes, it would be an excellent 'road' to take them for a ride.) The woods here are very pleasant. Unlike the usual uninteresting forestry plantations there are fine avenues of beech trees and oaks as you pass Grim's Ditch and head west. Where the road/ track swings right, go straight ahead along a narrow track; this links up with the main route again, giving a short and easy technical section between the trees.

From there on just keep following the road/track, knocking off the miles at a good rate, until you bear left by a barn and soon hit the road proper ahead on a bend, just below the Trig Point on the map at 650ft (198m). Ride straight ahead along the road here for about 50 yards (46m), then turn left down a track as the road bends sharp right. This leads into more woods and is excellent riding, but take it easy as we were surprised to meet a car coming the other way. The track breaks out into the open, becomes a hard concrete surface, and races up and down through open countryside to the south of Grim's Ditch. Go straight over at the next lane and, at the one a short way further on, follow the grass track bridleway on ahead towards farm buildings with a hill sloping up to the right.

Further on the track bears left towards the farm buildings of Manor Farm in a valley. Go straight ahead across coarse grass here, joining the rough and fairly indistinct track that goes north from Manor Farm through a gate that's hidden from sight in the far corner of the field. From here it's a steady pedal up the valley towards Chilmark Down. At the top of the next field the track bears right, but the bridleway goes ahead through a narrow iron gate on the left. It's uphill and can be seriously muddy and unridable in places, but it's not far up to the main A303. This is a very busy road, so take it easy when crossing.

If there has been much rain, the next section is likely to be gruesomely muddy; it probably only dries out after a long period of fair weather. A track leads straight into Stockton Woods ahead. After about 25 yards (23m) there's a much narrower track going off to the left which follows the side of the A303. When we rode here this was partly – though not seriously – blocked, and was difficult to spot. In dry weather it would make a good technical section with plenty of tree roots to guide your front wheel over; in wet weather there is some dismal mud!

After 200 yards (180m) or so look out for a track turning off to the right, following the side of the woods beside a field. Don't go straight on – the track ahead leads into an incredibly muddy area of woodland! The track up the side of the woods starts well, but as it heads back into the woods is likely to become progressively muddier. Don't despair – it's not far before you hit the main crossing track which is 'hard'! (According to the map you can get straight onto this track from the A303. This option may be worth checking out if the main route is likely to be muddy.)

Turn right onto the main track here, and then almost immediately left onto a wide track through an avenue of forestry. You're back on the Roman Road again, and it's another delightful ride. The road/track follows the woods of Snail Creep Hanging – an unlikely name – and then bears round to the right, leaving the course of the Roman Road. The riding surface is very good as it passes by massive rhododendron plants, which must be a great sight when they're in flower in spring. When you come to a T-junction at Great Ridge, take the right turning which continues northwards, breaking out of the woods at the top of Rowdean Hill with a fine view out over Well Bottom below.

From here it's a good, steady downhill through fine countryside, passing the Trig Point above Corton Down and coming to a crossing track by old farm buildings. Turn left then right by the side of the barn here, following the track northwards into the woods ahead until you start to go steeply downhill on a narrow chalk track. At first this is OK and provides some interesting technical riding, but further down the erosion is so bad that it becomes really difficult. Getting to the bottom without putting a foot down must be possible, but for most riders the sensible option is to get off and push.

At the bottom you hit the road just east of the hamlet of Corton. Ride straight ahead across the River Wylye, and on under the railway heading towards Upton Lovell. This is a very choice little hamlet with some delightful houses, and it's worth diverting left to the pub which comes at about the halfway stage of this ride. At first we were perturbed by the sign 'Only smart casual wear allowed'; but the lady publican couldn't have been more friendly to two extremely messy/muddy bikers at 2.30 p.m. on a Sunday, and the beer here is very good.

From Upton Lovell follow the road north, crossing the A36 and going straight ahead up the hill on the opposite side. Although tarmac with all the appearance of a road this is bridleway, going steeply up the side of Knook Horse Hill (the steepest climb of the ride) before joining a track that runs between farmland along the top of the down. The map shows the bridleway going straight ahead to join the B390 from here. It also shows another bridleway turning right to head east past Upton Great Barrow, *en route* for Clay Pit Hill. This is the way we went, and it caused the only major navigational problems of the ride. On the ground the track is signposted as a footpath, and certainly no horse could follow it. At first it's OK, even though it zig-zags round the side of fields in a way which isn't shown on the map. Further on it starts heading downhill through fields where any semblance of a track has been obliterated – ploughed up or sown over. The last section to the nearby road, just north of Auckland Farm, is most frustrating of all. While the map shows it going straight, the route on the ground zig-zags all over the place and is very difficult to find; moreover there are stiles rather than gates. Our deductions are: (a) if this right of way is used at all, it is only used as a footpath; (b) the farmer has diverted the route as he has seen fit, and has succeeded in making it incredibly difficult to follow.

The easy option appears to be to ride on to the B390 at Ansty Hill; follow the road to Chitterne; and then back south down to the turn-off above Auckland Farm. It's about two-and-a-half times the distance, but is likely to be considerably quicker. A hard track with a 'Private Road' sign goes up the hillside to the top of East Codford Down. The bridleway (unsignposted) turns steeply off it, then rejoins it on the top. Ride along the top towards the patch of woodland on Clay Pit Hill, then turn right with the track to head east past the Trig Point at 195 yards (178m). At the next gate go straight ahead, following an indistinct track on a slight downhill by the side of woods, with

MOD land coming into sight ahead and maybe the occasional Army helicopter dropping down to take a look at you.

At the bottom you'll come to an indistinct cinder crossing track, close by an MOD sign with the B390 a short way uphill to the left. Turn right here; this is the start of the final offroad section which takes you directly south-east towards Stapleford, just over 5 miles (8km) distant. It's an up and down track which is quite easy riding, passing through open country with a well hidden MOD airfield on the left and various signs telling you to watch out for tanks. Ignore the track forking to the right, and carry straight on towards the A303 once again, passing the huge fortifications of Yarnbury Castle, which is well worth a walk round if you're into ancient history. On the opposite side of the A303 the track turns to tarmac for just over 1 mile (1.6km) past Steeple Langford Down. Where it bends sharp right uphill towards Steeple Langford, follow the bridleway straight ahead on a wide grass track that joins a hard track which eventually brings you steeply downhill past a radio mast and back onto the A36 just west of Stapleford.

From here it's about 4½ miles (7km) onroad back to Wilton. The first mile (1.6km) or so is on the A36 which is not so pleasant. When you get to Stoford turn off the main road, crossing the River Wylye towards Great Wishford. From there bear left by the church, and follow the quiet country lane that runs due south beside the river – this is the way roads used to be – heading back into Wilton and passing the start of the outward bridleway just before the railway.

# Ride 13   STONEHENGE RIDE

**Area:** Wiltshire. From Stonehenge via Larkhill, Bustard Hotel, Redhorn Vedette, Compton, Enford, Everleigh Down, Bulford and Larkhill to Stonehenge.
**OS Maps:** Landranger 184 and 173.
**Start & Finish:** Stonehenge, near junction of A344 and A303 west of Amesbury, at grid ref 123425. Car park for ancient monument.
**Nearest BR station:** Salisbury or Grateley.
**Approx length:** 37 miles (60km). Allow 4+ hours.
**Ride rating:** Moderate.
**Conditions:** Mainly very easy tracks and fast riding. It's a good distance if you're riding fast.
**R & R:** Army style pubs and cafés at Larkhill; pubs at Longstreet and Bulford, plus the Bustard Hotel.

This ride takes you right across Salisbury Plain, and back again down the other side. Once clear of Stonehenge, which is sadly overwhelmed by roads and tourists, you're in a quiet and rather

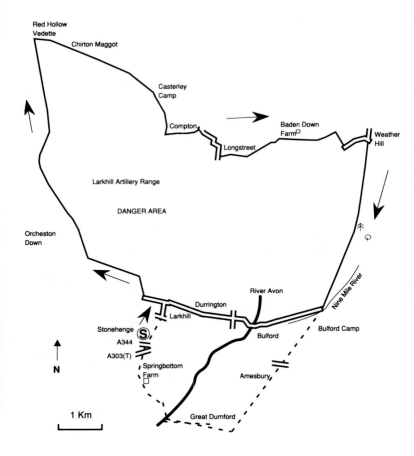

unreal landscape where the going is virtually all offroad for the first 31 miles (50km) and the tracks are excellent. The ride goes straight across the middle of the Larkhill Artillery Range, and some of the tracks will be closed when they're firing.

We set out on this ride with a fair amount of trepidation – a big circuit was planned, and it had been raining steadily for a week. How much mud would we encounter? For how long would we be reduced to dragging our bikes through slime, cursing and slithering at an average of 1 mph (1.6kph)? Thankfully these questions need not have bothered us – the tracks were for the most part in A1 riding condition, which makes this a great ride to opt for when your home patch is too wet. We wouldn't recommend it, however, if it's windy; Salisbury Plain is very exposed, and you and your bike could have a very hard time.

In fact we chose an almost perfect day – warm sun and barely any wind. This had brought the trippers to see Stonehenge in their hundreds; for those who haven't been there it's a sad and forlorn place, with the traffic on a couple of major A roads thundering close by which, together with the nearby car park, make it far too accessible and have completely removed any magical presence it may have had. The only good thing is that it does not take long to see! The car park is like a pitstop: park the car/coach, see Stonehenge, back in the car/coach and off again in five minutes. This means you should be able to find a parking space, though there may be queues.

From the car park look north, and go through a gate on the left side and onto a track which crosses 'The Cursus' and soon leaves behind the modern horrors of Stonehenge. The going is very good and gives an indication of things to come, crossing between fields before hitting tarmac and the start of the huge Army camp at Larkhill, where the artillery are based. At the road the OS map shows the bridleway going straight ahead. Don't try it! You're confronted by big padlocked gates, some very serious barbed wire, and a sign saying that dogs are on patrol. Reverse and retire . . .

Instead head west along the road. There's a fast downhill, and then, as the road levels out, you'll see a track on the right just past a belt of trees. This is the way to go, with the Army camp on the right and the first of many 'MOD Danger' signs on the left. Past a coppice of trees you'll hit a crossing track on a raised section. Turn left to follow this westwards – fast riding across an open landscape with no sign of the army or anyone else on a brilliant Sunday. The next turn comes after 2 miles (3.2km), and takes you northwards. It's easy to miss as we found out, going so fast that we overshot by some miles and found ourselves on the outskirts of Tilshead, way off course.

Keep following the main track, which in places is marked by poles which are presumably to guide tanks, and when you pass a copse of trees close by on the left slow up and look out for the Bustard Hotel – one of a rather forlorn group of buildings – 200 yards (183m) down the road to the left. Turn right here, following the metalled track/road north-west across Orcheston Down, and on as far as the Redhorn Vedette some 8 miles (13km) distant at the northern end of the plain. The OS map marks this track/road as bridleway, though we met a couple of well-behaved cars and it's tarmac most of the way. Past the gunners' Observatory – a low concrete building with slit holes for viewing – the track splits. Take the main track through the gate – which will be closed if they're firing – riding on through an eerie landscape, passing occasional burnt-out vehicles on the plain with endless DANGER signs all the way.

The state of the road deteriorates from here on, which is something of a relief as it's been too good to be true. At the far end of the plain you're off the end of the world and onto OS map 173. In truth it's really not necessary to have this map, which covers no more than an easy 1½ miles (2.4km) of the route. The track passes through another artillery range gate, and you come to the Redhorn Vedette building on the northern edge of the 'Danger Area'. Downhill ahead lies the Vale of Pewsey, with the downs rising beyond.

Turn right by the Redhorn Vedette, and follow the track eastwards between fields at Chirton Maggot, which brings you back down onto OS map 184. At the next Vedette building go straight ahead past Casterley Camp, joining a fast up and down track which heads southwards into Water Dean Bottom. You can't miss it when you're there; a very fast downhill gets a little uneven towards the bottom, and then the track continues quite steeply up towards a patch of trees on the other side. Stay in the bottom, and turn left on to the track which goes due east, following the bottom of the hillside. Shock! It's not at all what you're used to! It's muddy and wet! But even after all that rain it was no real problem, and we were soon out through the Compton farmstead and on the main A345.

As main roads go this seemed pretty mellow riding. Turn right (south) for less than 1 mile (1.6km), taking the first left turning downhill towards Enford. The road crosses the River Avon here – very pretty – and then a right turn takes you to the Swan Inn at the halfway point of the ride. Good beer and outside seating within sight of your bikes makes it an excellent place to stop. Ride on past the pub, and look for the first signposted bridleway track on the left. This leads on a rough but easily ridable surface on a gentle uphill, bringing you out into the open between fields above Rainbow Bottom. Follow the track eastwards, passing a dilapidated barn on the right, and then turning left at a T-junction with Coombe Field Barn farm over to the right. You're now on a wide, grassy track which follows the field edge, bearing east past Baden Down farm in the dip below, and steadily heading on a slight uphill to a big patch of trees at the top of Coombe Hill.

The track forks left and right. You can go either way; we elected to follow the left fork which is more direct, taking you along the side of another field and then quite steeply downhill to a big crossing track which is signposted as a byway, so look out for four-wheel-drive vehicles. Take a right here, and it's fast going to the road ahead. The track appears to go straight on, and you could no doubt find your way direct to the Old Marlborough Road offroad. However, to be safe we turned left (north-east) along the road for 1 mile (1.6km), riding uphill to the extensive woodland of Weather Hill Firs on the top, and then turning into the big open space on the right about 100 yards (90m) before the road bears sharp left.

The Old Marlborough Road goes south towards Bulford for just over 6 miles (10km), and is great riding. At first it's not too obvious which track to follow; there are five options radiating out ahead – the most obvious-looking one which goes ahead slightly to the right is the one. There's no tarmac, but the surface is very hard and this is fast riding as you pass the massive Sudbury Hill Fort over to the left; if you've time this would certainly be worth investigating, and looks a perfect place for a picnic. Keep on following the old road, making record time until you enter the artillery ranges again at Bourne Bottom. Suddenly the hard, wide, open track gives way to a narrower, wriggling track, passing through trees with some little ups and downs and even mud! The riding has been good, and even with puddles this variety makes a welcome change.

About 31 miles (50km) after leaving Stonehenge, you should find your wheels heading out of the Danger Area once again, and hitting the road on the outskirts of Bulford. From here it's 6 miles (10km) or so onroad back to Larkhill via Bulford and Durrington, with a couple of longish uphills on the way, before the final start/finish bridleway track takes you back to Stonehenge.

(N.B. This circuit could be extended southwards, through Bulford Camp and past Amesbury, following a bridle/byway to Great Durnford on the River Avon. From there the bridleway appears to cross the River Avon, joining a byway which heads north to Stonehenge.)

# Ride 14   LEITH HILL TOWER AND THE NORTH DOWNS WAY

**Area:** The North Downs, Surrey. From Newlands Corner along the North Downs Way, south to Leith Hill Tower, and back to Newlands Corner.
**OS Maps:** Landranger 186 and 187.
**Start & Finish:** Newlands Corner car park, off A25 on top of North Downs approx 3¾ miles (6km) east of Guildford, at grid ref 044492. Alternative start from Guildford BR Station, riding up to Newlands Corner via the 'Trackway'.
**Nearest BR station:** Guildford.
**Approx length:** 31 miles (50km), plus 3¾ miles (6km) each way to Guildford BR Station. Allow around five hours, plus time for pub stops and getting lost.
**Ride rating:** Easy.
**Conditions:** Some tricky navigation, and occasional patches of sand.
**R & R:** Principal pub stop at Coldharbour.

This is an excellent ride, exploring the countryside lived in by some of the most affluent of southern England, where the people have Porsches and BMWs, and the houses (all very desirable) are immaculately tucked away. Some of the tracks are sandy – so much so that they look as if the beach has been

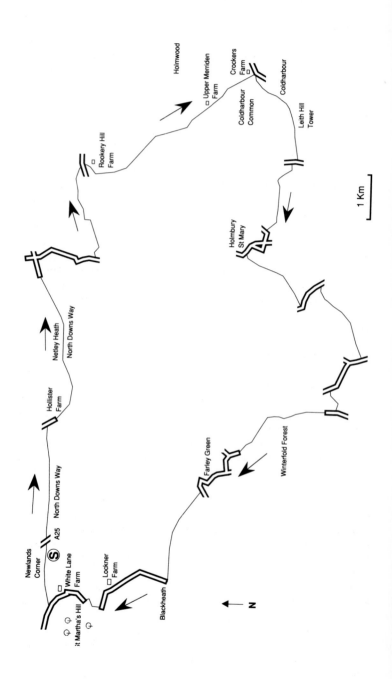

dumped on them – and while the first part of this ride is easily navigated with tracks that are straight and few, from Coldharbour back to St Martha's things get more confusing. There is a maze of tracks in this area, mainly going through woods with very basic bridleway signposting. Getting lost is easy and to be expected, and an OS map (1:25,000 Pathfinder is much clearer than the Landranger on this ride) and a compass will be necessary to keep you in the right direction. Even if you do get lost it doesn't necessarily matter – the tracks are mainly great, and it's very good territory for offroad biking with surprisingly few people out and about at weekends and friendly enough horseriders.

Start from Newlands Corner where there is a large car park at the top of the hill which is reached via the A25 (or from Guildford). From here cross the road at the top of the hill, and follow the North Downs Way straight ahead on an excellent cinder track. The going is fast, and on a Bank Holiday Saturday few people were using the trail – maybe they were all sitting on the beach.

The North Downs Way is clearly signposted and mostly easy to follow. At the first road crossing, go straight ahead, and then when you hit the road again (very quiet and very minor) follow it straight on for about ½ mile (0.8km), looking out for a bridleway track going to the right on a left-hand bend. Turn down this track, forking left for the North Downs Way and carrying straight on; where a more minor track forks left off the main track, take this route, following the North Downs Way eastwards along Netley Heath.

You will pass Hackhurst Downs on the right – a sign here says 'No Horses' since it is footpath area only – and carry on eastwards. From here some of the track becomes deeply rutted as it passes through trees, and there is a better secondary track running alongside, which makes the going easier but becomes confusing at times. Keep on ahead in a more north-easterly direction until you hit a lane running north to south from Effingham Upper Common. Turn right down this, and follow it on a steep downhill which takes you over the railway line at the bottom of the downs. A short way on there is a bridleway indicated on the left. Turn down here and follow the track round the side of a field where some of the going is heavy due to loose sand.

The track settles down in an easterly direction, passing through and continuing along a hard section past an isolated cottage where it bears right and then straightens out again. It soon brings you to a cluster of houses on the roadside above Westcott Heath, where you turn right down the lane and then left onto the A25 for a short distance. Cross the bridge over Pip Brook, and immediately turn right onto a track that follows the brook, passing some expensive houses on the way and crossing it by the side of one which has a waterfall in its garden. Past the houses the track starts to head uphill with fields on the left, finally coming out into the open with Sylvanus Wood on the left, a big field on the right, and Coast Hill Farm a little way off.

Follow the track along the side of the woods – again there is a secondary track in places, replacing the main one which is deeply sunken and could be incredibly muddy in wet weather. The track continues in the same direction on a more or less good surface, though a little pushing may be necessary in places, particularly in one part where Brighton Beach has been dumped on the track! Further on the track hardens and becomes faster, as it heads downhill along the side of Coldharbour Common towards the hamlet of Coldharbour where the very pleasant pub awaits you.

After the pub, it's time to check out Leith Hill Tower, a splendid landmark on the hillside at 968ft (295m) which on a clear day gives formidable views to the south. From the pub take the track going up the side of the hill, taking the right fork which brings you up to a clearing with a splendidly situated cricket green; at weekends in summer you'll more than likely be able to stop and watch a cricket match. Take the left fork past the cricket ground, and then head straight on through the woods, navigating towards the tower. In this part of Wooton Common there are tracks all over the place and it's easy to take wrong turnings, but keep on in the same ESE direction and you'll soon pick up signposts with a conspicuous tower motif to guide you on the way. Take care that you don't stray onto footpaths, and be prepared for quite a lot of walkers around the tower.

The tower is open in summer (National Trust) and has a small kiosk selling drinks and snacks; it's a good place to stop, ruminate, and plan the rest of the route. Going west from here there are masses of bridleway tracks in very ridable country, with lots of ups and downs and trees and woods all over the place. There is, however, no direct cross-country route, and all you can do is zig-zag in approximately the right direction. The route I took worked well enough, and gave a pleasant ride.

From Leith Hill Tower take the track due west that leads down to the road. Cross straight over, following the bridleway sign towards Burnhouse Copse, and then at the next bridleway sign turn right, which takes you along a track more or less parallel to the road. Look out for the second left turning by High Ashes Farm, and then follow the track all the way westwards towards Holmbury St Mary – a good ride which is mainly downhill through the woods towards Bulmer Farm. A short uphill brings you back to the road where you turn left; then turn right onto the B2126 through Holmbury St Mary.

This is a pleasant looking village with two pubs; by the second you turn left at the village green, following the dead-

*Holmbury St Mary – one of the few sections that are on-road in the mainly offroad ride from Leith Hill.*

end lane past a few houses and then heading into open country in the same direction. The track leads up to a five-way crossroads. Here you bear right to carry on in more or less the same direction, following the wide, fast, hard track ahead past Holmbury Hill until it brings you to a small car park by the roadside just south of Coverwood. Turn left downhill onroad here, taking the right fork for Ewhurst and a short way on looking for a bridle track that goes off to the right by the side of Radnor House. This is another good ride, dropping down through the woods, and then going through more open country before coming to the road.

Turn right here, following the left fork for about ¾ mile (1.2m) until you come to a pub by the side of Pitch Hill, in a pleasant position with a big garden and pond in the front, which makes it a good place to stop. Turn left down a bridleway past the side of Hurtwood Edge here, passing a few smart houses – a Rolls Royce pulled out of a driveway in front of me here, but had the courtesy to pull back and let me by. This track soon leads out to the road again where you turn right for a stiff uphill heading north. The road levels out by a left-hand turning, and here there's a bridleway going more or less straight ahead north across Winterfold Forest.

This is mainly fast riding, and at the next bridleway sign you should bear left towards Farley Green, turning left down a lane and right through the village. Just as you reach the green, an unmarked track cuts off across its left side. Follow this to the next road where you turn left, taking the next track on the right and following the right hand of two bridleway directions. From here the track bears west towards Blackheath. Some of it is sandy and some is good going, but with tracks and blue bridleway blobs all over the place navigation is none too easy. It should eventually bring you out to a car park a short way to the east of the village of Blackheath. Here you turn right along a dead end lane, to join the Downs Link which runs down a narrow track by the side of a house.

Head northwards on the Downs Link – a long distance footpath/bridleway connecting the North and South Downs – pushing and riding down the extremely sandy track towards Lockner Lodge where you cross the railway line. From here the track goes straight ahead over the road and past Lockner Farm, bearing right downhill and then coming up to a sign for the Downs Link where you turn right to start a steady plod uphill towards St Martha's. The track bears round to the right and becomes sandy and unridable near the top, eventually reaching the end of the Downs Link by a noticeboard next to an old concrete pillbox. Turn right a short way up the hill here (carry on if you want to see the church on the top, but walk), and then take the bridleway track which bears right downhill through the woods to join the lane below the North Downs by White Lane Farm.

Ride uphill, bearing round to the left as the lane, which is part of the North Downs Way, levels out. Some way past the footpath which turns off to the right, a bridleway doubles back in the same direction, just opposite a large house on the hillside. This takes you onto the 'Trackway' on top of the downs, a fast track on level ground which brings you back to Newlands Corner in record time.

If you want to get down to Guildford BR Station from here, ride back along the Trackway to the road, going straight ahead at the next crossroads, which leads to a continuation of the Trackway across fine open country on the top of Pewley Down on the outskirts of Guildford. When you reach the road, head downhill, keeping on down and crossing straight over into the High Street (watch the one-way system) where you can bear left downhill towards the station, an extra distance of just under 4 miles (6.4km).

# Ride 15   DOWNS LINK TO AMBERLEY

**Area:** Surrey and Sussex. From St Martha's Hill to Amberley.
**OS Maps:** Landranger 186, 187, 198, 197.
**Start & Finish:** Start from just below the church on St Martha's Hill, on the North Downs Way to the south-west of Guildford, at grid ref 032483. There is a car park nearby.
**Nearest BR stations:** Guildford, Amberley.
**Approx length:** Downs Link 30 miles (48km); from the southern

end of the Downs Link to Amberley via the South Downs Way 15 miles (24km). Allow 4 hours for the Downs Link, plus a further 3 hours to Amberley.

**Ride rating:** The Downs Link is easy; the additional leg to Amberley makes it a long, and quite hard ride.

**Conditions:** Mainly fast, flat riding on the Downs Link; more variety on the way to Amberley which features two long climbs.

**R & R:** Pubs and cafés can be found in the various towns and villages passed on the Downs Link; at the end of the Downs Link Steyning is recommended; on the South Downs Way there are pubs at Washington and Amberley, where there is also a café and restaurant.

The Downs Link is a footpath and bridleway which follows the course of an old railway line, linking the North Downs Way at St Martha's Hill in Surrey with the South Downs Way at

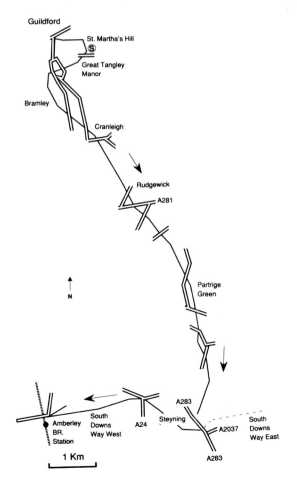

Steyning in West Sussex. It covers 30 miles (48km) with good tracks and little in the way of hills, but to make it a little more challenging we have extended this route along the South Downs Way as far as Amberley, where there is a convenient rail connection to get you back to base.

Dr Beeching closed the line which now forms most of the Downs Link in 1966, just over 100 years after it had been opened. I suppose it's indirectly thanks to him that we can ride along it today. In other respects the railway is a great help on this end to end ride though, since you can start the ride from Guildford which has fast connections to London and not too many hassles when it comes to taking bikes, and you can finish it at Amberley which will get you back to London, if that's where you want to go.

The Downs Link has a special railway arch waymarking symbol; when you're on the old railway line navigation is predictably straightforward, but when you deviate off it you need to watch for the signs and follow the map. First find the start of the route. From Guildford railway station take the A280 out of town towards Horsham. Past the Yvonne Arnaud Theatre and River Wey boating centre, take the road turning left just over ½ mile (0.8km) from the station. This leads you onto the Pilgrim's Way, a signposted trackway going up through trees and onto the North Downs Way.

From here the bridleway passes just below the church on St Martha's Hill, close to where the Downs Link officially starts. The church here is in a fine position and worth a visit, but don't ride your bike up to it. I pushed mine up, and was still tackled by an aggressive clergyman with words to the effect of 'No bikes, be off!'. I replied that I was really keen to see the church and so he could hardly refuse.

Just below the church there's a Downs Link noticeboard by an improperly sited concrete bunker. To start with the sandy tracks are a problem, with the route leading downhill into Tillingbourne Valley where it joins a hard track, passing the Lockner Farm riding stables before crossing the A248. From here it carries straight on, joining another narrow sandy track which is a difficult ride (or, more likely, a push) on a gentle uphill by the side of a hedge, before bearing right on a wiggly track through woods on the edge of Blackheath. This is a big area of heathland and pines where you need to keep a careful look out for the railway arch symbols to avoid going off course.

There's more sandy track riding here to slow you down, before the route passes Great Tangley Manor on its way to Wonersh Common and Chinthurst Hill, from where there are fine views over the surrounding country. A short way on the route reaches the old railway line, dropping down the embankment by a bridge. Here you turn south (left), and it's mainly easy navigation and fast riding all the way to the end of the line, though there are a few exceptions when the route leaves the old railway, usually because it's been gobbled up by modern developments.

Past Bramley the Wey and Arun Canal runs close to the track; it was originally built to link the Thames with the south coast via the River Wey and River Arun, but was closed by the coming of the railways in 1868. The track then runs through open country across Run Common, passing an old signal on the way into Cranleigh where the railway disappears for a short while. The route bears around the west side of the town (which calls itself the largest village in England), passing the Recreation Centre and playing fields on a tarmac lane which brings you back onto the railway.

Another forlorn signal is passed, and the impeccably restored Baynards Station which is now privately owned. Just past here are the gates of Baynards Park with its tree-lined avenue, and then the bridleway and footpath routes split to divert past a blocked bridge and cutting. Don't take the footpath route which at first seems most obvious. It goes straight into South Wood, where there are stiles and other obstacles. The bridleway route goes left to cross under and over the road bridge, turning into South Wood and rejoining the railway and the footpath a short way on, just across the Surrey/Sussex border.

Past Rudwick the Downs Link crosses the A281, and then goes over the River Arun on a two-tier bridge bound for Slinfold. Crossing the A29 and A264 it suddenly turns off the railway line by the road bridge, heading along past Weston's Farm to Christ's Hospital where, for a short while, it runs alongside the modern railway line. The famous public school where the boys wear those odd blue coats is set in enormous grounds with playing fields as far as the eye can see. I did this ride in high summer, and at this stage was badly in need of a drink, so took a quick tour of these grounds looking for a friendly outside tap. Don't bother – there aren't any!

Back on the old railway, the next stop is Southwater where there are more off-railway diversions, crossing the A24 via a handy underpass and continuing along the railway line. From here on the countryside gets better, with the line passing through the old railway platforms of West Grinstead Station. By Partridge Green it diverts onto the B2135 for a short while, rejoining the track by Homelands Farm with views of the South Downs opening out ahead. It crosses the River Adur, coming to Henfield where the route once again temporarily leaves the track, bearing south-west to cross the River Adur again, this time close by Stretham Manor, and then reaching what is now the end of the line on the outskirts of Bramber at Wyckham Farm.

From here a fast track leads down to the road which goes on

*Towards the southern end of the Downs Link – it's well used by recreational riders on fine weekends.*

to the big A283 roundabout, passing close by Bramber Castle (English Heritage), a complete ruin, but worth a look round. There's nothing much else to Bramber, but you may care to ride into Steyning which is a pleasant small town with good buildings, and it has an excellent tea shop in the main street, as well as a choice of pubs. From the roundabout the route goes south for a while along the busy A283, with a bridleway leading off to the right (west) to follow the course of the old railway across flat country, closing with the River Adur. The end of the Downs Link comes by the foot/horse/cycle bridge which crosses the Adur; here it joins the South Downs Way, with a Downs Link noticeboard marking the spot.

The nearest railway station is Shoreham, about 3 miles (4.8km) distant, if you want to make for home. After a relatively easy pedal down the Downs Link I wanted more, and opted to finish the ride off in a harder fashion, riding westwards along the South Downs Way to Amberley.

## South Downs Way to Amberley

After the flat riding of the Downs Link, hill climbing comes as a bit of a shock with an immediate big climb up Annington Hill to the Steyning Bowl. From here there's a gradual pull uphill to Chanctonbury Ring – a mystical ring of trees – which is a great ride if you're going the other way. However, what goes up must come down, and you're soon flying down the hillside on a fast track that leads down to the A24. Take it easy here; despite having ridden this section several times before, I inadvertently took a left hander by the Trig Point at Cross Dyke, following the even faster track down to the A24 at Muntham Farm, way off the official route.

The dual carriageway A24 is not pleasant to cross without an armoured car; a safer way is to follow the side road north to Washington where there's an agreeable pub, and then take the horse/foot/cycle bridge that crosses the A24 by the church. From here there's a long ride up Barnsfarm Hill, riding across the top of the downs on a good track, and then staying high all the way past the Trig Point at 633ft (193m) on Rackham Hill, ready for a brilliantly steep downhill into Amberley. This passes Downs Farm over to the left, with fine view of Amberley Wild Brooks and Castle to the right, before you join a narrow lane which heads on down by the side of the Chalk Pits Museum. At the road, turn left with Amberley station a few hundred yards further on. From here you can take the train, or if you want somewhere to stay head for Arundel.

# Ride 16    RIVER ARUN

**Area:** West Sussex. From Arundel via Slindon, Stane Street, the South Downs Way and Houghton to Arundel.
**OS Map:** Landranger 197.
**Start & Finish:** Arundel, on A27 between Chichester and Brighton, at grid ref 018071. Extensive car parking available.
**Nearest BR station:** Arundel or Amberley.
**Approx length:** 15 miles (24km). Allow 3 hours, plus time to stop and look around.
**Ride rating:** Moderate.
**Conditions:** Be prepared for some mud if it's wet, some ups and downs, and a tricky ride by the River Arun.
**R & R:** Pubs, cafés, etc. in Arundel; pubs at Slindon, Houghton and Amberley; café at Amberley.

This is an excellent ride, starting and finishing in the historic city of Arundel and taking in a section of the South Downs Way, with offroad riding for 90 per cent of the route, culminating in an interesting though somewhat technical ride along the banks of the River Arun. Be warned that parts of the ride have the potential to be seriously muddy, so think twice before you start after a spell of wet weather.

Arundel is a very interesting place with lots to look at, including a large church and a splendid castle which dominates the town from the hillside. From the Information Centre find your way to the main roundabout at the intersection of the A27 and A284. About 50 yards (46m) along the A27 going west (Chichester direction) cross over to the north side of the road, and go up the unmarked driveway ahead between the lodges on the corner.

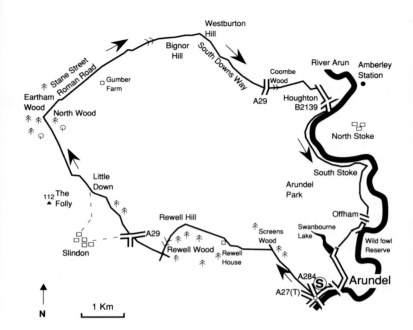

A short way on, take the bridleway track that's signposted off
to the left. This leads straight into Screens Wood, following a
wide track through the trees which is likely to be seriously
muddy if there's been any rain – you have been warned!
Further on the track breaks out of the trees and becomes more
bike friendly, turning left out of the woods by a padlocked gate
and crossing a field to join a track across open country on the
way to Rewell House. This section is all fast riding on level
ground, leading past the back of Rewell House into Rewell
Wood on a hard track. Keep straight on over the first crossing
track, and then go past the second forestry crossing track with
its sign saying 'No Horses'.

Some way on you come to bridleway signs pointing right
and straight ahead, just below Rewell Hill. Go straight ahead,
following the track round to the left and onto an increasingly
fast downhill. The track breaks out of the woods on a fast,
bumpy surface, re-entering the woods and coming to a dark
hollow. Signposting is somewhat lacking here and the way is
not too obvious; turn sharp right for more downhill riding,
following the woodland track on past a summer camp site, and
you should come out onto the A29 just east of Slindon.

Go straight over here; it's a tricky road to cross, with a blind
bend and cars going really fast in both directions. Go up the
short lane ahead, and look for the bridleway that goes straight
ahead into the woods. (If you want to visit the village of
Slindon, which has a pleasant pub, turn left along the road
here; a bridleway reconnects with the route.) Follow the narrow

track through the trees. This is another section that can be muddy, as it leads out to open country over Little Down where you should take care to keep heading north, before following the track left (westwards) to join a narrow tarmac lane close by the Trig Point at The Folly on the opposite hillside. Ride north-wards along this lane for 100 yards (90m) or so, forking left onto the bridleway that follows the track ahead past a gate. This is good riding, leading along a dead straight trail with tall trees on either side, heading into North Wood with Eartham Wood beyond.

After riding on this track for 1 mile (1.6km) or so you come to an ancient five-way signpost, showing the route of the Roman Road known as Stane Street, which once ran all the way between Chichester and the Roman Villa at Bignor, connecting them to settlements beyond. To follow Stane Street, take the track signposted for Bignor. Although a bridleway it's fairly narrow – let walkers or horseriders come by – and riding is made difficult by old gnarled roots lying across the surface. After a time it breaks out into the open across a field, passing Gumber Farm in a hollow and steadily heading uphill, with the radio masts at the top of Burton Down showing the highest point of the downs in this area.

Keep straight on ahead ignoring crossing tracks, and what remains of Stane Street will eventually bring you up to the car park on top of Bignor Hill. Turn right here for a fast pedal eastwards along the South Downs Way. As with any ride along this well used LDP, remember that the sections near car parks can get congested so take it very easy with walkers. A good track leads steadily uphill with fine views on both sides of the downs, before swinging sharply and steeply down to the farmstead at the bottom of Westburton Hill (it can be extremely muddy down here), and then steadily uphill again until the track levels out and brings you to the A29.

This is a very busy road. The easiest way to get across is to turn right down the verge, and after 75 yards (69m) or so cross straight over to the South Downs Way sign on the other side. This leads you on a hard chalk track heading steeply down by the side of Coombe Wood, with great views ahead over the Arun valley to the continuation of the downs beyond Amberley, where the chalk cliffs rise out of the plain. This is a steep, fast descent taking you down towards the village of Houghton where there's a pub a short way up the road to the right, or turn left to cross the bridge into Amberley where you'll find a café and restaurant, as well as the famous Chalk Pits Industrial Museum.

To continue cross straight over the B2139 to a dead-end lane. This lane leads downhill past some houses to a narrow track that follows the side of the River Arun – a short way along there's a clearing under the cliffs on the right-hand side which

*Part of the South Downs Way section, the hilliest part of the ride to and from Arundel and the best views.*

makes a good place to stop for a picnic. This part of the route looks short and easy on the map; in practice it's pretty slow going. The riverside track is narrow and tortuous – few horses would risk coming along here – and on summer weekends it's likely to be popular with walkers, so take it easy. Some way on the bridleway heads up the hillside away from the river, following the side of fields which is much easier riding. The track leads on to the tiny select hamlet of South Stoke – check out the wonderful architecture of the buttressed old barn here – and then across the open plain to Offham.

At Offham the track joins the road, passing the Black Rabbit Inn which is sited in an extremely pleasant riverside position. Further along the road the Wildfowl Reserve is a popular place with visitors, and then after 1 mile (1.6km) or so you're back beneath the battlements of the castle and heading into Arundel, which is as nice a place as any to finish off a ride.

# The Lake District

*A return to the Lake District with a choice of six offroad tours that range from easy to hard. The routes visit the major lakes and probably have the best scenery that England can offer, but remember how popular the area can be in high season, ride sensibly, and always give the walkers priority.*

## Ride 17    WINDERMERE

**Area:** The Lake District, Cumbria. From the northern end of Ullswater to the northern end of Windermere, and back.
**OS Maps:** Outdoor Leisure 5 and 7.
**Start & Finish:** Penrith town centre at grid ref 515303, or Pooley Bridge at grid ref 471243.
**Nearest BR station:** Penrith or Windermere.
**Approx length:** 42 miles (68km). Allow 7–8 hours.
**Ride rating:** Moderate/Hard.
**Conditions:** Mainly good riding surface. Two big climbs!
**R & R:** Cafés at Pooley Bridge; pubs at Troutbeck, at the top of the Kirkstone Pass, and on the road back to Pooley Bridge.

*From Penrith:* Penrith is a pleasant, bustling, small Lakeland town which is worth a look around. From the information centre in the middle, head out on the A6, signposted towards Clifton and Hackthorpe, going over the big roundabout and crossing the River Eamont. Go through the hamlet of Eamont Bridge, and take the next turning on the left, signposted to Pooley Bridge, which takes you over the top of the M6 motorway. Carry on over the railway line, passing a turning to the left and riding on through the hamlet of Stockbridge.

A short way on, turn left onto a narrow lane signposted to Cellernon and Askham. This winds steadily uphill bearing left. Ignore the first bridleway turning off to the right, and take the second a short way on riding up a track towards a farmstead. Ride through the first gate, and just past the second gate bear right across a grassy field, heading through another gate and on up to open grassland by the side of Heughscar Hill. From here there's a clear track marked by cairns; keep left, and it will lead you to a four-way bridleway signpost.

*From Pooley Bridge:* Pooley Bridge is a small village at the head of Ullswater, likely to be busy in summer. From the car park,

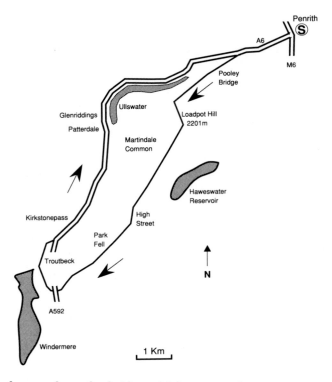

head away from the bridge which crosses the River Eamont, forking right on a corner by the small church to take the direction signposted to Howtown. At the next crossroad (signposted right to Howtown) carry straight on over, riding up a narrow lane and passing a large campsite on the left by the side of Howe Hill. Go through a gate here and out onto open moorland, climbing steadily up the track until you come to the same distinctive four-way bridleway sign by the side of a large cairn at the bottom of Heughscar Hill.

*The Ride:* From the bridleway sign take the direction to Howtown, following a clear but rocky trail across the fells. This soon brings you to a strange circle of stones known as the Cockpit where you bear right with the track. A little further on High Street, the Old Roman Road, clearly goes up the hillside, heading up Barton Fell with Arthur's Seat to the right beyond. Don't go up this way. Despite being clearly marked on the map, the track soon peters out into nothingness. There's a much better track which heads up to join the same route from the corner of Barton Park Woods – keep on towards these woods which are conspicuous ahead.

   The track drops down into a ravine, crossing a stream at the bottom before heading up the other side – change down as you go down to get up this short climb! Just past here fork off on the track which goes uphill to the left, which is easily followed past the cairn at Arthur's Crag. It is also easily ridden (if you don't mind a longish uphill), and after 1½ miles (2.4km) or so rejoins High Street which has once again turned into a recognizable track. Follow it on upwards, heading south past the Lord's Seat – from here it steepens as it snakes right and left, up to the high point at Loadpot Hill 2,200ft (671m) – a short way on are the conspicuous remains of a chimney which makes a good place to stop with fine views all around on a clear day.

From Loadpot Hill, High Street continues south and is more or less easy to follow as it goes down and up, down and up, down and up past the high points of Keasgill Head, Red Crag and Raven Howe. Just keep following the most obvious track, and ride as much as you can – if you're good, that means all the way! At one point the track bears right through a hole in a wall, and from there on follows a wide track between walls for some way. Occasionally there are small bogs to cross – judging the 'sink factor' of these is tricky – once I got it wrong and ended up going in down to my handlebars!

Past High Raise the scenery becomes increasingly spectacular. From Ramsgil Head you can see Haweswater down to the right; and to the left the hillside is cut away in monumental fashion to give a view down Riggindale Beck towards the southern end of Haweswater Reservoir. Following the 'Straits of Riggindale', High Street heads south to the 2,717ft (828m) high point of the ride where there's a giant tower of a cairn that can't be missed, which is a good spot for quiet reflection. From here, follow the track that heads on south.

A few hundred yards from the big cairn it dips steeply downhill over some rocks, and here the track splits. The most obvious route goes ahead and then bears left up to the mighty top of Ill Bell and is footpath. High Street, which is the bridleway, bears off to the right on a narrow grassy trail, heading downhill on the left (east flank) of the Troutbeck Valley which is ahead of you. After so much climbing, this should be a great descent, but unfortunately most of the track is pretty steep and narrow, so much so that in places it's easier to walk than ride. The good point is that fine views of the valley open out ahead; and when you finally get to the bottom and go through the gate, there's an excellent fast track running along the west side of Hagg Gill (the stream here is a good place to stop and cool off) beneath the hill named The Tongue.

Keep on until you come to a gate, with another gate set in the wall to the left and a derelict building (the first you come to) on the other side of the stream. Here you turn left to cross the stream over a small footbridge, following a track that runs along the side of the stream. Carry on following it along the side of the stream, joining a better, well-defined track which heads on

*Magnificent country on the heights above Ullswater with High Street stretching ahead towards Windermere.*

south away from the river, passing farm buildings at Long Green Head with farmland in the valley over to the right. A short way on you pass above the campsite and caravan park at Limefit Park. You can choose to fork left downhill to join the road here, though I opted to push further along the track that continues on the hillside, passing woods on the right and then taking the next right fork downhill, bearing sharp right by a house and then left downhill on a dark, slippery, rocky track before joining the A592 road close by Church Bridge.

*To Windermere:* Having come this far is around 22 miles (35km) offroad from Pooley Bridge, and a good four or five hours' riding. If you want to link up with Windermere and the BR station, simply turn left along the A592 – it's about a 2½-mile (4km) ride.

*To Pooley Bridge/Penrith:* The return is around 20 miles (35km) to Pooley Bridge, onroad all the way, but is nevertheless pleasant riding. Turn right on the A592 and head north. If you want to visit the pub at Troutbeck there's a short offroad section. Turn left onto a track just past the church; ignore the first right turning; cross a stream; and turn right uphill through the right hand of two gates which brings you up to some houses perched on the hillside. Turn left up a tarmac track here, turning right onto the road at the top, and the hotel/pub is about 200 yards (180m) further on. To continue push on in the same direction, which brings you back down to the A592.

Despite being an 'A' road, the A592 is comparatively quiet with few cars to bother you. It's a very long drag uphill from

Troutbeck, slowly churning those pedals, from 413 to 1,434ft (126 to 437m) at the top of the Kirkstone Pass. (But it's not that bad, and by no means such a severe climb as the Kirkstone Road, which comes up from Ambleside, and is known as one of the toughest climbs in the Lakes by the local road riders. The top section is fittingly known as 'The Struggle'.) At the top there's a pub/café which may be a handy place to stop, before a breathtakingly fast downhill towards Patterdale – you're likely to go faster than the cars, but the road is too windy to overtake them. This downhill goes on and on, levelling out past Brothers Water, and carrying on through Patterdale – where there's a hotel/pub – before reaching Glenridding with a choice of pub or cafés.

From here the road follows the west side of Ullswater which is pleasant riding, clocking off the miles with fine glimpses of the lake. Before you know it you're back in Pooley Bridge, and if you want to go on to Penrith it's another 6 miles (10km) or so of easy cycling. That makes a full distance of 47 miles (76km) – a serious and very full day out, but definitely a ride to remember.

# Ride 18    ROUND ENNERDALE

**Area:** The Lake District. A tour of the area between Windermere and Coniston.
**OS Map:** Outdoor Leisure 7.
**Start & Finish:** The car park in the centre of Hawkshead, on the B5286 west of Windermere, at grid ref 352981.
**Nearest BR station:** Windermere.
**Approx length:** 19 miles (31km) following the offroad route. Allow 3 hours, plus time to get lost and stop at the pub.
**Ride rating:** Moderate.
**Conditions:** Riding is mainly quite easy, but navigation through some of the forestry areas is confusing.
**R & R:** Pubs and cafés in Hawkshead; pub and hotel at Near Sawrey; pub at Satterthwaite; seasonal refreshments at Grizedale Forest Centre.

The centre of Hawkshead is a handy place to start from, but likely to be seething with trippers in the main summer season. If you've a mind to stay in the area the nearby Youth Hostel at Esthwaite Lodge on the west side of Ennerdale is comfortable and well situated for bikers, who can combine this ride round Ennerdale with the offroad ride round nearby Coniston (No.19) to make a grand tour of the area. Generally the scenery here is not of the best as many of the hillsides are covered by forestry, but by lakeland standards the riding is very accessible.

From Hawkshead take the road signposted to Near Sawrey

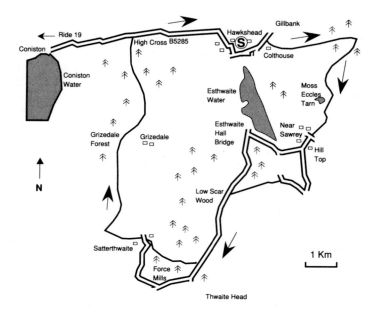

and Ferry (the ferry which crosses Windermere), but almost immediately turn off on a minor road to the left towards Gillbank. This bears right and left past some houses and a sign for a religious 'Meeting House', coming to a few more houses at Crofts Head after ½ mile (0.8km) or so. Just past a large house on the right, the bridleway goes uphill through a gate at an acute angle. Follow this good track on a steady uphill at Colthouse Plantation, climbing above Hawkshead and going through a few more gates before entering the forest, where the track can be very muddy in wet weather if it's chewed up by forestry vehicles.

After a while this track heads downhill through the woods, before coming to a clearing with a wide forestry crossing track. Ignore the hi-tech bridleway gate straight ahead with a signpost to Bell Grange, and turn right on the forestry track, following it round to the left on a slight uphill, bearing right on the bridleway track and following the small wooden signposts pointing to Sawrey, not to the Ferry. Past a gate you come out of the trees with the tarn at High Moss on the left. From here the track drops downhill across a magical landscape, bearing left to pass Wise Eeen Tarn, heading up through another gate, and then dropping downhill past Moss Eccles Tarn with distant views of high hills beyond.

Follow the hard track through a third gate, keeping downhill and bearing left to head steeply down into Near Sawrey. Past the farmyard here there's a small hotel which does excellent teas in the summer, and off to the left there's a good pub – the Tower Bank Arms. This is virtually next door to Beatrix Potter's old home at Hill Top (National Trust), now open to the public and a shrine to her many admirers. From Near Sawrey there are two potential routes to the next village which is Satterthwaite – a short onroad section, or a much longer offroad.

## Onroad

The narrow, minor roads connecting these two hamlets are very pleasant for bike riding with comparatively few cars, so it's no hardship to take this route. Turn right on the road at Near Sawrey, and then first left down a narrow lane leading to the east side of Esthwaite. Bear right at the first fork for Esthwaite, bearing right again for Esthwaite Hall Bridge where you turn sharp left (due south) for Thwaite Head and Satterthwaite. Follow the road for about 3 miles (4.8km), taking the first right to Force Mills where you turn right to Satterthwaite, a distance of around 7 very pleasant miles (11km).

## Offroad

The offroad route follows bridleways, which according to the OS map take a more or less direct route through the forestry which covers the area. However, as with riding in so much forestry land, one is confronted by a number of problems:
1. Once you leave the road, signposting is poor or non-existent.
2. The bridleways are often in very poor condition for bike riding, due to cut branches dumped all over the tracks.
3. There is a confusing mass of tracks all over the place, with most of the forestry's own tracks unmarked on the OS map.
4. With trees all over the place you can't see where you're heading.

From Near Sawrey follow the lane towards Ees Bridge, but take the first fork to the left which brings you to the road at Eel House Bridge. Turn right here, and after a few hundred yards you'll find a bridleway sign off to the left where the woods come close to the road past Long Slack. The route which follows is anything but simple, since the bridleways are such a mess. Rather than go into long, complicated instructions I will leave you to find your own way over the top and through the woods to Satterthwaite, and rest assured that you will almost certainly get lost!

## From Satterthwaite

A bridleway track signposted for Coniston leads westwards out of the village, turning directly off the road. Follow this track on a good surface past a playground, through a gate, bearing right past a river until you come uphill to the edge of the forest where there's a crossing track T-junction. Turn right here, following a wide, fast forestry track on a hard surface, up and down towards the Grizedale Forest Centre where you come to a blue cycleway sign. Fork right here if you want to visit the Forest Centre; fork left to carry on, following the same fast track northwards up and down through the woods – you can go pretty fast here, but be considerate to walkers who tend to string out across the track.

When you come to a sign showing the blue cycleway going straight on, and the red cycleway bearing left to High Cross, follow the red route, which continues as fast riding on hard tracks through open forestry land, eventually coming downhill to the road at High Cross. From here it's 1½ miles (2.4km) back to the start point at Hawkshead on a fast downhill; alternatively, if you want to combine this with a ride round Coniston (Ride 19), turn left from High Cross to follow the road on a super fast downhill, which weaves its way towards Coniston, some 2½ miles (4km) distant.

# Ride 19   CONISTON

**Area:** The Lake District. A ride round Coniston Water.
**OS Maps:** Outdoor Leisure 6 and Landranger 96.
**Start & Finish:** Car park on the east side of Coniston village, at grid ref 303977.
**Nearest BR station:** Kirkby in Furness.
**Approx length:** 17 miles (27km). Allow 3–4 hours.
**Ride rating:** Moderate.
**Conditions:** A hard climb up towards the Old Man of Coniston. Possible navigation problems going into the forestry area on the east side of the lake.
**R & R:** Pubs and cafés at Coniston; pub at Torver.

This is a fine ride round Coniston, with most of the distance covered offroad. The hills past the Old Man of Coniston on the west side of the lake are spectacular, while on the east side the route leads through lonely moorland and then on through a huge area of forestry. Here, as with so many forestry areas, navigation can be hazardous! This circuit can easily be combined with Ride No.18, making a great 34-mile (55km) offroad tour for a full morning's and afternoon's riding.

Head south out of Coniston on the Torver Road, and after a short distance turn right uphill onto the Walna Scar Road which is signposted. Follow this road straight on uphill – it soon narrows and becomes viciously steep, before levelling out and winding up towards the Old Man of Coniston, a large rock outcrop towering above. Beware of the quarry lorries carrying huge lumps of stone down from here; they use and need all the road, and you should get out of the way if you see one coming.

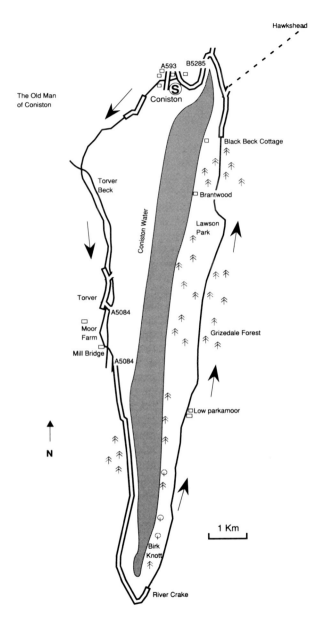

Carry on through a gate, leaving the tarmac and joining a good but rough track, ignoring the quarry track which goes steeply off to the right and passing the signposted footpath to the top of the Old Man, which also goes off to the right. You may care to leave your bike to climb up here to enjoy the spectacular view over Coniston on a clear day. From here the track gets worse as it starts to bear right uphill; ignore the first

*Tower Beck – a spectacular sight after heavy rain on the way back down to the lakeside at Coniston Water.*

grassy track off to the left, and then take the second unmarked track, which leads on a good grass surface between ferns towards Tower Beck with its spectacular waterfalls crashing down after heavy rain.

From here take the track which bears south-east along the side of the beck, becoming more obvious to follow as it bears left round the side of the spectacular waterfalls and then bears right down through a narrow shale gulley (impossible to ride) to reach the sturdy bridge that crosses the beck. This brings you down past a secluded house where you continue on the main track downhill to Scarr Head. Here you join a lane, turning left to ride down to the main road at Torver.

Turn right here past the two pubs, taking the first left signposted to Blawith (A5084). After about 75 yards (69m) turn right onto a tarmac bridleway track. Just before you reach the gate to Moor Farm turn off to the left, following the bridleway sign through a gate by a stile, going round the right-hand side of a field. Bear left through an opening in the hedge, keeping left down to the side of the stream which is still Tower Beck, and following it on a pretty track until you come down by the side of a house with a beautiful garden at Mill Bridge. Turn left to cross over the bridge here to rejoin the main A5086, turning right onto the road by the side of Coniston.

This is pleasant lakeside riding, and the road is wide enough so the cars don't seem too much of a problem. Follow the road southwards for 2 miles (3.2km) or so to Water Yeat at the bottom of the lake. This takes you off the large scale OS Outdoor Leisure map and onto Landranger 96 for a short while. Turn left here to cross the River Crake towards High Nibthwaite on the east side of the lake, going offroad once again by the phone box on the bend. Here there's a footpath sign pointing up to the right along a track. Turn up here; the footpath bears off to the left, and the track carries on uphill to become bridleway at Low Parkamoor.

Follow the track round to the left as it heads uphill on a good surface, bearing away from the woods at Birk Knott and continuing along the easy to follow, easy to ride track into open moorland, high on the hillside with fine views of Coniston opening out to the left. Carry on until the track splits, following the less distinct left-hand track downhill to the old farmhouse at Low Parkamoor. From here on the way is not too obvious, despite the bridleway being clearly shown on the OS map. The track passes close by the front door of Low Parkamoor, and then heads on up the hillside on a narrow grassy track, going north towards the edge of Grizedale Forest.

Keep straight on and you should join a track leading downhill to the main forestry track; if you come up against a high wire fence blocking the route, you have strayed too far to the east. Once on the forestry track, it's fast pedalling in a NNE direction towards Lawson Park where the bridleway bears left to take you down behind Brantwood – John Ruskin's old home and open to the public – towards Black Beck Cottage. From here, after a steep and sometimes slippery downhill, it rejoins the road. Turn right, bearing left to follow the road round the top of Coniston back to your start point, or if heading for Hawkshead turning right for a long uphill.

# Ride 20   BUTTERMERE

**Area:** The Lake District. A ride round Buttermere and beyond.
**OS Map:** Outdoor Leisure 4.
**Start & Finish:** Grange, just off B5289 south of Keswick in the North-West Lakes, at grid ref 257177. Alternatively start from Gatesgarth Farm at grid ref 196150, or at Buttermere at grid ref 175170.
**Nearest BR station:** None within easy reach.
**Approx length:** 30 miles (48km). Allow 4 hours plus stops.
**Ride rating:** Hard.
**Conditions:** Some technical offroad sections, but great country and fine views. Three big climbs.
**R & R:** Pub and cafés at Grange and Buttermere.

This ride divides into three offroad sections, sandwiching two long onroad sections. However the onroad riding is very pleasant, taking you through some of the Lake District's most spectacular countryside with mind boggling descents – you've never been so fast – and comparatively few cars to worry about. The offroad riding is by comparison TOUGH!

Grange is a picturesque little place which brings in the summertime trippers, boasting a café, a tea house, a shop, a chapel, a hotel and not much else. Apart from two roadside bays there is nowhere easy to park, which may make Gatesgarth Farm or Buttermere better alternative start points for this circuit. From the B5289 ride over the bridge and bear left and right through the hamlet, looking out for a bridleway sign pointing down a track to the left before you've gone far. Take

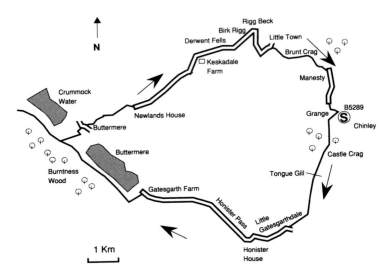

this direction, following it straight ahead and ignoring a fork off to the right, heading up through woods and then down to the side of the River Derwent close by a campsite, following the bridleway as indicated by a blue arrow pointing uphill. From here the track goes up, and steadily gets worse. As you head up Broadslack Gill towards Castle Crag the going gets rockier and rockier, and this old road can only be ridden with extreme difficulty – nevertheless, persevere by pushing and panting, keeping on up in the knowledge that you will be greeted by the usual incredible lakeland views at the top, with Derwent Water behind and Borrowdale spread out before you.

At the top you join a grass track, and from here on it's mainly downhill and mainly ridable, although rocky sections conspire to make some of the going difficult. Where the main track appears to bear right around the hillside, take the narrower track which goes downhill to cross the bridge over Tongue Gill. Take it easy as you go, as this is part of the 'Allerdale Ramble' and on a weekend you may meet quite a few walkers. Beyond the footbridge the track starts to head downhill, and becomes easier, eventually coming into sight of the road at Seatoller. Here you go through a gate where the footpath goes straight down to the road, while the bridleway bears round to the right, following alongside the road and joining it some way on.

Once you come onto road at Little Gatesgarthdale you have much of the worst part of the climb behind you, but there's still some way to go until you reach the Youth Hostel at the top of Honister Hause. From here there is a most amazing descent onroad along the Honister Pass. It seems to drop down incredibly steeply before levelling out on an endless descent, taking you virtually all of the way to Gategarth Farm and Cottage at the south-eastern end of Buttermere. (This is an alternative start for the ride, with better parking.) Now you are ready for the second offroad section.

Turn left through a gate, following the track ahead which runs across the bottom of Buttermere with the might of High Crag towering ahead of you. Past another gate the bridleway forks left uphill for Scarth Gap Pass, which looks to be a very serious undertaking, and right along the shoreside of Buttermere. Follow this latter route, which is relatively easy riding close by the shoreline, although occasional rocky sections do make riding difficult. On a summer weekend your progress will almost certainly be slowed by walkers. Some way along, the bridleway bears left to go slightly uphill through Burtness Wood, while a 'Permissive Path' continues by the lakeside. Take the bridleway, and then take the first turning which bears right downhill to bring you back down to the lake.

A short way on you come to the waterfalls at Sourmilk Gill, where there's a bridleway signposted going left steeply uphill

*Heading out from Grange with some difficult offroading
to come, plus some of the best views in the Lakes.*

to Red Pike, which again looks like a serious undertaking. From
here I opted to follow the bridleway straight ahead, with a
fairly rocky section leading to the shores of Crummock Water in
splendid isolated scenery. From here I had been advised that it
was possible to follow the bridleway that is shown on the OS
map all the way past Gale Fell and Great Borne, coming down
to Bowness on the shores of Ennerdale Water on the other side
of the hills. Then follow the track through the woods of
Ennerdale Forest, passing isolated Youth Hostels at High
Gillerthwaite and Black Sail Hut, and return via the bridleway
that goes over the Scarth Gap Pass. In practice this did not seem
like such a good idea. After a short way I had decided that it
could be a most vicious circuit – the bridleway that starts to
head uphill from Crummock Water round the side of Gale Fell
is alternately rocky, steep and boggy, and really not at all easily
ridable.

I abandoned that option, retracing my wheeltracks from
Crummock Water to the bridleway at Scale Bridge (left through
a gate) that leads on a good, flat track to Buttermere where
there's a hotel, a tea shop and a Youth Hostel, plus plenty of
dawdling trippers on a summer afternoon. (A second
alternative start point for the ride, with better parking.) This
was the start of the second road section, taking the long uphill
on the minor road that weaves its way uphill to Newlands
Hause – a long but steady climb with dramatic scenery all the
way. From the top there's a very fast downhill in the lee of
Knott Rigg, before the road flattens out and follows several
twists and turns before it comes to the turning to Little Town
over on the right in the valley.

This turn down a narrow lane is almost impossible to miss –
there's a really unusual lilac-painted clapperboard house on the
corner, which looks as if it's flown straight in from the southern
states of the USA! Turn right down to Little Town and, if
you've a mind, take the right turn signposted to the small
church – a pleasant diversion to a pleasant spot set in charming
surroundings. Carry on along the road to Little Town, heading
past a stile on the right as you go uphill past a few houses with
the bridleway going up through a gate just beyond – it's marked
'Footpath', but is clearly bridleway. The track bears right and
left uphill, keeping to the right side of the hillside on a good,
ridable surface before crossing the stream below Yewthwaite
Crag and continuing up the other side. For some way here it's
unridable, getting better as you near the top with Derwent
Water coming into sight ahead as you cross a footpath that
leads left up to the hill called Cat Bells and right steeply up to
High Ground.

Go straight on here, joining the track that leads down the
hillside from Hause Gate. It's easy enough to follow as much of
it is marked by railings, but the first part is ferociously steep –
one would imagine impassable by horses – and all the way
down is tricky until you come to the lower sections, where it
joins the road running along the west side of Buttermere. Turn
right here, and a short way on you'll come back into Grange
with its welcoming café at the end of this fine on and offroad
ride.

# Ride 21    ULLSWATER

**Area:** Lake District. A tour of the fells to the west and south-
west of Ullswater.
**OS Map:** Outdoor Leisure 5.
**Start & Finish:** Pooley Bridge at the northern end of Ullswater,
at grid ref 472243. Limited car parking.
**Nearest BR station:** Penrith.
**Approx length:** 23 miles (37km). Allow 5 hours plus stops.
**Ride rating:** Moderate/Hard.
**Conditions:** Very rough round the bottom of Ullswater – stop
and wait for walkers. Otherwise good up and down riding. The
climb up to Boredale Hause is hard all the way.
**R & R:** Pub and cafés at Pooley Bridge; serious food in opulent
surroundings at Sharrow Bay (get changed); pubs at Patterdale
and Howtown; small seasonal café at Side Farm.

This ride could be started from Penrith which has the
advantage of a BR station, adding another 10 miles (16km) or so
onroad with an offroad option. For convenience, I started from
Pooley Bridge giving a testing five-hour 23-mile (37km) circuit.

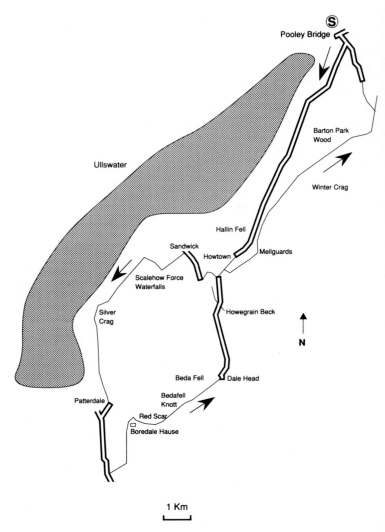

1 Km

Lester Noble of Orange, who suggested the route, reckoned he could 'ride it' in half that time. For me, despite a considerable amount of walking and pushing, it was still a rewarding circuit with plenty of spectacular scenery.

From Pooley Bridge, head out on the Howtown road, going south on the east side of the lake, past the Sharrow Bay Hotel. Carry on through Howtown on this pleasant, quiet road, crossing the cattle grid and zig-zagging uphill beside Hallin Fell. At the top the road drops downhill, passing a church on the left, bearing round the side of Howegrain Beck. Where the road goes straight on – signposted as a dead-end with a foot-path leading to Patterdale – take the right fork to Sandwick.

Just before you reach the few houses that make up this lakeside hamlet, bear left off the road up a track which is signposted as bridleway leading to Patterdale. This is the start of the track that runs round the perimeter of the south-eastern end of Ullswater. At first it's comparatively easy riding, dipping down to cross a beck in a sylvan setting at Scalehow Force Waterfalls. From there on parts of the track get tricky and may prove unridable according to your expertise; in summer you should also watch out for walkers and give way to them as necessary, and really this track is more suitable as a footpath than a bridleway.

Further on around Silver Crag the going gets quite difficult and a certain amount of portaging is necessary, but this only lasts a short time before the track widens and improves, leading you quickly down to Side Farm where in summer they sell welcome ice creams and other provisions, with a pleasant sitting-out area where you can study the route. From Side Farm go straight on, through a gate and along the track until you reach another gate at the end of a tarmac lane. To the left a sign shows the way up Boredale Hause, but I'm told that this way really is unridable, and besides you may not want to miss the pub at Patterdale.

Ride on down the lane, bearing right to cross Deepdale Beck and hit the main A592 road – the hotel/pub is a short way to the right. To continue, ride on along the road in a southerly direction for about 1 mile (1.6km) to Deepdale Bridge – you can't miss it as there's a telephone box by the roadside with bridleway signs pointing both right and left. Take the left hand track by the side of a house, going through a gate and crossing a field from where you can clearly see the track snaking up the side of Dubhow Crag, turning right for a short distance and then going upwards to the left. Go through the gate at the end of this field, and cross the bridge to join this track – left for about 25 yards (23m) (ignore the footpath going on ahead); right for about 30 yards (27m) (ignore the track going south); and then left and on up.

This is a long hill. Lester Noble tells me he rides the whole way up it; I preferred to push, and in some parts it is steep even then! At the top you come to a flat, level area called Boredale Hause, with the ruins of a few old mine workings, which is a good place to stop and reminisce. From here on a compass is handy to make sure you're heading in the right direction. Head due east from Boredale Hause, and then take the right hand of two tracks going south-east. This leads you round the side of Red Scar, heading along the edge of Beda Fell, and should not be confused with the track that heads north-east down the side of Hawk Crag to Boredale Head. (This route comes into view on the opposite hillside as your own route also bears round to the north-east.) Keep on heading steadily upwards to the top of

Bedafell Knott – it's a long way but, when you get up there, the views are incredible. A track appears to go on along the ridge, but you want the one that goes down the other side into the Bannerdale Valley, opening out a magnificent view to the south and leading down to the farmstead at Dale Head. The track passes a lonely ruin, and then heads on downhill on a mainly grass surface – most of it is easily ridable but parts can be tricky and it's not the sort of downhill where you can really open up.

At Dale Head go through the old farmyard, joining the lane which takes you along the valley to the farmstead at Winter Crag. Go on past the old chapel, with fabulous views behind, until you come out on the road close to Hallin Fell, which you rode past on the outward route. Turn right here, and then right again by the small church, joining a bridleway which goes directly up a steep short hill. At the top push on in the same direction which leads you up and over a hillock to a fast track that runs down towards Howtown. At the cattle grid by the bridleway signs, you can either go down to Howtown – where there's a pub with a walkers' bar which should be suitable for your battered and muddy state – or carry straight on as directed over the stream. If you go to Howtown don't take the easy route and ride onroad back to Pooley Bridge. The offroad section which follows is probably the most enjoyable of the ride, so backtrack to follow the offroad route.

Go through a gate by a smart house at Mellguards, joining the track which runs by the side of a wall, more or less parallel to the lake. Mostly it's quite fast going until you come to a right and left fork – the left says Pooley Bridge and is downhill; the right says Moor Divock and is very much uphill. Despite this, the Moor Divock route is the way to go as the Pooley Bridge fork takes you down to the road some 3 miles (4.8km) from the village. Ride on up by the side of Auterstone Crag, beneath the might of Arthur's Fell, a spectacular rock overhang, and continue to follow the clear track through ferns and across the moor. It soon levels out, and is fast riding past Barton Park Wood and on to 'The Cockpit' circle of stones.

From here you turn left to join the main track by a four-way bridleway sign (straight on if you want to ride back via bridleway towards Penrith), turning left for a fast and furious final descent towards Pooley Bridge, skipping and hopping at maximum speed before you reach the gate at the bottom. After that it's straight on down the lane for a ½ mile (0.8km) or so before you're back in Pooley Bridge.

# Ride 22    SKIDDAW HOUSE

**Area:** Cumbria. From Mosedale via Peter House Farm and Caldbeck to Mosedale.

**OS Map:** Landranger 90.
**Start & Finish:** Mosedale, at grid ref 354321.
**Nearest BR station:** Penrith, 13 miles (21km) from Mosedale.
**Approx length:** 23 miles (37km). Allow 4–5 hours.
**Ride rating:** Moderate.
**Conditions:** Quite testing in places.
**R & R:** Tea and cakes at the Mosedale Meeting House most days. Pub grub at the Sun Inn, Bassenthwaite Village, 1 mile (1.6km) off route. YHA Skiddaw House open 1 May to 31 October.

Hiding in the eastern lee of Skiddaw itself lies Skiddaw House, once the centre of a large sheep farm, now a seasonal Youth Hostel. One can understand why the accommodation is only on offer from 1 May until the end of October if you pass that way in winter. Make no mistake, this can be a supremely picturesque and rewarding tour on a still day with the snow on the ground, but when the wind blows from the north or north-west, conditions can become Arctic and all sources of water freeze.

The route is described in a clockwise direction from Mosedale in the hope that you will have the wind at your back

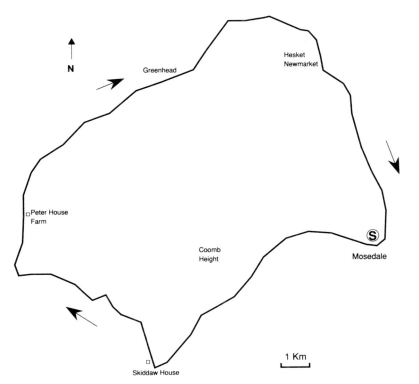

for the final leg down the Caldew valley, but of course you can start from any point that suits you.

## Mosedale to Peter House Farm

If you use the roadside parking between Mosedale and Swineside, return to the hamlet, then head north to Calebrack. The road is often wet, even when it's not raining! This is due to water draining off the high fells, and the ford at the Carrock Beck sometimes carries a fair amount of water. On the steep hill beyond the ford there's a sign imploring you to 'Try Your Brakes'. This must be a joke, I'm usually out of the saddle and struggling to reach 3mph (4.8kph)!

The little 'white' road towards Calebrack turns out to be tarmac, but there's an offroad shortcut at the Linewath turnoff to amuse you. At Calebrack a splendid disused mine road skirts the northern flank of the Caldbeck Fells, eventually coming out at Fell Side, but unfortunately there is no legal right of way. It's a classic old green road, especially above Potts Gill, and we had used it several times before very recent researches revealed its private status. (Sorry, we thought it was an old county road.)

The legal tarmac alternative which isn't too bad, winds around to Hesket Newmarket then back down to Fell Side, along to Greenhead. Then you do actually join an old county road across to Longlands. It gives you access to great views as far as the Solway Firth and a terrific descent down into the farm. The final stretch of tarmac takes you to Peter House Farm, but take your time as you climb past Over Water. The last time there were close to thirty-three wild geese in the surrounding fields, and I'm led to believe this is not unusual.

## Peter House Farm to Mosedale

Look for the signpost for Skiddaw House at the red gate, although someone will no doubt paint it a different colour between now and your visit. There are several gates to deter the less determined as you climb through the highest pastures, then when the skinny tarmac veers down to Dash Farm we go straight on for the big push up to the waterfall of Whitewater Dash.

The crux comes before the col. Bedrock Skiddaw slate pokes through on the final corner at the waterfall providing a loose broken surface – exactly when you don't want it. If you ride it you're better than me, but I'll do it next time; I'm going to wait until there's a dusting of snow to anchor the flakes of slate, take my time, and just toddle round. The high point, 1,631ft (497m), comes well after you cross the beck, on the side of Little Calva, then it's down to Dead Beck and on to Skiddaw House.

The view from Skiddaw House is great at virtually any time

*Wild country and big hills, and the views from Skiddaw House are great at almost any time of year.*

of year. You are hemmed in by huge hills on every side, and could well imagine you were many hours, or even days from the rush of the modern world. The fact is you're only half-an-hour from Mosedale, or perhaps a little more! And about the same from Keswick, although it will take you a lot longer in the opposite direction. The run down to Mosedale gets better and better. Technical bridleway with soft stoppers to start with; then wide form but broken track beneath Coomb Height; then high speed tarmac for the last 1 mile (1.6km) to Mosedale. Don't go unprepared. Even on the finest days the huge monolith of Skiddaw can produce its own weather system which can be quite severe.

# The Peaks and Pennines

*While it's one of Britain's most popular National Parks, the Peak District is poorly served by offroad routes for bikers and its footpaths are strictly out of bounds. Despite the lack of usable trails we've put together four great circuits that show off the immense difference between the White (south) and Dark (north) Peak areas, and a little further north have added two fine circuits across the Pennines.*

## Ride 23   CASTLETON

**Area:** The Peak District. A hilly circuit out of Castleton.
**OS Map:** Outdoor Leisure 1.
**Start & Finish:** Large car park with all-day parking on A625 on west side of Castleton, at grid ref 149829.
**Nearest BR station:** Edale.
**Approx length:** 26 miles (42km). Allow 5 hours plus. It could take at least 1 hour longer if you go all the way round the two reservoirs and return via Peveril Castle.
**Ride rating:** Moderate/Hard.
**Conditions:** Mainly good tracks, but some unridable sections with plenty of difficult uphills.
**R & R:** Pubs, hotels, shops and cafés in Castleton.

A great ride in spectacular scenery, and one of the few bridleway circuits in the Dark Peak area which, as with the whole Peak area, is badly off for bridleways. Many of the Peak footpaths have 'No Bike' signs, and you must abide by them. There are a lot of ups and downs on this ride, but fantastic views with some excellent riding, a small amount of pushing, and the attraction of beginning and starting in Castleton, one of the Peaks' prime honeypot villages.

Start from Castleton where there's a large car park, plenty of pubs, cafés, a Youth Hostel, an Information Centre, and a fine castle built in the days when the kings of England hunted here. It's a nice enough place to stroll around, and if you like the idea of going underground it has a famous series of caverns – Peak, Speedwell, Blue John and Treak Cliff.

Head out eastwards along the A625, bound for Hope, where you take the left turning for Edale. Cross the River Noe at

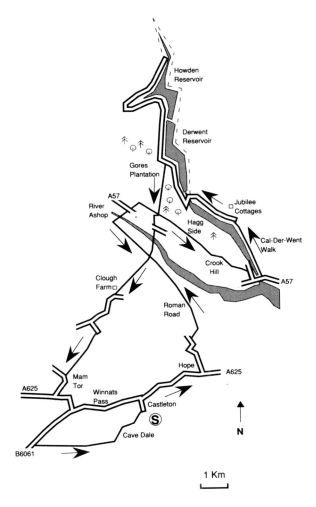

Killhill Bridge, ride under the railway, and a little further on
where the road goes right and left over Townhead Bridge bear
off right onto a track that leads up to Fullwood Stile Farm. Here
it turns left and commences a long and steady ascent into open
country. Pass through a gate to join the bridleway, following
the old Roman Road that goes up the side of the hill on a good
surface that is ridable all the way. Eventually it levels out, and
starts to follow the contours of the hillside, with fine views
back down the valley towards Castleton, though the day I rode
it started incredibly misty and foul.

The Roman Road becomes a fast track which closes with the
massive woods of Woodlands Valley on the right, where you
pass a Guide Post which is a tall stone block, ignoring the
footpath turning at the gate and going on to the next gate where

there is a clearly marked bridleway crossroads. Turn right here downhill, bound for Haggwater Bridge. At first you can let rip down the side of a grassy field, but from there on the track becomes difficult riding as it winds its way down through the woods on a zig-zag track with much of the surface washed away by the constant rainfall, leaving an unforgiving rocky surface.

Eventually you come down to a gate ahead. This is where the OS map shows the bridleway going on before doubling back; I found it padlocked, so I carried on down to the left on the rough old track, coming to the bottom of the valley and riding along the side of the woods to pass a bridleway sign showing I was indeed on the right track. Turn right over Haggwater Bridge here to cross the River Ashop, bearing left and taking the track which heads uphill towards the A57 road – a hard push on a rocky trail, but not far. Cross straight over the road, and take the track which goes on uphill straight ahead. At first this is tarmac and easy riding, but once it reaches the driveway to Hagg Farm (YHA), it becomes a rough unforgiving track where the flies in mid-August bothered me greatly!

After a hard push, or very hard ride, the track breaks into open ground, winding round to the left on a clear track until it comes up to bridleway crossroads at the top by the edge of Woodoak Coppice. Turn right here along the edge of the woods by Hagg Side, riding along the edge of a field, and carrying straight on ahead where you come to the bridleway leading left down through the woods towards Derwent Reservoir by Ridges Coppice. Ignore this and keep on along the side of the woods until the track breaks into open ground across Bridge-end Pasture, where it is easily followed as you head through a gate and on a speedy downhill towards the extraordinarily shaped Crook Hill ahead, with glimpses of the reservoir in the valley.

The bridleway bears round the left of Crook Hill – the way is really easy to follow, eventually joining a hard track running along the side of a wall. This leads you down to Crookhill Farm, where you turn left through a gate and bear left through the farmyard, carrying on downhill at a fast rate on a tarmac lane which brings you to a minor road close by the southern end of the Derwent Reservoir.

Turn right here, and then a short way on turn left over the bridge for a short distance on the A57 road. On the other side of the Derwent Reservoir turn almost immediately left onto a track which leads you to the bridleway that follows the perimeter of the reservoir, dubbed the Cal-Der-Went Walk. This is fast going, although there are a few ups and downs and you've got to take care with walkers, and it soon leads you to the only remaining part of the old village of Derwent (the rest was drowned to make the reservoir), joining a lane which runs on by the side of the reservoir towards the first great dam.

*The big dam between Howden and Derwent reservoirs, a
fine monument of Victorian architecture.*

Just past an aqueduct – a rather ugly long black pipe that
crosses the water – the lane heads downhill towards the dam
by Jubilee Cottage. A track goes straight on ahead into the
woods, and if you want to carry right on around the Derwent
Reservoir all the way to the top of the Howden Reservoir this is
the route to take. This extra loop will add about 9 miles (14km),
taking at least an extra hour. On a nice day it would be
recommended, but take note that at this stage of the ride there
is still some way to go and some big peaks to tackle. If you want

to follow it, the bridleway keeps pretty close to the west side of the reservoir past the Howden Dam, and then goes all the way to the top of Howden Reservoir near Cranberry Clough. Here there's a footbridge to take you over the River Derwent, although the locals say that this northern end of the reservoir normally dries up anyway. A bridleway leads back down the east side of the reservoir, joining the road by Upper Wood. This leads on down past the Howden Dam, where you can join the bridleway that goes up the side of Gores Plantation, close by Gores Farm, about 1 mile (1.6km) north of the first dam.

I opted to do without the extra circuit, and crossed the reservoir at the first dam, following the road past its mighty base where there's a picnic area. Continue on up past the Cycle Hire Centre, and then turn right onto the reservoir road, which I was glad to see is closed to cars on Sundays and Bank Holidays. Ride north past the top of the dam, and after about 1 mile (1.6km) the road bears left past Gores Farm to head around an inlet, where you bear left uphill on a clearly signposted bridleway. It's a good pull up through the woods of Gores Plantation, but ridable most if not all of the way. The track soon levels out and carries on by the side of the woods, following a mainly good surface which takes you down past Lockerbrook Farm – which looks like some sort of artists' community – passing through a gate with a handily situated waterfall for refilling your bottle.

The track climbs a short way before levelling out again, bringing you back down to the bridleway crossroads at Woodcock Coppice. Turn right here on a good downhill, passing through a gate before zig-zagging down the hillside to Rowlee Farm where a tarmac track takes over and leads you on down to the road (A57). Cross straight over here, carrying on downhill on the track ahead and crossing the River Ashop at Rowlee Bridge before heading on along the track which starts to head uphill. When you come to a left fork going uphill the other way, take this turning and ride on up – slow, steady and quite hard – the side of Blackley Hey. Where the track levels out you simply follow it ahead round the twists of Blackley Clough, and on to the bridleway crossroads where you originally turned right off the Roman Road down to the Haggwater Bridge.

The quickest way home from here is straight back the way you came, and a pleasurable ride it would certainly be. However, I opted to push on for the might of Mam Tor – a hard end to the ride which elevates it to the status of a classic. Turn right at the bridleway crossroads, following the track downhill into Jaggers Clough where the surface becomes more and more difficult as it gets steeper and steeper before hitting the bottom. At the bottom, follow the track which bears left uphill on a hard surface, before heading gradually down the hillside towards Clough Farm on the other side – it was here I overtook a whole pack of horses whose owners warned me, 'Our horses don't like bikes!'. They were moving very slowly, so I just hopped off and ran past carrying the bike.

Turn left through a gate to go past Clough Farm, ignoring a track that goes off to the left. The bridleway continues past the farm, soon coming to the minor road below. Turn right along the road here, following it on for 1 mile (1.6km) or so. When it bears left beneath the railway look out for a track that goes off to the left a short way on. Signposted to Backtor Farm this is the start of the bridleway that painfully leads you up towards Mam Tor. Ride on up past the farm, going through a gate where a sign warns cyclists coming down the hill the other way to take it easy – good advice as the bends on the way down would be completely blind. Follow the bridleway signpost which points left up towards Hollins Cross, following the washed-out track up the side of the hill at an angle that is not easily ridable.

Continue on up until you come to a gate in a wall; go through and follow the track on in the same direction gaining height along the hillside – the going becomes a little easier and it soon bears left to bring you up to Hollins Cross where there is a memorial. From here you get an incredible view out over Castleton and the surrounding countryside, looking forward to Mam Tor which is the next stage of the journey. The bridleway along the ridge up towards Mam Tor is pretty good, though you may find some pushing necessary until you eventually hit the heights at 1,696ft (517m).

Note that the bridleway doesn't go right to the top of Mam Tor, but cuts round the right side of it (the north side) by a fence before dropping down to the road just short of the summit. The track up to the Tor isn't marked as a bridleway or footpath, but you can push your bike up to the Trig Point on top of it, and when you go down the other side a series of steps leads down to the road where it's a fast downhill to the A625. Here you turn left, and then right by the lane that runs down to the Treak Cliff and Blue John Caverns. The next left will lead you quickly down into Castleton onroad via the spectacular Winnats Pass, and is the route that I would recommend to finish off the ride.

However, if you want another 40 minutes' or so offroading, there is a back route which gets you down to Castleton. Ignore the Winnats Pass turning and bear right along the B6061 road towards Sparrowpit, taking the first track that you see off to the left, which has a Caravan Park sign, opposite a hill named Snels Low. You soon pass Rowter Farm to the left while riding on a fast surface, keeping on through a couple of gates as the track runs between old walls. After about 1 mile (1.6km) a track comes in from the right, and the main track bears left. At the next gate look for a bridleway sign pointing left and right, which is well obscured by a pile of wood. From here on is the only part of the ride where I had problems with navigation. The left turn leads you across a field on a slight downhill following an easily defined grass track, but look out for a gate in a wall down to the right.

This is the turn off for the bridleway which leads you down along the bottom of Cave Dale, a deep fissure which is ridable at first, but becomes impossibly rocky as it heads more steeply downhill, after passing through the second gate just above Peveril Castle. This state of affairs only lasts for 200 rather unpleasant yards (180km) during which you feel at a marked disadvantage to walkers, before it once again becomes ridable (though watch out for castle visitors), bringing you down to the top end of Castleton after a technically tricky end to an energetic and exciting circuit.

# Ride 24   HIGH PEAK AND TISSINGTON TRAILS

**Area:** The Peak District. A ride along the two major disused railway lines of the Peaks.
**OS Map:** Landranger 119.
**Start & Finish:** The Parsley Hay car park at the northern end of the Tissington and High Peak Trails, at grid ref 148637, just off the A515 to the south-west of Buxton.
**Nearest BR station:** Buxton or Cromford.
**Approx length:** 50 miles (80km). Allow 5–6 hours.
**Ride rating:** Easy ride, but it's a good distance.
**Conditions:** Mainly good, fast railway track.
**R & R:** Pubs, cafés in Ashbourne; a few pubs on the road route between the bottom of the High Peak Trail and Ashbourne; cafés and pub in Hartington.

The High Peak and Tissington Trails follow disused railway lines through the Peak National Park, and are open to walkers, horseriders and cyclists. They are not really 'offroad' – the condition of the tracks is mainly so good that you could ride them on a road racer, but this circuit still makes a pleasant and easy day out for the mountain biker. Unless the weather is really foul, you can expect to meet quite a lot of people on these two Trails – in particular the Tissington Trail is popular for young kids learning the rudiments of cycling. So take it easy, and have an enjoyable ride.

You can start this circuit from Parsley Hay or from Ashbourne, and follow it either way. I recommend riding clockwise from Parsley Hay where there's easy parking if you're arriving by car, though you may prefer to start and finish with all the facilities of the market town of Ashbourne.

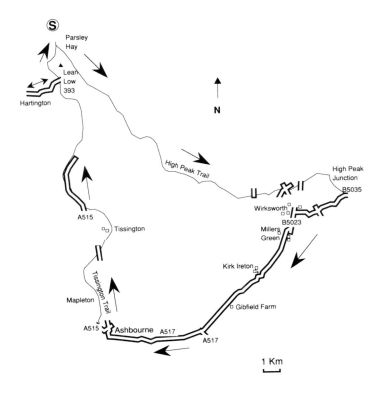

From Parsley Hay head south along the High Peak Trail, forking left after ¼ mile (0.4km) or so – the right-hand fork is the start/finish of the Tixall Trail, leading down to Ashbourne. The High Peak Trail is extremely easy to follow, going along the old railway line to the south-west, following embankments and cuttings and crossing the occasional road or lane. The going is fast, with much of the surface cinder track and occasionally tarmac as the route passes old disused railway stations. After a couple of hours or so you should come to the station at Middleton Top, where there's an Information Centre and a small museum. It's worth buying a guide to the trail here to read up on points of historic interest concerning the railway line, and with a pleasant outside picnic area Middleton Top is a good place to stop for a while.

Past the station there is the first steep downhill of the ride, with a fine view of Matlock opening out to the north just before the final very steep (8:1) and very fine downhill brings you to the end of the Trail at High Peak Junction. Here there's another railway museum in a very pleasant setting by the side of the Cromford Canal. The only way to reconnect with the Ashbourne end of the Tixall Trail is an onroad ride of 15 miles (24km) or so, but if you want to avoid the A6 there is a short

*Cinder tracks can give high speeds on these old Peak District railway lines, but go slow for walkers!*

section of bridleway to start off the route. The problem is that you have to head back up that steep hill – a slow, steady climb – looking for a bridleway sign on the left about two-thirds of the way up. This takes you onto a bridleway track passing under the hill via a bridge; turn right along it, and when you come out at the edge of the trees follow the track round to the right (not straight on) and left, riding on a fast surface which soon brings you down past a caravan site to the B5035.

From here there are all kinds of options to get you onroad to Ashbourne. The area is criss-crossed with footpaths, but bridleways don't appear to exist – nevertheless you need a map to deal with the maze of roads and lanes. I chose an up and down route through pleasant, quiet countryside that took about 90 minutes. Follow the B5035 into Wirksworth, a pleasant and architecturally pleasing Derbyshire village. Ride on through Wirksworth, bearing left downhill on the B5023 bound for Duffield. Less than 1 mile (1.6km) from the centre, take the right fork for Millers Green and Kirk Ireton, which is reached by a series of up and downs on narrow country roads.

At Kirk Ireton bear right past the church, and then turn left at the top of the High Street, taking the road to Blackwall, which is nothing more than a few houses and a bright red letter box. Keep on along in the same direction, following the road downhill until you come to what appears to be a major road junction. The right turn here effectively leads to nowhere, going to Carsington Reservoir construction site, and you turn left along this big, wide road, passing Gibfield Farm after a few hundred yards, and carrying on straight ahead at two junctions to join the A517 about 1½ miles (2.4km) further on.

Turn right towards Ashbourne here; the A517 is not too bad as A roads go, and soon leads into the town. Follow the signs for the town centre – it's a pleasant place to stop in, with some interesting shops, cafés and pubs. From the square in the centre of Ashbourne, start to head uphill on the A515 Buxton Road, but after less than 100 yards (90m) fork left for Mapleton, following the signs for the start of the Tixall Trail. This is a fast track similar to the High Peak Trail, mainly tarmac or hard surface, but the difference is that from Ashbourne it's a steady uphill virtually all the way to the end of the line. This is no bad thing – you can still keep up a fast pace. As there are walkers, hired bikes and kids learning to ride on this most popular trail, speeding downhill in the other direction at 20–30mph (32–48kph) is really not on.

Keep following the course of the railway line, passing the old stations and then riding through open country. There's no shelter here in wet or windy weather, so dress accordingly. The line finally reaches the top of the Trail at Parsley Hay having rejoined the High Peak Trail. Just short of here you may like to turn off the Trail at Hartington Station, turning left downhill for 2 miles (3km) into the quaint village of Hartington which has three tea shops (all closed by 5 p.m. when I visited!), a pub, a cheese factory open to the public, an award winning cheese shop, and nearby the impressive Youth Hostel at Hartington Hall which has plenty of room for secure bike storage.

# Ride 25    HIGH PEAK TO MONSAL TRAIL

**Area:** Peak District. A ride connecting the High Peak and Monsal Trails with some good trans-Peak riding in between.
**OS Map:** Outdoor Leisure 24.
**Start & Finish:** The Black Rock car park and visitor centre, just south of Cromford off the B5036, at grid ref 293557. Plenty of free parking.
**Nearest BR station:** Cromford.
**Approx length:** 38 miles (61km). Allow 5–6 hours, plus time for stops.
**Ride rating:** Moderate. Mainly easy riding, but it's a good distance.
**Conditions:** Fast riding on the 'trails', with some tricky sections in between.
**R & R:** Pubs at Cromford, Grange Mill, Winster, Monsal Head, Ashford in the Water, Youlgreave; Cafés at Cromford, Steeple Grange, Winster, Haddon Hall, Ashford in the Water, Youlgreave.

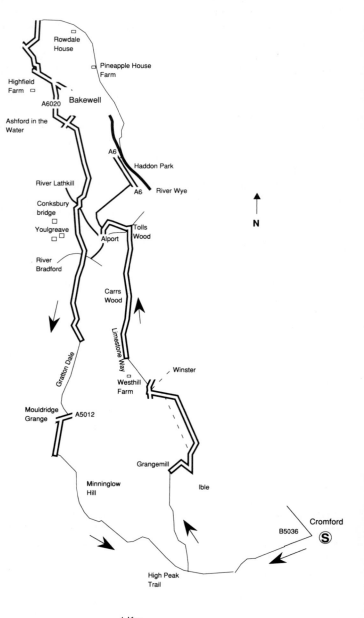

This ride spans a good chunk of the eastern side of the White Peak area, connecting the High Peak Trail in the south with the Monsal Trail in the north. Both these 'trails' follow old railway lines and offer effortless fast riding, while the land in between has plenty of variety with a good network of bridleways and minor roads to provide the link. The White Peak scenery is less dramatic and much less demanding than the Dark Peaks to the north, but on this route it provides an enjoyable day out with plenty of places to stop for pubs and picnics.

The Black Rock car park is a convenient place to start, though there are numerous other parks along the High Peak Trail. If starting from Cromford you're faced with a steep climb on the B3056, which must also rate as one of the busiest and noisiest B roads in the Peak District.

Once on the High Peak Trail, you'll find it's a cinder track in excellent condition, having closed as a railway line in 1967. You can make fast progress on a bike, but that depends on the number of walkers and other cyclists  who are out there with you. A surprisingly steep uphill leads up to the Middleton Visitors Centre (a train once ran away here!) where cycle hire is available, and then another steadier uphill brings you into open country past a huge quarry just before Moor Farm. The Trail crosses a lane by quarry works, and then follows by the side of another lane going due west. Just before the Trail bears right away from this lane, a bridleway turns off to the right through a gate; you can't miss it as the turn is just after a secluded farmhouse on the right, and just before an ugly, modern quarry works building.

Follow this track up the side of a field towards Griffe Grange, bearing left through the gate in the top corner of the field where it can be muddy. The track carries on along the side of another field, bearing right by the entrance to New Harboro' Farm where it joins a rough, hard track on a bumpy downhill. This brings you onto a much better track, heading north with a few ups and downs until you come to a grassy field ahead, just beneath a line of marching pylons. The course of the bridleway isn't obvious: go through the left gate, following an indistinct track across the field and then passing the big quarry on the left. This will bring you downhill to the road juction at Grange Mill, where a bridleway sign points back to show you have been riding in the right direction.

Cross straight over. (You may like to stop at the pub on the corner, but it's early in the ride yet.) Almost immediately turn right up a narrow line with a dead-end sign, passing old farm buildings with a 'Beware Bull' sign and then riding steeply uphill past Tophill Farm on the left. This is a delightful, ramshackle place, with the obligatory old railway carriage in the yard which no doubt once saw service on the High Peak Trail. At the next crossroads turn left, passing Whitelow Farm, which has more modern buildings, and bombing along a delightful fast track through open country across Bonsall Moor. I found it so delightful here that I overshot the next turning, riding on towards Brightgate. I then backtracked, but compromised by missing out the bridleway which follows the hillside, and took the very minor road up the side of the moor.

Another quiet road leads west, with a good downhill to the road junction at the B3056. Here you turn right and almost immediately fork left, crossing the next lane onto a track which is part of the Limestone Way. (You can divert to Winster here – it's a smart little place with some fine Georgian houses, olde worlde pubs and cafés, and the ancient Market House which is open to the public, care of the National Trust.) This is one of the few sections of the Limestone Way that is bridle/byway. Most of its route follows footpaths and roads, covering 26 miles (42km) between Matlock and Castleton. If you don't mind doing without a bike, it's a really enjoyable walk for another occasion – either a one-day non-stop marathon, or a much easier two-day stroll with Monyash the halfway point.

The first part of this Limestone Way byway leads downhill on a sunken trail. I found it littered by boulders which looked as if they had been purposely placed there, or maybe fallen off the back of a tractor – they certainly had to be avoided. Crossing a road (left turn to Elton where there's a Youth Hostel) the Limestone Way joins a narrow lane on a fast downhill to rejoin the B3056. This is a good descent, but be prepared to slow down as there are a few bijou houses on the way which means possible cars, not to mention walkers, tackling the Limestone Way. At the bottom the Limestone Way bears left through a gate onto a track that leads up to the rocky pass called Robin Hood's Stride. A National Park sign here says 'No Bikes', so do as they say and leave your bike behind if you want to investigate further.

The route carries on along the B3056. This is a wide road with few cars, and is mainly a pleasant, fast downhill through wooded countryside. Crossing the bridge over the River Lathkill, turn immediately right onto the side road signposted to Alport, following the dale with glimpses of the river weirs on the right. Alport is about ½ mile (0.8km) on; it's worth turning downhill to the left to check out this picture-postcard hamlet with its little houses lined up by the side of the river.

To continue, cross straight over the Alport road, and go steeply up a narrow track that leads over the hilltop above the dale. At first the track is fairly good, but when it comes to a gate by a big modern barn on the right it can degenerate into seriously muddy conditions. The only bridleway signpost here points left to Youlgreave; in fact bridleways go straight on ahead and 90 degrees right. You take the latter direction, passing the back of the barn and then following the wall by the side of Haddon Fields. It's reasonably good going and quite easy to follow, eventually heading down the hillside and going through a gate, to join a rough track that leads down to a car park by the side of Haddon Barn. When I rode down here there was a huge party of walkers coming up the other way, so take it easy if required.

Here you're on the A6, right opposite the main entrance to Haddon Hall, an imposing medieval pile overlooking the River Wye in a fine park. It's home to the Duke of Rutland, is open to the public between spring and autumn, and will no doubt serve you a nice cream tea. From here you have to ride a short way along the A6, looking out for the right turn to Haddon Park Farm which is signposted as a bridleway, although the sign is pretty small. The tarmac lane here crosses the River Wye and then bears right up the hill, passing part of the Monsal railway line (the London Midland service) which was diverted through a huge tunnel to pass underneath the Haddon estate and keep the Duke happy. This must have been a mammoth feat of engineering in 1860, and is in bitter contrast to today's philistine politicians who refused a tunnel for the M3 extension.

There's no access to the line here, and besides it is totally overgrown, but you can see the start of the tunnel which is now bricked up. If you've got time to spare, the bridleway follows an interesting route for a couple of miles, via woods and the hillsides above Haddon Hill towards Rowsley. However, the bridleway you want is back at the bottom of the hill, where it's signposted by a gate. At first it looks uninviting, with no obvious track or trail, but the going is quite easy as it crosses grassland above the riverbank. Passing a solitary house up the hill to the right, it then turns uphill by the side of a wall which brings you to a gate on the edge of Cook Woods. A hard track leads left here to join the south-eastern end of the Monsal Trail.

The Monsal line closed to trains in 1968, and the trail, unlike the High Peak and Tissington Trails, is only partly open to horseriders and cyclists. You can ride it for 4 easy miles (6.4km) or so, until the famous Monsal Dale viaduct bars the way. This giant bridge opened to a storm of protest in 1863. Ruskin declared, 'The valley is gone and the Gods with it, and now every fool in Buxton can be in Bakewell in half an hour ...'. Despite his views it's a fine piece of engineering which has blended with the landscape and is well worth a look at today.

A small sign on the platform at Ashford Station (now a private house) tells cyclists this is the last place to get off the line. Cross the bridge which goes over the line, and follow a lane down past Thornbridge Hall, a massive and most impressive looking house which now acts as a local education centre. The quiet road winds on downhill – one of the incredible things about this ride is that there don't seem to be

*The start of the Monsal Trail, with easy riding towards
the famous Monsal Dale viaduct.*

as many uphills! At the B6465, take the left turn signposted to
Ashford; alternatively if you want to see the Monsal Dale
viaduct from below, it's about 1 mile (1.6km) to the right, with
a pub close by. Ashford is quite a big place with a choice of
pubs and cafés, and from there you follow the A6 for a short
way uphill, heading towards Bakewell before taking the first
right turning down a lane by the side of Moorland View Farm.

This is pleasant riding, leading on an easy uphill to a T-
junction where you turn left for Youlgreave. More easy up and
downhills lead to a severe downhill at Conksbury Bridge. I
overdid it on the sharp left turn here and skidded onto the
wrong side of the road, so take it easy. Conksbury Bridge
crosses the River Lathkill in a delightful setting before a short
uphill; then the first left turn leads to Youlgreave which soon
comes into sight across the fields. Youlgreave is a big village
which has a Youth Hostel, famous summer 'well dressings'
(hangover of pagan rituals), and one of the best church towers
in the Peak District. There's a convenient pub opposite the
church at the first crossroads; from there you carry on downhill
to cross the River Bradford, where it's worth leaving your bike
to investigate the intricate series of weirs and waterborne
wildlife westwards up the dale. There's also a handy café on
the hillside about ½ mile (0.8km) further on.

From the river it's a long uphill heading south on a very
narrow lane; few cars pass, but it's infuriating if you have to
pull onto the verge to let them by. At the top of the hill you
unsurprisingly start to go down by the side of the woods at
Rock Farm, with fine views over the countryside ahead. Bear
left at the next junction, and then look out for the bridleway to

the right by the phone box at Dale End, close by the attractive looking Dale End House. With the exception of the High Peak Trail this is the last bridleway section of the ride, and in some ways it's the worst, while in others it's the best. Turn through the gate and ride past the Lime Kiln on the right, which comes complete with information board. Another gate leads you into the steep-sided Gratton Dale, and it's here your problems may start.

To begin with it's very popular since it is extremely pretty. When I rode through on a Sunday morning there were a lot of walkers, and I counted half a dozen bikes. Secondly, it is seriously muddy in wet weather. Thirdly, the southern end of the dale becomes very rocky and is tricky to ride. All three factors can make it a 'pushathon', which is acceptable as the surroundings are the finest of the ride. Bear left with the dale, crossing the stone wall and following the hillside round to the left. The track here becomes really unridable, but eventually leads up to a gate at the southern end of the dale. Here the track coming down Long Dale from Middleton looks a lot better riding, but would need careful checking out.

A fairly steep climb leads up the hillside ahead, bearing left when you see Mouldridge Grange (no more than a farmhouse) on the hilltop. The way is not too obvious, but keep on across the grassy field and then turn right when you can by the wall which brings you out onto the A5012. Turn right for a short way downhill, and then left onto a narrow lane which leads up to the High Peak Trail by Nine Miles Plantation. You'll see the newly refurbished embankment ahead, coming to a small car park where you turn left onto the Trail. Most of the way from here is a steady uphill gradient, though the exceptions are a long downhill past the Intake Quarry and the very steep descent from Middleton Top. However, you can only go as fast as the traffic: walkers use the High Peak Trail for a quiet stroll after Sunday lunch, while most bike riders take it pretty easy and are often accompanied by wobbling debutante children. Respect their right to be there; the Trail is not a race track and courtesy and consideration are what gets mountain biking a good name.

When you get back to Black Rock, it's worth checking out the rocks themselves. They are popular with local climbers and afford a fine view over Cromford to the north, where the big house on the far hill was built by Arkwright, who invented the spinning jenny. He never lived there, but you can visit the remains of his mill by the end of the canal. You may like to ride on to the end of the High Peak Trail, 1½ miles (2.4km) further on at High Peak Junction after a brilliant downhill which is great if there are not many walkers. There's a small museum here, which is open in the summer season, with a footpath leading along the canal towards Cromford. If you don't mind pushing, this leads to Arkwright's old mill which has an excellent café.

Cromford itself hasn't much to recommend it and has largely been ruined by through-passing traffic, but there is a bridleway which connects it to the High Peak Trail. Retrace your wheeltracks for about a third of the way up the hill, and then turn left off the Trail to cross under the line and join the bridleway, which follows the contours of the hill into town. You may like to push on along the A6 into nearby Matlock Bath; it's not my cup of tea and it suffers from desperate traffic, but it is a major Peak tourist spot.

# Ride 26    CHINLEY TO MATLEY MOOR

**Area:** The Dark Peak. A tour of high moorland.
**OS Map:** Outdoor Leisure 1.
**Start & Finish:** The War Memorial just over the railway bridge to the north of Chinley, at grid ref 041824. Roadside parking here. Alternatively, cheat by parking up at the top of the hill where the route goes offroad at Trial Hills.
**Nearest BR station:** Chinley.
**Approx length:** 13.5 miles (22km). Allow 3 hours depending on your uphill speeds, plus time to stop at the pub.
**Ride rating:** Moderate.
**Conditions:** There are some big hills. The final climb over the top from Birch Vale to Chinley is serious indeed. Very exposed on the tops.
**R & R:** Pubs and cafés in Chinley; pubs at Birch Vale and Rowarth.

Though quite short this is a real mini classic. It packs in spectacular views, long steep descents, some very serious climbs, and a tremendous variety of tracks – and there's an attractive pub at the halfway point. I rode it on a grim winter's day, accompanied by a raw northerly wind and occasional buckets of rain. I enjoyed it then, and you could enjoy it even more if the weather is kinder.

Chinley is an unexciting out-of-the-way place a few miles to the north-west of Chapel-En-Le-Frith, which has all the facilities that a small town can offer. To find the start point, turn right up a slight hill over the railway bridge, and the fine War Memorial will be before you. From here turn left for a long, taxing uphill that takes you along the side of Dry Clough and Throstle Bank on a road marked 'Unsuitable for Motors'. If you've arrived by car you could cheat and drive to the top; however, this misses a great final downhill, and as this ride is packed with hard climbs it seems silly to miss out on this one.

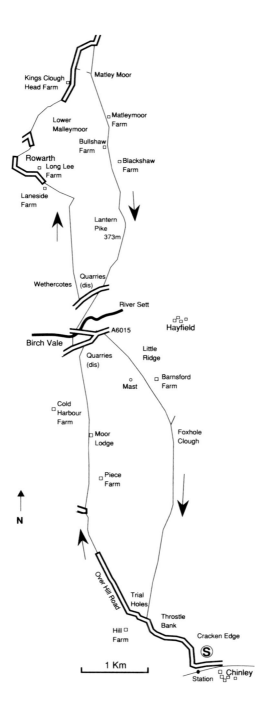

Matley Moor

Kings Clough
Head Farm

Lower
Malleymoor

Matleymoor
Farm

Bullshaw
Farm

Rowarth

Long Lee
Farm

Blackshaw
Farm

Laneside
Farm

Lantern
Pike
373m

Wethercotes

Quarries
(dis)

River Sett

A6015

Hayfield

Birch Vale

Little
Ridge

Quarries
(dis)

Barnsford
Farm

Mast

Cold
Harbour
Farm

Moor
Lodge

Foxhole
Clough

Piece
Farm

N

Over Hill Road

Trial
Holes

Throstle
Bank

Hill
Farm

Cracken Edge

S

Chinley
Station

1 Km

The narrow road soon leads away from Chinley, with fine views over the flat country to the west opening out over Toddbrook Reservoir. Past the small farmstead at Throstle Bank the road levels out, coming to a left-hand hairpin which leads back downhill. Here you go straight ahead, going offroad on a good track which is the start of Over Hill Road, heading northwards round the hillside. The going is more down than up, and the surface is mainly good as you speed past empty moorland, crossing straight over the Laneside Road (the right turn here is a bridleway), to join a rougher byway that snakes downhill on a rocky surface before officially leaving the Peak National Park at Moor Lodge.

Here the rough track joins a smooth lane, taking you steeply and very rapidly downhill past big quarries on the left. A few cars pull out here, so keep those fingers ready to haul on the brakes. This leads you down onto the main A6015 road at Birch Vale, 2 miles (3.2km) to the east of the conurbation of New Mills. Turn left along the road here, and after just over 100 yards (90m) look for a track going down the hillside on the right. The sign just says 'Keep to the Bridleway', so you know you're on the right track, going steeply downhill away from the house on the left to emerge in a yard by the side of the River Sett. Turn right out through the gates here, and then go left on the road for about 50 yards (45m), taking the first right turn up a track by the back of a fine crescent-shaped terrace of workers' houses.

This track leads quite steeply up by the side of woods – the surface is rough and broken, so at first it's difficult riding. It follows the side of a wall and becomes easier going as it leaves the trees, climbing steadily through open country and leading up to a road by a house. There's a bridleway sign pointing straight ahead here – I opted to make it the return route, and turned left up the hill onroad with great views out over the Birch Vale valley below. At the top of the hill the road goes straight on and begins to dip down the other side, while a track turns off to the right, which takes you back into the National Park. Follow this track through the farmyard at Wethercotes, pedalling straight on along a good surface on the byway that heads north.

The route bears left, hitting an unexpected sandy patch with good views to the north-west. It then heads downhill on an old broken track – once this must have been a fine old road with the remains of its smooth surface still to be seen, but now it requires concentrated technical riding as it leads you down past Laneside Farm, which when I passed by had been transformed into a bijou hideaway, complete with Porsche 911 in the drive. Join the lane here and bear left away from Long Lee Farm where I met the first of a number of (friendly) horseriders on that bleak winter weekday – I guess there must

*Good riding and some excellent tracks in the High Peaks,
not far past Kings Cloughhead Farm.*

be quite a few horseriders around when the weather is kinder,
so be polite and take care.

Follow the lane round to the right, crossing the stream by the
pub, which is in a delightful setting at Rowarth, and looks a
good place to stop. Just past here a bridleway leads off to the
right by the back of a few houses, following a crumbling track
on a slight uphill and then bearing left up the road to the
charming L-shaped terrace of houses which completes the
hamlet of Rowarth. It must be an exclusive place to live as
there's a gate across the road! At the corner of the L, turn right
along a signposted bridleway which leads you steeply uphill on
tarmac, with more great views over the beautiful Dark Peak
dips and hills ahead. Near the top of the hill watch for the
bridleway sign which points straight ahead through a gate; the
tarmac lane which is signposted as a footpath bears left on a
dead-end trail towards Cloughhead Farm.

The rough bridleway track leads steeply down the hillside,
crossing a stream in the valley bottom and then following the
track to join a dead-end lane at Low Matleymore. Here you're
right in the middle of fine moorland with little chance of being
bothered by cars, as you pedal on a steady uphill going
northwards past Kings Cloughhead Farm. A short way on
there's a spot of bother with the OS map. An inviting
unsignposted track to the right is shown as footpath, but this is
the way to go. The map shows the bridleway backtracking from
where the road bends left further uphill, but when you get there
you'll find there's no access short of hopping over the footpath
stile, and then following faint tracks across open moorland,
riding parallel with the road to rejoin the main track.

Follow this track on through a gate, heading south and joining an old road which bears left between walls past Matleymoor Farm. Past the five-way signpost by Blackshaw Farm the bridleway surface deteriorates, going through a gate and heading on a slight uphill across spongy moorland (take the left fork, though they both join), and coming to a gate at the foot of Lantern Pike by a National Trust sign. From here the bridleway follows the side of the wall beneath Lantern Pike; it's worth leaving your bike and walking the short way to the 1,224ft (373m) summit, which gives a spectacular view over the surrounding Dark Peak area and makes a good place for a picnic on a fine summer's day.

The views need to be good, as the track which leads on southwards round the side of Lantern Pike is not. It is badly eroded and prone to serious mud stirred up by horses' hooves; if it's been wet you may end up pushing more than riding this mainly downhill section with Birch Vale ahead. The going improves near the bottom, and eventually you emerge on the lane by the roadside house where you turned left towards Wethercotes on the outward leg, rejoining the bridleway that heads on down past the crescent of houses on the outskirts of Birch Vale.

Turn left along the road here, riding the short way up to the main road, and crossing straight over by the pub on the corner. The road ahead has a dead-end sign as far as cars are concerned; as far as you are concerned it's the start of the last and most serious uphill of the ride. Don't be fooled by thinking the radio mast must be on the top of the hill – this is one of those uphills that just keeps on going, fooling you whenever you think you've made it to the top. At first it goes straight as a die up the hill on tarmac, soon leaving the few houses behind. Riding up this hill is simply mind over matter, though one wonders what it would be like in the other direction – an incredible descent for sure. It eventually brings you to a signposted gateway which once again takes you back into the National Park, going offroad for the coming long section across the moor.

From here on the riding surface deteriorates, and some parts can be very muddy in wet weather. You're up high in the middle of nowhere, so this is not the place to be caught by foul weather when there are only sheep for company. The views are the best of the ride, looking out over Kinder Reservoir towards the mighty ridge between Mam Tor and Hollins Cross, with Castleton beyond. The track is mainly easy to follow, winding its way across the hillside in a more or less southerly direction, with a few parts that are tricky to ride as ruined old stone walls show the way. At long last the track levels and then begins to head downhill, leading through a gate where the riding surface improves to bring you quickly down to the road by a spinning windmill close to the Throstle Bank farmhouse. From here it's an extremely fast descent back down to the War Memorial at the end of a really great ride.

# Ride 27   WORSTHORNE MOOR AND HEBDEN BRIDGE

**Area:** South Pennines. A tour out of Hebden Bridge.
**OS Map:** Outdoor Leisure 21.
**Start & Finish:** Hebden Bridge Information Centre, at grid ref 992272.
**Nearest BR station:** Hebden Bridge.
**Approx length:** 25 miles (40km). Allow 4 hours.
**Ride rating:** Easy/Moderate.
**Conditions:** Mainly easy riding on good tracks. Navigation on Moor Lane going west from Hebden Bridge requires some care.
**R & R:** Pubs and cafés at Hebden Bridge; pubs at Heptonstall, Mereclough, Worsthorne (also fish and chip shop), on road past Brown Scout, and at Horse Bridge.

You may be closer to the South Pennines than you think. This ride is within easy reach of such major towns as Burnley, Blackburn, Halifax and Huddersfield, and while the surrounding industrial landscape may be pretty grim, this ride encompasses an unspoilt area of moorland with fine tracks and country roads that provide a good circuit. The riding is generally easy, there are some interesting places on the way, and Hebden Bridge makes an excellent starting point.

Hebden Bridge is billed as the capital of the South Pennines, built in a dramatic hillside setting on the profits of weaving, in the days when Hebden Water and the Rochdale Canal linked it to the outside world. Nowadays it is accessible by both railway and motorway, and is a popular place on the tourist circuit for those checking out this area. The OS map shows that its surrounding countryside is laced with a confusing mass of footpaths; there are also a few long bridleways and plenty of quiet country roads which this route attempts to make the best of, though with map in hand you may customize it as you wish.

From the Information Centre in the centre of the town, head out westwards, following the A646 bound for Todmorden. At the first traffic lights opposite a pub, turn hairpin right, joining a minor road that heads steeply up the hillside. As it bears round to the left it gives fine views over the nineteenth-century terraces and mills of Hebden Bridge, before you head away by taking the first left fork and riding on uphill to Heptonstall. This is a small weaving village, and very quaint too. In my experience the grocery store on the right does excellent filled rolls, and then you ride on up the cobbled main street, coming to the top of the hill and open country.

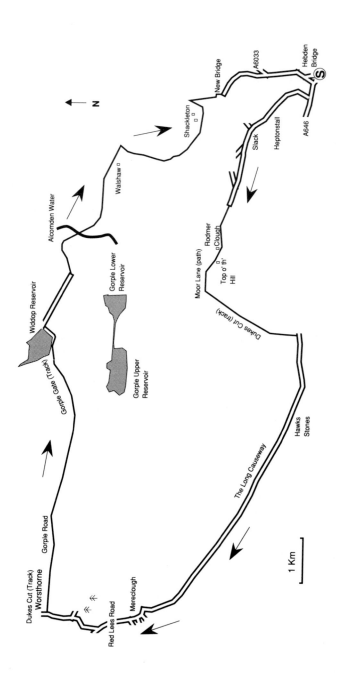

The road carries on through quiet farmland, taking the left fork at Slack to head westwards. Less than 1 mile (1.6km) further on, just past a phone box, take the track which bears off to the right where the road starts to bend left downhill. This is Edge Lane, and you follow it on for about 1 mile (1.6km) past occasional houses, looking out for the bridleway which bears left down the hillside into the valley. This turn is signposted to a garden centre but is easily missed, as the main track carries on to Gorple Lower Reservoir, heading into wilder country as it bears round to the north, which takes you in the wrong direction for this circuit.

In the bottom of the valley the route turns right along a driveway, bearing left to pass by the side of a smart modern conversion of an old farm building. A concrete track leads on to a brief uphill which brings you to the side of the aptly named Top o'th' Hill – another old house converted for modern use – before Moor Lane bears left and begins to head south towards the road, passing ruined farm buildings beyond an old track to the right. Here you should stay on the hard gravel track, before passing the radio mast where there can be a fair amount of mud.

Turn right along the road here, which is known as The Long Causeway. This was once a Roman Road, and is straight for 5 miles (8km) or so to Mereclough. It passes through attractive scenery with easy ups and downs and few cars to bother you, so it's enjoyable and fast riding. Just before Bank Top Farm the modern road leaves the route of the Roman Road, diverting in a loop around the hillside. Here you can take the offroad option, by following the unmarked bridleway track straight ahead down to Bank Top Farm. I asked the farmer which way to go from here; he directed me round the right side of his house and straight down the steep grassy hill, telling me to watch out for the Roman Centurion who is known to haunt the old ruined bridge at the bottom! There's no track here and the way is not very clear; asking for more advice, I skirted left round the back of Stiperden House Farm, and then followed the driveway back up to the road. All in all it would have been a lot easier (and quicker) to have stayed onroad!

The Long Causeway brings you to Mereclough, passing a pub and joining Lees Road to wind towards Worsthorne on the outskirts of Burnley. This is an unremarkable though pleasant enough place with a pub, a fish and chip shop, and an imposing church in its centre. To continue ride up the dead-end road by the left side of the church, passing the allotment gardens. This leads into the Gorple Road, an old trackway crossing Worsthorne and Heptonstall Moors in a west-east direction, which is easily followed all the way. As you leave civilization behind, the tarmac disappears and a rough surface takes over. Gorple Road wends its way up and down past

Wasnop Edge, Ben Edge, Wether Edge and so on; it would have been enjoyable, but the day I had chosen was grim and grey with a stiff, cold headwind which made riding quite unpleasant.

Past Gorple Stones the track narrows and deteriorates, passing above Gorple Upper Dam in wild surroundings and joining the Gorple Gate track. At the south-west side of Widdop Reservoir it goes steeply downhill and deteriorates still further, becoming difficult to ride in a few places. Once by the south side of the reservoir it improves again, passing Cludders Stack and opening out into a wide modern track built with uncomfortable broken stones. This leads you over the dam, and onto the road by Widdop Lodge.

Follow this road downhill for 1 mile (1.6km) or so eastwards – it's in the middle of nowhere, and you're unlikely to encounter many, if any, cars. Where it bears right by Brown Scout, follow the signposted bridleway track off to the left by the side of a footpath. (If you carry on down the hill here, you'll find the Packhorse pub.) This leads through fine iron gates on a concrete track which gives fast riding on the route of the Pennine Way. Bearing right downhill, the route leaves the Pennine Way which goes left northwards on footpath, heading south and dipping down to cross Alcomden Water at Holme Ends. It goes up the other side to continue on a rougher track which follows the contour line of the hillside past New Laith Moor, which is fast riding past New Laithes Farm, bearing left and right between the buildings at Walshaw Farm.

Here the route turns southwards, running above the steeply wooded valley of Hebden Dale with the well known Hardcastle Crags to the right and open moorland on the other side. It continues as fast going to the farmstead at Shackleton, where the OS map inexplicably shows the bridleway coming to a dead end. You have to go somewhere, so I recommend that you walk your bike and follow the wide track on a steep downhill through woodland, taking the right-hand hairpin at the bottom to join a tarmac lane down to the car park at Horse Bridge, close to the road. Turn left here, following the narrow road uphill on the hillside above Hebden Water. Joining the A6033, a fast downhill takes you back into Hebden Bridge, where the delights afforded by numerous pubs, tea houses, shops and cafés await you.

# Ride 28    ALSTON MOOR

**Area:** Cumbria. A tour across the North Pennines.
**OS Maps:** Landranger 91, 87, 86 (if returning on road).
**Start & Finish:** On the roadside at Kirkland, about 5 miles (8km) due east of the A686 at Langwathby, at grid ref 646326.

**Nearest BR station:** Appleby-in-Westmorland.
**Approx length:** 28 miles (45km) returning offroad, 26 miles (42km) returning on road. Allow at least 4–5 hours.
**Ride rating:** Hard.
**Conditions:** Most of the old mining tracks are in pretty poor condition, and where the tracks fade out navigation can be tricky. Two long climbs.
**R & R:** Pubs at Garrigill, Hartside Height, Melmerby and Ousby.

Mountain bike visitors to Cumbria flock to the Lake District, but seldom check out the country on the other side of the M6 motorway. Ten miles (16km) to the east of Penrith the Pennines rise dramatically in an uninterrupted chain. Here there is some

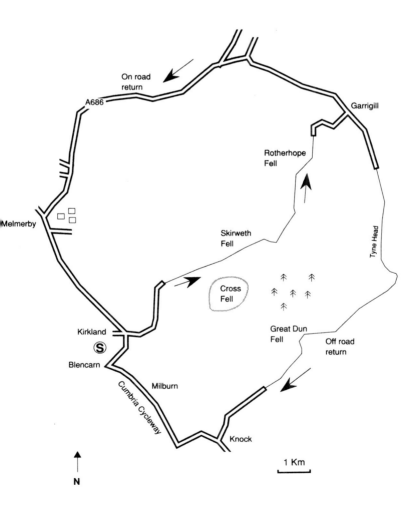

wild country, with a couple of handy bridleways that traverse the Pennines, crossing Skirwith Fell and Knock Fell on the way. Compared with the summertime crowds in the Lakes you will find this is quiet country, with riding that's as tough, demanding and exhilarating as almost anywhere in the UK.

We started this ride from Kirkland, a small hamlet at the foot of the Pennines, where the roads stop, and wilderness starts. It's handily sited on the Cumbria Cycleway which in this area links Skirwith, Kirkland and Blencarn before heading south to Knock and Dufton. It's onroad riding, but is still very enjoyable.

You can park in Kirkland by the roadside next to the phone box on the small green. From here turn left up an avenue towards the Pennines, passing some picturesque, award-winning holiday cottages, and then going on to a rough track which begins to lead up the side of Kirkland Beck. The going is almost immediately quite difficult, leading on a fairly steep uphill on a loose surface, before the track levels out again for a while and then begins to climb steeply up the side of High Cap, weaving in and out of disused mine workings.

Fine views soon open out behind, with the peaks of the Lakes clearly in view if the weather's clear. Above the first set of mine workings, care needs to be taken as the track appears to bend round to the left. This goes nowhere, and the unmarked bridleway route continues straight ahead by the side of a cairn over the moorland, with no more track and consequently some pretty demanding riding. Navigation here requires a mixture of compass and common sense. It's not a place to fool around as the top is very exposed with no help to hand, and lots of hard rock to fall on. The high point of the ride at Cross Fell where the Trig Point is at 2,930ft (893m) will frequently still have snow late into the spring.

Passing the screes beneath Cross Fell, the route once again joins a track which starts to head downhill. The track here is all that remains of a miners' road, though now the surface is only broken rock which requires good technical riding if you are to ride it all the way. Apart from a single tin hut on the way up, there's not a single building on this bleak moorland landscape until you come to a battered slate building which now acts as a bothy. Try the door and you'll find it's open, though on our visit the room inside had been left in a real mess and was pretty uninviting – you'd have to be pretty desperate to want to stop there, but in a snow or rainstorm, or if caught by the dark it could be a lifesaver.

Dropping down across Skirwith Fell, the track is joined by the Pennine Way. It comes and goes in terms of ridability, passing numerous mine workings and eventually joining a newly constructed track at the top of Rotherthorpe, built to provide vehicle access to the nearby radio mast. This provides a fast downhill as it zig-zags down the hillside towards

*Heading up the side of High Cap on the west side of the Pennines, with the Lake District spread out behind.*

Garrigill, but watch out for the 'speed humps' designed to divert rainwater into gulleys.

Garrigill is a quiet little place with a pub in a pleasant setting. From here you have two options to get back to Kirkland – either offroad or onroad. We had planned to go offroad, but started late and had underestimated the time required for the Pennine crossing. The offroad route we intended to take was south (right) from Garrigill, following the dead-end road uphill through Howgillsike and West Ashgill to join a bridleway track that follows Tyne Head southwards to cross the River Tees. It then bears south-west along the side of Trout Beck below Hard Hill, where the track stops though the bridleway continues. This would probably be hard riding, both in terms of navigation and turning your legs, until you reach the resumption of the track below the radio mast at Great Dun Fell. From there it passes Green Castle with a downhill all the way past Knock Pike to the hamlet of Knock on the Cumbria Cycleway, about 5 miles (8km) down the road from Kirkland.

We opted for the onroad return, following in the wheel tracks of biking friends for whom this was a regular trip. They had told us that despite being billed as an 'A' road, the descent down the A686 was truly memorable. From Garrigill the country road leads uphill and downhill on the south side of the River South Tyne where the Pennine Way continues along the banks, crossing the waters to come to the attractive hamlet of Leadgate from where you bear left on an endless uphill to join the A686. As 'A' roads go this is a good one, being just two lanes and not over heavy with traffic. However, the uphill climb goes on and on and is really pretty dull until, glory be, you hit the top at Hartside Height where you'll also find a pub.

This is also the start of an incredible downhill that wiggles and winds its way to Melmerby. It is a really fast one, and there's a temptation to use the whole road for cornering, although do remember that motorized traffic uses this route too! All too soon you hit the botttom at Melmerby where there's a handily sited pub on the left, which was happy enough to serve two bikers. You also turn off the main road here, following the lane ahead and keeping left through Row and Townhead, from where a track leads straight across to join the Cumbria Cycleway on the outskirts of Kirkland at the end of this high energy ride.

# Wales and the Borders

*Wales has some wonderful rides, most notably in the middle and south and in the border area. Out of season riding here is about hills, more hills, and not too many people; this selection of ten rides shows off some of the best on offer on both sides of the border.*

## Ride 29   MYNYDD MAWR

**Area:** Berwyn. From Llanrhaeadr-ym-Mochnant via Llanarmon Dyffryn Ceiriog and Llangadwaladr to Llanrhaeadr-ym-Mochnant
**OS Map:** Landranger 125.
**Start & Finish:** Llanrhaeadr-ym-Mochnant, on the B4580 12 miles (19km) west of Oswestry, at grid ref 128262. Car park in the village.
**Nearest BR station:** None within easy reach.
**Approx length:** 13 miles (21km). Allow around 2–3 hours.
**Ride rating:** Easy/Moderate.
**Conditions:** Much of this ride is onroad with lots of ups and downs. The short offroad section is potentially strenuous. Extending the ride across the wilderness towards the River Dee would make it a serious, long distance affair.
**R & R:** Pubs and cafés in Llanrhaeadr-ym-Mochnant; pubs and shop at Llanarmon Dyffryn Ceiriog.

This was a ride which didn't work out as planned. I had intended riding a mega circuit with a long crossing of the Berwyn wilderness, but deep snow on the hilltops and seriously cold winds (in spring time!) called for a change of plan. The result was a much shorter circuit, much of which was onroad, but this is delightful riding, following a switchback of narrow lanes through forgotten countryside with some brilliant views. A highly recommended short circuit for those who like to take it quite easy.

Llanrhaeadr-ym-Mochnant (LYM) is one of those Welsh villages with a seriously unpronounceable name. It's also well away from any big towns, and right on the borders of an impressive area of wilderness. With the Afon Rhaeadr flowing through its middle it's a delightful one-street place which appears to be quite busy, with a choice of pubs and cafés to choose from, plus several B&Bs if you want to stay overnight.

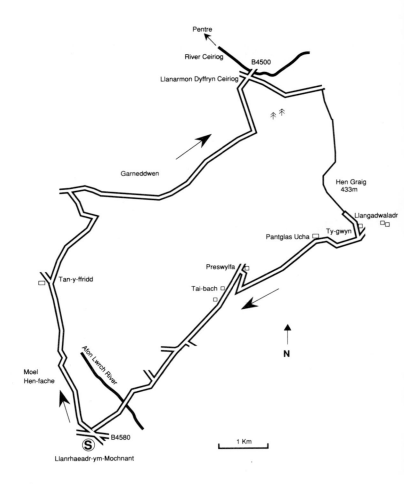

My route was based on the premise that I was about to undertake a seriously long circuit, and for that reason I opted to start with 7 miles (11km) or so onroad to the next village of Llanarmon Dyffryn Ceiriog (LDC). From the small car park on the east side of the village, head uphill past the police station, and then take the first turning on the left. This leads northwards on a narrow, switchback country lane, taking you up and down through really beautiful countryside as you follow the side of the Afon Lwrch river. Take the right-hand fork at Tan-y-ffridd, steadily gaining height, going right again at Tyn-y-ffridd where there's a large farmstead. A moderately serious uphill takes you up onto the ridge to the south of Garneddwen. When I pedalled along here in mid-April there was deep snow with more to come – the views were still pretty good, with the Berwyn wilderness stretching to the north.

At the end of the ridge the road leads steeply down towards

*The ridge to the south of Garneddwen can be a bleak place in cold weather, even with tarmac under your wheels.*

LDC. This is a great descent, and with few cars around you can really go fast. LDC is a charming little place, blessed with a small village shop/PO, two pubs and a church by the side of the River Ceiriog, though one suspects it may be popular with car-borne trippers in summer. From here I had planned to strike out across the Berwyn wilderness, following the dead-end lane signposted to Pentre which is as far as I got. From here a track leads westwards over high ground before dropping down to rejoin civilization in the River Dee valley on the other side, joining the B4401 just outside Cynwyd (where there's a Youth Hostel). I'd then planned to head south to Llandrillo, following a dead-end lane up Cwm Pennan and onto a track which joins the B43912 to make the connection back with LYM, a distance of some 40 miles (64km). With deep snow on the hills and a biting Siberian wind, discretion played the better part of valour and I turned back; it was without a doubt the right decision, and that ride lies waiting for another time.

To continue the circuit back to LYM purist mountain bikers should stick with the official bridleway which heads steeply up the hillside on the south-west side of LDC, joining the track that leads south across the hilltops close by Hen Craig. Navigation is not easy here; keep on the west side of Hen Graig and follow the track down the steep hillside to a sheep pen (big sheep country), joining a track that follows a stream towards the Lwnt farmstead. It can be muddy here, and with hawthorns on both sides it's also a bad place for punctures, as I discovered.

Follow the track out onto the road by Ty-gwyn. Some interesting bridleway tracks head eastwards from here if you want to go exploring offroad, while narrow country lanes lead back towards LYM, winding and wriggling their way through the hills with plenty of ups and downs; in particular there's a really good downhill as you pass the small chapel on the hillside above Preswylfa. From here it's around 3 miles (4.8km) back to the start point at LYM. It's a good ride in itself, and if you want more you can extend it in a number of directions with interesting potential for offroading on bridleways that head northwards round the side of Moel Hen-fache.

# Ride 30   LAN FAWR RIDGE

**Area:** Montgomeryshire. From Montgomery via Lan Fawr and Chirbury to Montgomery.
**OS Maps:** Landranger 137 and 126.
**Start & Finish:** Montgomery, on the B4388 south of Welshpool, at grid ref 223965. Parking in and around the town.
**Nearest BR station:** Welshpool or Newtown.
**Approx length:** 21 miles (34km). Allow around 4 hours.
**Ride rating:** Moderate.
**Conditions:** Good riding, but be prepared to take care with the navigation. The steepest climbs are onroad.
**R & R:** Pubs and café in Montgomery; pubs at Old Church Stoke, Priest Weston, Chirbury.

This is a real little classic, starting in the wonderful small Welsh town of Montgomery, crossing Offa's Dyke Path through low country, and then climbing to follow the magnificent ridge of Lan Fawr with marvellous views over Wales to the left and England to the right. I rode it in foul weather with biting winds and heavy rain and enjoyed it; in fine weather it should be a great ride.

Montgomery is a delightful little place, a town that's no bigger than many villages, overlooked by a fine old castle on the hillside, above which it is well worth climbing. The town square boasts a handful of shops, an interesting art gallery, and a tea shop cum café, which on my visit was a great place to finish off the day. If you're into antiquities, take time out to visit the church on the other side of the road, and see if you can locate the 'phantom' robber's grave.

Turn right out of the main square, turning down the hill and out of town on the south-bound B4385. Just before a right bend, look out for a bridleway track on the left, going through a gate in a fence and following the track along the side of the recreation ground. This leads to an ornamental park; turn right along a tarmac track between the two large ponds, and follow it between woods and out of the park until you reach a cattle grid by the crossing for Offa's Dyke long-distance footpath.

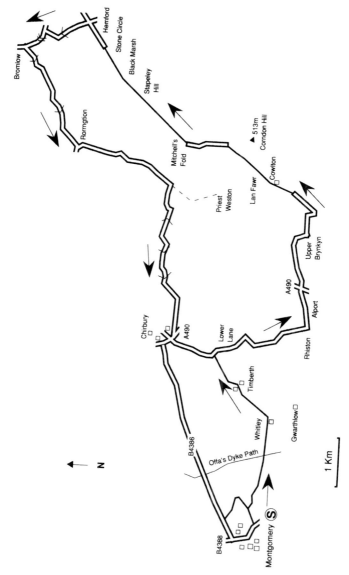

The OS map shows the bridleway turning right to follow the LDP here, but it's a miserable way to go in wet weather, following the side of fields with no very obvious way out onto the road at Gwarthlow Farm. Better to go straight ahead along the tarmac lane to Whitley Farm – this is not shown as a right of way, but joins with a bridleway immediately behind the farmhouse. Turn right through the gate, and cross the farmyard to the next gate, joining a track that follows the side of fields to the large farmstead at Timberth. Go straight ahead through the farmyard here, following a track downhill and then bearing left

*Fine scenery on the mid-Wales borders with mainly good, hard tracks to ride on.*

to follow the side of the woods up on the hillside. The way here is not too obvious, but just keep going on across the next grassy field and you'll come out onto Lower Lane, hopefully by the bridleway gate.

Turn right along the quiet country road here, taking a left turn at the T-junction at Rhiston. This soon leads across the main A490 at Alport; go down the steep hill ahead, joining a rough and sometimes muddy track to cross the river valley, and then going steeply up the other side for a short way to come out on a smooth tarmac lane by Upper Brynkyn. This leads you to the road; turn left by the house on the corner, and start to head uphill until you come to the pub at Old Church Stoke, which looks a welcoming place with fine views from its garden towards Montgomery and its castle. Past the pub bear left and then sharp right by a phone box, to head steeply up the side of the hill. As you approach the top look for an unmarked narrow tarmac lane on the left, which is the start of the ridge ride.

Ride along this lane which leads fairly steeply up between high hedges, eventually coming to a gate and joining a rough track by the side of the solitary house in a magnificent position at Cowlton on the hilltop. From here there are tremendous views over the surrounding country, but it's also very open to the weather and I was forced to take refuge in a dilapidated barn while a good dose of wet Welsh rain lashed the hillside. From here on the track is mainly good riding and easy to follow, keeping along the ridge past Lan Fawr and the forestry by Corndon Hill, before dropping downhill to cross the road above Priest Weston. On the other side the track becomes less distinct, bearing right by the ancient Stone Circle at Mitchell's

Fold and following a slight uphill to the top of Stapeley Hill with more superb views on all sides.

When the track starts to go down the side of Stapeley Hill, take care with your navigation. It's a fast and enjoyable descent, and before you know it you'll rush on down past the south side of the huge block of partly felled forestry ahead – this is the wrong way to go, and once at the bottom there's no easy way out from the area called Black Marsh. Slow down and look out for the correct bridleway route which swings left to follow the top western side of the forestry, and then bears right down through the woods on a rough, bumpy track that can also be seriously muddy.

Beyond the forestry the route goes onto OS Landranger 126, joining a tarmac lane which leads to the road ahead above Hemford. Turn left at the crossroads here for the start of a long up and down section on ultra-narrow country roads, many of which look almost forgotten as if they rarely ever see a car. A steep, winding descent leads into the valley, passing the pub above Bromlow which appeared to have been shut up for good on my visit. Beyond Bromlow follow the signs to Rorrington with more ups and downs back onto OS 137, then either going southwards straight ahead to the pub at Priest Weston below the Lan Fawr ridge, or turning right to Chirbury from where it's just over 2 more miles (3.2km) along quiet roads back to Welshpool.

## Ride 31    LLANFAIR CAEREINION

**Area:** Montgomeryshire. From Llanfair Caereinion via Llanllugan, Mynydd Clogau, Bwlch y Garreg, Cefn Gwyn and Llanllugan to Llanfair Caereinion.
**OS Maps:** Landranger 125 and 136.
**Start & Finish:** Llanfair Caereinion, at grid ref 103061. Small free car park up the hill going south on the B4389 towards Newtown.
**Nearest BR station:** Welshpool.
**Approx length:** 21 miles (34 km). Allow 4 hours.
**Ride rating:** Easy/Moderate.
**Conditions:** Mainly easy riding with good tracks and straightforward navigation, though the narrow roads on the way out can be confusing.
**R & R:** Pubs and cafés in Llanfair Caereinion; pub at Carno.

Llanfair Caereinion is a pleasant enough little place, on the main A458 Mid-Wales road a few miles west of Welshpool. Turn over the bridge that crosses the Afon Banwy, and then follow your nose up past the church to a small signposted car park on the left. When you return there's a a handy café here on

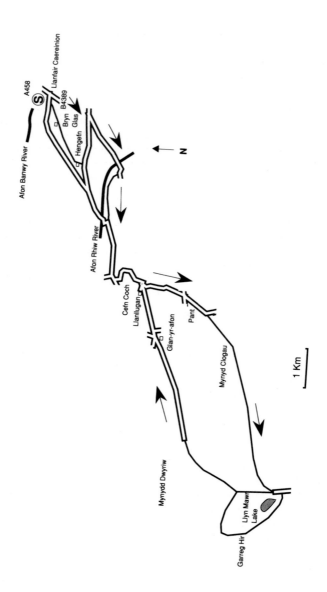

the corner, as well as a choice of pubs and a fish and chip shop nearby.

Turn left out of the car park, heading up the hill. After a few hundred yards fork right off the B4389, following a minor road signposted to New Mills. Just a few yards on, an unmarked track bears off to the left; this is the bridleway, leading on a steady uphill on a good, hard surface. On the right it passes immaculate gardens at Bryn Glas with fields away to the left, snaking right and left more steeply uphill to join an old road that runs along the top of the hill between hedges – good going when it's dry, potentially quite muddy when it's wet.

Go straight ahead through the farmyard at Hengefn, opening and closing the gates as you go. On the far side a hard track leads on uphill past hen coops, before heading down to join the road with a fine valley panorama ahead and the distant peaks of the hills of Mynydd Clogau where you're bound ahead of you.There are all kinds of variations on the route to get to these hills, but I was pretty happy with the way I found, which mixed peaceful country lanes with an excellent offroad section.

When the farm track hits the road, turn left by the house on the corner and follow the road eastwards. The OS map shows a bridleway going due south downhill here, but it's by no means obvious, so ride on for ½ mile (0.8km) or so to the first right turning which goes steeply downhill. Follow this narrow lane down into the valley. At the bottom the road bends left to cross a stream by a well-hidden caravan park/camp site shown on the OS map, and then bears right uphill. Where the road bends sharp left a track goes straight on along the side of the valley – this is the next bridleway section. Follow the track past the farm on the right, following an old road with a beautiful view over the valley and the Afon Rhiw below. Mostly the going is good, until you come to the final section of track which follows an avenue of trees. When I rode it this part was impossibly muddy, with a mini torrent flowing down the middle after recent heavy rain; the answer is simply to go up the hillside a short distance, following hard ground above the track until you see the gate ahead and the road.

Turn west to follow the road towards Cefn Coch, turning off after just under 1 mile (1.6km) to follow a narrow lane steeply downhill into the hamlet of Llanllugan. Follow the road straight through and uphill the other side, heading south over the crossroads to Pant. Less than ½ mile (0.8km) further on, just past a left turning, take the bridleway track that forks off to the right towards Mynydd Clogau, the start of a long offroad section.

From here on it's really good riding. The track is in excellent condition as it passes through a wild landscape on a steady uphill, bearing towards the south-west. It runs for just over 3 miles (4.8km) and is easy to follow to its south-western end

*Riding in the Carreg Hir area, where you normally see few folk around.*

where it starts to head downhill, passing a farmstead on the hillside below to the right as the lake of Llyn Mawr comes into view. Here the track crosses a cattle grid to join a tarmac lane, with a number of options for the return route.

The simplest way is immediately to turn sharp right downhill along the driveway that goes towards the farmhouse. This joins the bridleway track which passes the back of the farm buildings to head due north. Another option is to find a pub – the nearest is at Pontdolgoch (grid ref 938012) which is due south 2 miles (3.2km) off the route, but may provide an interesting diversion. The third option is to seek out something a little more challenging. For some tastes the track across the moorland may seem too easy, but if that is how you feel there are plenty of bridleway routes heading across more wild terrain with no such easy tracks to follow.

The bridleway which runs along the south side of Llyn Mawr heads towards the highest point of the whole area, Carreg Hir at 1,591ft (485m). The turn-off is through a gate a short way down the lane from the farm, with a sign indicating that only cars with hang-gliders are welcome. A good track leads on for a short way past Llyn Mawr, but from there you follow an indistinct track through the grass by the side of Carreg Hir in fine surroundings. The going is OK, though with its bumps and lumps and a slight uphill some may prefer to walk it. From there on navigation gets a little tricky. After coming to high ground you cross what appears to be a really good track that is shown on the OS map reconnecting with the return trail. However, something went wrong for me here and I ended up dragging the bike along a steep hillside through waist-high bracken, and then fording a deep stream cutting, floating with the occasional dead sheep, to find my way back to the trail. If you've got time to spare you could spend a pleasant few hours exploring the tracks and trails that go out towards Mynydd Dwyriw here; if not you'd do better on the easy route.

Once back on the right track the going is straightforward, though the condition of this northbound track is poor in places, with some enormous holes which require slamming on the brakes and careful riding. Much too soon the offroad comes to an end, at the start of a long downhill passing a camp site and coming to crossroads at Glan-yr-afon. Once again there are all kinds of options for the return route from here. I chose to follow the river eastwards towards Llanllugan – this route passes a beautiful waterfall, and in the spring there's one long lane which is lined with daffodils from end to end.

Past Llanllugan, rejoin the outward route for a while, following the road uphill and then bearing east and north-east towards Llanfair Caereinion – it's all agreeable and easy riding on very quiet roads. You can either ride on direct to the start point from here, or at the top of the final downhill by the phone box go a bit higher to rejoin the outward bridleway. This is the route I would recommend, finishing more offroad than on with a good downhill back to Llanfair Caereinion.

# Ride 32   LONG MYND

**Area:** Shropshire. From Church Stretton via Little Stretton, Plowden, the Long Mynd and All Stretton to Church Stretton.
**OS Map:** Landranger 137.
**Start & Finish:** Large car park on the south side of Church Stretton, at grid ref 452937.
**Nearest BR station:** Church Stretton.
**Approx length:** 18 miles (29km). Allow about 3 hours.
**Ride rating:** Moderate.
**Conditions:** Mainly good riding. It's a steep and very long offroad climb to the top of the Long Mynd.
**R & R:** Pubs, cafés, etc in Church Stretton; pubs at Little Stretton and All Stretton.

Here's another mini classic which takes you in a big circuit from the honeypot tourist town of Church Stretton, along the magnificent Long Mynd ridge with only gliders for company. The route is approximately 50:50 onroad/offroad, and apart from a seriously long uphill to the top of the Long Mynd is easily ridden most of the way.

Church Stretton is a popular place with the tourists, in the shadow of the huge Long Mynd ridge and easily reached by rail or car with the A49 main Shrewsbury road passing close by.

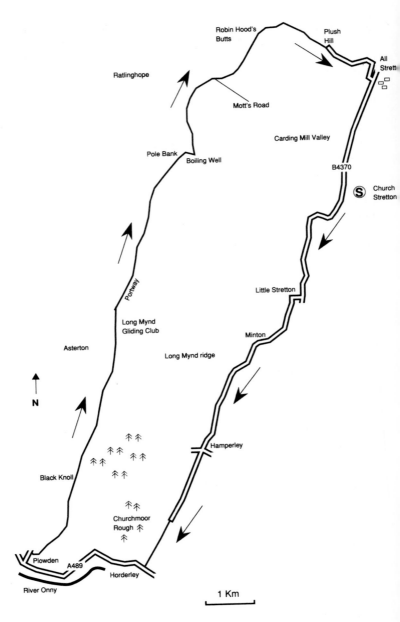

The town has a large municipal car park which makes a good start point, and its fair share of antique and tea shops, plus the handy Long Mynd Cycles if you need spares or feel the desperate urge to get a new bike.

Turn left out of the car park into the main street, and then right along the B4370 towards Little Stretton. Thankfully the nearby A49 takes 99.9 per cent of the traffic, as the B road winds through pleasant countryside and past bijou cottages on its way through Little Stretton. From here take the dead-end road uphill through Minton and on to Hamperley, passing through a farmyard and eventually leaving the road to follow a rough track along the side of fields. The bridleway continues south-west along the side of the woods at Churchmoor Rough, and for a short distance the way is none too obvious. Keep on ahead, and then on down by the side of a rough, bumpy field, bearing right down a lane by the farmstead by the side of the A489 at Horderley.

Turn right for 2 miles (3.2km) along the main road here. It follows the valley of the River Onny and would be much more pleasant if it was a country lane, but nevertheless the traffic is not too bad. As the A489 goes downhill look out for the right turning at Plowden, going quite steeply uphill on the narrow road that leads north towards Asterton.

A few hundred yards up this hill the bridleway doubles back up the hillside on the right, passing through a gate. This is the start of a long, steady uphill to the top of the Long Mynd – the going is good, though steep, and the views over to Wales get better and better as you go higher. Carry on through the sheep pens, bearing left with the main track to climb past Black Knoll. Once on the top the track levels out into a series of gentle ups and downs, with extensive woodland on the right-hand (south-east) side of the ridge. After two miles (3.2km) along the top of the ridge you approach the Long Mynd Gliding Club, with several signs warning you to keep to the trail. As gliding clubs go it's in a fairly spectacular position, and often there's a fair amount of activity here. The club's driveway leads out onto the Portway, an ancient road which is now sadly a modern road that continues along the top of the ridge. It's the kind of road that occasional cars potter along, out for their 'Sunday afternoon drive in the country'.

The Portway is none the less pleasant riding, and continues past the Trig Point at Pole Bank, the high point of the ride at 1,693ft (516m). Just past here you can cut the ride short at Boiling Well by taking the right turn going steeply downhill into Church Stretton. It's better to turn left towards Ratlinghope for some more offroading (this road was closed to cars when I rode here in the spring), before forking off right on the first bridleway track. This leads across open moorland, bearing right downhill past Mott's Road (a direct bridleway route to Church Stretton via the Carding Mill Valley), and then swinging east at Robin Hood's Butts for a really good downhill, speeding across open grassland towards the valley below. At Plush the track hits the road which winds steeply on downhill into All Stretton. From there it's just over 1 mile (1.6km) along the B4370 back to Church Stretton.

# Ride 33   TALGARTH TOUR

**Area:** The Brecon Beacons. A tour of the eastern area.
**OS Map:** Outdoor Leisure 13.
**Start & Finish:** Talgarth, on A49/A4078 east of Brecon, at grid ref 155336. There is a large free car park on the outskirts of the town.
**Approx length:** 52 miles (84km). Allow about 7 hours, excluding stops.
**Nearest BR station:** None within easy reach.
**Ride rating:** Moderate/Hard.
**Conditions:** Variable, but mainly ridable. Some severe uphills.
**R & R:** No pubs directly on the route; Talgarth has limited facilities.

This circuit has some taxing offroad riding, taking in a couple of the big hills of the Brecon Beacons. A good part of the total distance is onroad, but the roads are mostly so quiet and delightful that riding on them is a pleasure. I originally rode this route clockwise, but came to the conclusion that it would be better to do it anti-clockwise which is the way I have described it. This has the advantage of giving a wonderful offroad downhill from the top of Mynydd Llysiau, though you miss the long onroad downhill through the Mynydd Forest. Whichever way you do it there are some fierce uphills; it really is quite a tough marathon, with no pubs or other diversions directly on the route to distract you from the serious business of offroad riding.

From the centre of Talgarth head south on the road signposted to the Mid-Wales Hospital. Follow this minor road all the way to Pengennffordd, joining the main A479 for about ⅓ mile (0.5km) before forking left onto a byway track just as you come to the woods – if you reach the pub, you've gone too far! Follow the track past buildings at Pant-teg-uchaf, passing more woods on the left and joining a tarmac lane after about ½ mile (0.8km) offroad. Carry straight on ahead here, passing the riding centre and then turning right at a T-junction. A short way on there's a track up to the left, unmarked except for a National Park sign telling you to 'Keep your dog under control/sheep about/etc'.

An optional offroad route to get to here from Talgarth is to follow the byway that skirts the side of the gliding club, and then follow another byway past the remains of the ancient hill fort at Castell Dinas. This is fine when you're fresh into a ride, but is quite hard and really not rewarding when there's still so far to go.

The track is the start of a long uphill up the side of Rhiw Trumau, which for most riders is likely to be a 'pushathon' up to the cairn that marks the top at 2,028ft (618m). Don't despair

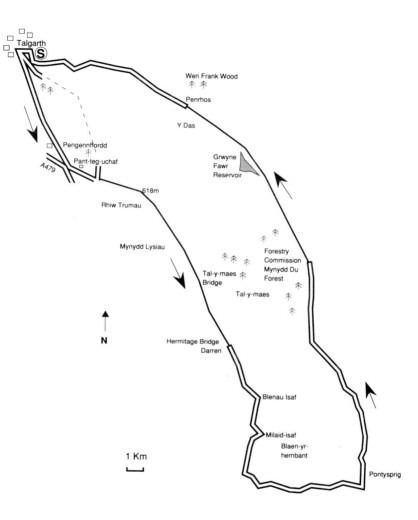

— it is not a good downhill if you're coming in the other direction, and there's a classic to come on the other side. After heading up the rubble track between trees, the bridleway goes on uphill through gates to a sheep pen where it bears right up the side of the hill on a badly eroded but easily followed track. It's steep going here, but the view over the valley to the right below gets better and better as you gain height.

Before long you're up at the conspicuous cairn. Turn left to go through the 'gap' that leads over the top here, ignoring the track which heads south-west down the hillside, even though it looks inviting. On the other side of the ridge a rubble track leads downhill for 100 yards (90m) or so before coming to an effective dead end; here you turn hairpin right to join a really magnificent grass track which heads off along the side of the valley beneath Mynydd Lysiau, steadily losing height on a perfect gradient for easy, fast riding in a magical landscape.

Keep on going downhill, drawing level with a great swathe of ugly forestry on the opposite hillside which makes the landscape a little less magical. For a time the track becomes really narrow and is slower going as it runs beside a wall, before becoming a grassy track once again as it heads on down to the old stone Tal-y-maes Bridge. On the other side of the stream, continue to follow the track in much the same direction, with a brief burst of uphilling before going through a gate and joining a tarmac track by the side of woods at Tal-y-maes.

Carry on down the valley, passing the farmstead at Darren over to the right, close by the Hermitage Bridge, keeping on in the same SSE direction and eventually joining the road proper by a bridleway sign marked by a horse insignia. From here on the road is delightful, becoming an old track that can hardly see more than a few cars a year. Past a house with smart gardens on the left, take care to take the left fork downhill, passing a small chapel in an idyllic riverside setting – a grand place for a picnic if no one is about, and no sacrilege as the chapel now serves as part of an outward-bound centre.

The fairytale road weaves on past a few well-hidden houses, bearing right after a house on a corner called Blenau Isaf, as it heads south with a few ups and downs. Follow the road round to the left as it hooks uphill past Milaid-Isaf, keeping on south to pass a bridleway sign pointing up a track to the left. This bridleway leads steeply uphill and then across wild ground past Blaen-yr-hernbant to the Forestry Commission Mynydd Du Forest. If you can find the way down past the old disused farmstead at Ffordd-las-fawr it's possible to ride on through the woods to emerge on the road just below Penwyrlod. Amazingly, the Forestry Commission do have the occasional blue bridleway blob to help guide you through these woods, but as with so much forestry many of the bridleways have simply disappeared. Finding the correct route is a nightmare, and I gave up after a wasted hour.

Better then to stick to the road, which becomes more of a proper road but still stays quiet as it bears east eventually to reach a multiple crossroads by a solitary phone box, just above Pontysprig. From here you follow the road going north through the Mynydd Du Forest, gradually gaining height as you head through the forestry. This is certainly a good downhill in the other direction, but being on tarmac is comparatively easy to ride uphill. Keep riding up this road which becomes a byway track as it crosses the river, heading on uphill from the picnic site by the side of the woods. Don't follow the lane along the valley floor here – it leads to the base of the reservoir dam, and there's no way up from there!

The byway which continues uphill to the dam at the east end of Grwyne Fawr Reservoir is stony but easily ridable. For a brief diversion you can ride across the top of the dam here to check out the view, then carry on following the track by the side of the reservoir, heading out into wilder country on an old road now in a poor state of disrepair. Keep following this track as it steadily gains height and bears round to the left, becoming muddier and less rocky under your wheels and eventually leading to the top of Y Das by a cairn, with splendid views over the landscape to the north-west.

From here the track bears right to plunge downhill on a track that is at first too steep and rocky to ride. It zig-zags down the hillside and, as it drops, riding becomes more possible, with the track bearing round to the west to head down towards Wen Frank Wood on a grassy surface. If you think it's tricky coming down, you'd better believe it's worse going up! Eventually the unmarked route passes between a wide avenue of trees near the bottom of the hill, leading straight ahead to a tarmac lane in the middle of nowhere at a place called Penrhos. Turn right here and then first left, crossing a cattle grid to continue on a quiet lane which brings you rapidly downhill towards Talgarth, passing the Mid-Wales Hospital.

## Ride 34   SARN HELEN

**Area:** The Brecon Beacons. A tour of the central area.
**OS Map:** Outdoor Leisure 11.
**Start & Finish:** Brecon Beacons Mountain Centre, to the south-west of Brecon off the A470, at grid ref 976262.
**Nearest BR station:** None within easy reach.
**Approx length:** 30 miles (48km). Allow around 5 hours, excluding stops.
**Ride rating:** Easy.
**Conditions:** Mainly good tracks. Navigation through forestry from Garwnant Forest Centre is tricky.
**R & R:** Café/picnic area at Brecon Beacons Mountain Centre; pubs at Ystradfellte and Penderyn.

This is a fine circuit round the central area of the Brecon Beacons. There's a fair amount of onroading, but apart from an unpleasant stint on the A470 this is all enjoyable riding, and there are excellent offroad sections along the ancient Roman Road of Sarn Helen and the drovers' road on the side of the Glynn Tarell Valley.

The Brecon Beacons Mountain Centre is a good place to start and finish this ride. If you come by car there's plenty of parking space, and inside the building you'll find books, maps and an information centre with helpful staff; while downstairs there's

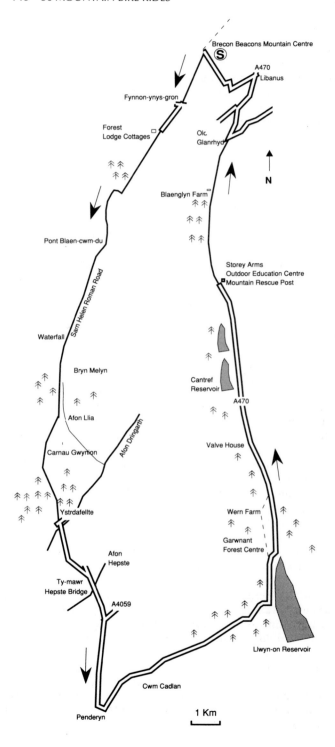

a café/picnic area with outside seating and really fine views across to the mountains, with a garden which is a good place for kids to play in. The Centre is open every day of the year except Christmas Day from 9.30 a.m.–5 p.m. (4 p.m. in winter). Alternatively, you could start this ride from Brecon itself, making your way to the Mountain Centre by minor roads and a final stretch of bridleway, adding some 5 miles (8km) to the total distance.

Turn left out of the Mountain Centre, keeping left along the side of the woods and following a track over open grassland, which is fairly easy going. This soon brings you to the road ahead at Fynnon-ynys-gron. Go straight over here and along the lane ahead, riding through the gate by Forest Lodge Cottages and joining Sarn Helen, the old Roman Road. This is excellent riding and easy to follow, skirting the side of the mountains as it passes Forestry Commission woods on the right.

The track bends round in a loop, following a fine avenue of hawthorns which are ablaze with red berries in the autumn. Swinging round to the south the track climbs uphill for a while, before bending left and dropping downhill to Pont Blaen-cwm-du, a fine place with stark hills on the left and rolling valleys away to the right. The track bears sharp left over a bridge here, heading uphill on a rough surface which is more like a river in flood after heavy rain. It's interesting to ride, though you'll be excused for a little pushing. At the top the track continues to follow the contours of the hillside on a good surface in a magical setting, though during my ride there really was water, water everywhere, nowhere more so than when crossing the waterfall marked on the OS map. This proved a tricky place to stay dry.

After some more easy climbing to Bryn Melyn, the Sarn Helen track keeps straight on to join a quiet road just past Rhyd Uchaf, ending a fine start to this ride. Head south along the road which is a biker's delight – straight, more downhill than up. When I rode it only a shepherd's Land Rover and a car parked by the verge were there to remind me that the world of automobiles still existed. The road bombs on through a wild landscape, following the course of a river on the left (Afon Llia), and then passing a cattle grid and entering forestry where a track off to the right is the continuation of Sarn Helen.

From here Sarn Helen goes all the way to Neath, which I am told is a fine ride, except that the return involves a lot of miles onroad. I had toyed with the idea of following Sarn Helen round to the edge of the Coed y Rhaiadr forestry, where the OS map shows a connecting bridleway heading eastwards through the woods to rejoin the road. This was discounted in favour of staying on the road by my own extreme anti-forestry feelings, and the advice of the Warden at the Mountain Centre – 'You'll definitely get lost.'

Keep on south along the road past the forestry with its marked picnic area. A short way on the road bends sharply left on a downhill, and here you go straight ahead up a track, shown as byway on the OS map though signposted as a footpath. Follow this round to the right on a grassy surface heading up between drystone walls. After an easy uphill the track swings left between the twin rock outcrops of Carnau Gwynian with old mine workings in their sides, heading on through a gate and then bearing left (don't take the less obvious track going straight ahead) across heathland and rock Pillow Mounds. This brings you down to a gate in a very muddy corner of a field, and then to an overgrown grassy track which heads downhill into the small hamlet of Ystradfellte.

After around two hours' riding I was delighted to reach this place at 1 p.m. looking forward to visiting the PH which is clearly marked on the OS map. However, when I arrived the pub was closed, and looked as if it had been closed for some time! Ystradfellte is also a famous centre for exploring the half dozen or so Brecon Beacons waterfalls – they're all located to the south, and can be found with an OS map, but must be approached on foot.

To continue the ride, follow the road past the church and over the Afon Dringarth, and head steeply uphill before the road levels out with a series of easy ups and downs through more forestry. Coming once again into open country, this quiet road then starts a fast downhill, passing Ty-mawr and crossing the Hepste Bridge to join the main A4059. Turn right onto this road for about 1 mile (1.6km) – there's little traffic, and it's mainly downhill into Penderyn which gets it over quickly. Here there's a pub in an uninspiring setting if you want to stop; just opposite the pub you turn left onto the narrow lane with a rusty old sign pointing to Cwm Cadlan.

This is another really quiet road – just one car and one lorry passed me in 4 miles (6.4km) or so. It heads steadily uphill past the cattle grid to cross open moorland, before heading rapidly downhill through forestry to reach the Llwyn-on reservoir, a great ride on a deserted road. When you come to the crossing road that runs along the side of the reservoir, a short path leads down to the 'beach' here, which is a really pleasant spot to stop on a fine day if the water's not too high. To continue, turn left (northwards) along the road which is also extremely quiet. After just under 1 mile (1.6km) you come to a turning signposted to the Garwnant Forest Centre, and have the option of turning off for a ride through the woods, or just keeping along the road to join the A470.

The Forest Centre could be worth a visit, though was closed when I called by. The picnic area is good, and there's an impressive range of outdoor activities for kids. A track runs along by the side of the Centre which is shown as a bridleway

*The first easy climb of the splendid Sarn Helen circuit,*
*with Pont Blaen-cwm-du not far ahead.*

on the OS map, though the signs only indicate a footpath and tell you that it's part of the Taff Trail. An easy ride through the woods brings you past Wern Farm, which is in a disused and ruinous state, from where the official track bears right downhill to a stile beside an overgrown gate. Go through here, and ignore the Taff Trail footpath signs which point left to another stile on the edge of the woods, this time with no gate. The bridleway here appears virtually disused. As far as I could make out it goes down the right side of the field, following a sunken track before bearing left and then right towards the road on an embankment. It passes a fine old iron gate which is almost hidden by trees, joining an overgrown track by the side of the river. This leads to a narrow bridge, and from there up to the road by a padlocked gate. Despite the lack of signposting I was fairly sure this was the correct bridleway route, in which case this gate should be unlocked!

(An optional route is to push on through the forestry from Wern Farm, where there's a clear track going north through the woods. Though not marked as a right of way, the OS map indicates that it can be followed for just over 1 mile (1.6km) until it meets up with a bridleway crossing track. This turns right at Valve House, and right again to bring you over the reservoir dam to the A470 at the southern end of the Central Reservoir. Having not tried this track I cannot recommend it – like so many forestry trails it may disappear while you get hopelessly lost; on the other hand it may be a classic, easy to follow ride which saves you a mile (1.6km) or so on the A470.)

Unfortunately, the A470 is the only way to go north from here. It's a fairly busy road, and since it's mainly uphill it takes a comparatively long time to cover the 3 miles (4.8km) and a bit that are needed. However, there are many worse roads in Britain, and you soon go offroad once again! The point to look out for is just after a stretch of woodland where the road swings left past a parking place. On the opposite side of the road there's an isolated white building which is the Storey Arms Outdoor Education Centre; cross the road here, and you'll find the start of the track by the public phone box.

Ignore the gate on the right which is a footpath, and follow the track ahead along the side of the valley which is the old drovers' road. At first this runs parallel to the road on a great downhill section, before bearing off to the right and getting well away from the road on the opposite hillside. The riding along the partly walled track is delightful, and all too soon you hit tarmac at Blaenglyn Farm, though it's still a bridleway.

This leads to the road at Old Glanrhyd. If you want to go to Brecon, turn right here and follow the quiet country lanes for 5 miles (8km) or so to the town. For the Mountain Centre, turn left, which brings you back onto the A470, though this time it's downhill and in no more than five minutes you reach Libanus where the sharp left turning for the Mountain Centre is clearly signposted. From here it's a steady climb on a quiet country road, which after 10 minutes or so of pedalling should bring you up to the common called Bedd Gwyl Illtyd. If you've made it in time, turn right over the cattle grid for a welcome cup of tea at the Mountain Centre – but why, oh why, can't they serve it in pint mugs?

# Ride 35    BRECON AND THE 'GAP'

**Area:** The Brecon Beacons. A ride across the 'Gap'.
**OS Map:** OS Outdoor Leisure 11.
**Start & Finish:** Marketplace car park in Brecon, at grid ref 046285.
**Nearest BR station:** None within easy reach.
**Approx length:** 30 miles (48km). Allow around 5 hours, excluding stops.
**Ride rating:** Moderate.
**Conditions:** Mainly good tracks and reasonably straightforward navigation. You go high, but it's steady climbing.
**R & R:** Pubs and cafés in Brecon; pubs at Talybont, Pencelli and Llanfrynach.

This is a ride with brilliant views and some very good tracks, heading through one of Britain's nicest National Parks. The people are also very friendly. An elderly Brecon local pointed out the 'Gap' which allows you to cross the pass between the two big peaks of Cribyn and Fan y Big, going into rapturous

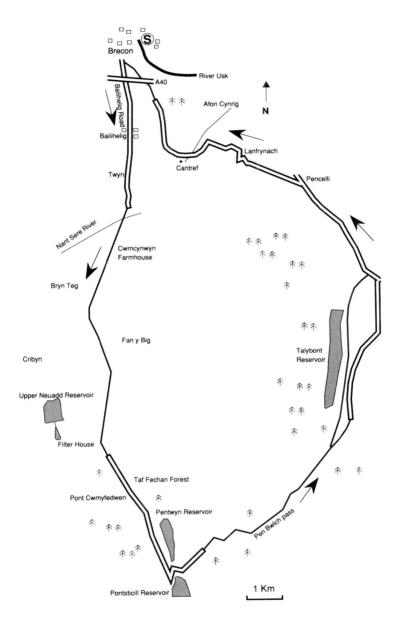

detail about the offroad route that he used to ride on his motorbike some thirty years previously. The Roman Road that leads up to the 'Gap' has deteriorated in the meantime, but is still ridable nearly all the way as you set out on this excellent circuit.

Note that market day in Brecon is on a Tuesday, when the marketplace should be avoided unless you want to trade in sheep. Otherwise it's usually pretty empty, and is a good place to start this ride from. Before leaving you may wish to check out the Information Centre which sells relevant maps and other publications. However, be warned that when I paid a visit the assistant couldn't tell me anything about the tracks and trails in the neighbourhood beyond the incorrect information, 'I'm sure you're not allowed to ride them on a bike'.

Ride through Brecon following the Cardiff direction out of town. This takes you over the bridge across the River Usk. A short way on past traffic lights, turn left by a small church down the Bailihelig Road, which is unmarked except for a signpost pointing to the Hospital. Ride on past the hospital, heading uphill onroad and across the dual carriageway A40. Keep following the road on a moderately steep uphill heading due south, passing a large farm at Bailihelig and some way on passing a B&B at Twyn with fine views of the 'Gap' ahead of you. It looks intimidating from down here, but is not as bad as it looks.

Further on the road bends left downhill. Take the next turning on the right (marked as a byway on the OS map), heading on downhill across the Nant Sere River, following the tarmac lane as far as a gate, by a track going down to the left to Cwmcynwyn Farmhouse. Go straight through this gate ahead, starting the long ascent up the side of Bryn Teg on a rough track. At the next gate, by a National Trust sign, you go into open sheep-grazing country, following the track uphill and ignoring a narrow track that bears off to the left by a wall, heading down into the valley. Keep on up the main track which is an old Roman Road, with a surface that gets rockier as you gain height but is mainly ridable. The track leads straight up to the 'Gap' between Cribyn and Fan y Big. For walkers there is a mighty natural horseshoe here extending to Pen y Fan which makes a classic ridge walk.

As you get higher the track gets wetter, and at times is like riding up a stream. Towards the top the track bears round to the left and steepens up rock steps, the only part so far that is unridable. Go on through the 'Gap', taking in the fine view behind before heading off on a long steady downhill going south on a fairly good surface. Upper Neuadd Reservoir is passed down on the right; at the southern end of the reservoir the track dips steeply down and up to cross a crevasse by Filter House, before going through a gate and following the track by the side of the woods ahead.

Keep on along the track until you reach the road at Taf Fechan Forest. Follow the road – a very quiet lane – on a fast downhill through the woods, crossing Taf Fechan at Pont Cwmyfedwen and carrying on in the same direction. Keep straight on ignoring a left turning, with Pentwyn Reservoir coming into view on the left. More downhill brings you past a

*The 'Gap', looking back towards Brecon. From here*
*Upper Neuadd Reservoir is soon passed ahead.*

solitary converted chapel, with a parking/picnic place on the left which is a good spot to stop and check the map and have some lunch.

A short way past here, take the turning which doubles back to the left, crossing between the Pentwyn and Pontsticill Reservoirs. Keep on the lane ahead, passing the Dolygaer Outdoor Pursuits Centre, as you head uphill going east-north-east. The lane turns to a rough track, steadily gaining height on a variable surface before passing through a gate at the end of the woods. There are no signposts, so follow the most obvious track which bears off to the right here, before resuming the ENE direction across open country. This route eventually brings you up to 1,706ft (520m) bearing left to the north through the Pen Bwlch pass with brilliant views of the Dyffryn valley down to the right.

From here on the riding is really excellent, as the big Talybont Reservoir opens out ahead. Follow this fine, fast track towards the forestry. Just before you reach it, a track bears left downhill by a ruined building, a turning which is easily missed. This is the offroad route to Talybont; if you miss the turn you will come to a gate, with the track running on ahead by the side of the forestry. From here it becomes a road heading on a long, long downhill towards Talybont; you're unlikely to meet many cars, so this route can be equally enjoyable.

The offroad route is, however, the real thing. Head downhill from the ruined building, and where the track forks left and right take care to go right, following a narrow, fast track along the contour line of the hillside, going through thick forest with the reservoir far below to the left. The track soon passes above the northern end of the reservoir, carrying on through the woods as it takes you on a bumpy downhill towards Talybont. A short way before the village the track turns left over a disused railway bridge to cross the old line, bringing you past the Brecon and Monmouth Canal to the White Hart pub. This is in a pleasant position with canal boats gliding by, and is the first pub on the ride, some 3-4 hours from the start at Brecon.

From here it's mainly onroad back to Brecon, but most of the roads are narrow country lanes which seldom appear to see cars, so it's still enjoyable riding. Turn left through Talybont where there is another pub, following the road for just over 2 miles (3.2km) to Pencelli, which also has a pub. From here you could follow the road to join the main A40 into Brecon, which is fine if you're in a hurry, but I would recommend a quieter option. Turn left by the phone box in the middle of Pencelli, going up a short track to cross the bridge over the canal. Turn right along the lane here, and follow it all the way to the next village, which is Llanfrynach, the only place I saw any cars on this part of the ride – and they weren't moving.

Make for the church in Llanfrynach – there's a pub here too – turning left and left again for Cantref. Follow the pretty lane for 1 mile (1.6km) or so by the side of Afon Cynrig, riding uphill by Cantref Church, which is hidden in trees with some nice looking big houses on the way. Past here ignore the left turn signposted to Brecon, bearing right and then following the road past the rather unpleasingly modernized farmhouse at Tir-y-groes with a conspicuous footpath sign opposite. Keep on along the lane until it turns sharp left with a track going straight ahead. Follow this track, which is the last offroad section of the ride, into Brecon, heading on a bumpy downhill before crossing the A40 and bearing left to come out opposite the hospital on the Bailihelig Road. Take care here; there's no obvious place to stop and cars from the hospital can whizz by unexpectedly. From here turn right and retrace your tracks onroad back into Brecon, which boasts a bike shop even if it has few inspiring places for tea.

# Ride 36   RADNORSHIRE HILLS

**Area:** Radnorshire. A tour of the Welsh borders including the Hergest Ridge.
**OS Map:** Landranger 148.
**Start & Finish:** Kington on the A44 west of Leominster. Start from Information Centre, grid ref 296566.
**Nearest BR station:** None within easy reach.
**Approx length:** 28 miles (45km). Allow 5 hours.
**Ride rating:** Moderate.

**Conditions:** Very good riding, but care needs to be taken with navigation. Plenty of climbs, but nothing too hard.
**R & R:** Pubs and cafés at Kington; pubs at Gladestry and Painscastle.

While riding in the Brecon Beacons it's worth exploring the Welsh hills to the north, particularly those at the eastern end bounded by the English towns of Kington and Hay-on-Wye. They are much more forgiving than the Beacons to ride, with excellent tracks and narrow lanes criss-crossing the moorland countryside and joining the various hill ranges in this very quiet part of Britain. This route gives some excellent hill riding, together with a panoramic trip along the Hergest Ridge on the way to and from Kington. I rode it over a couple of days in foul weather with so much rain that I had to give it up on the first occasion, but it still had the makings of a classic. It can be adapted and modified to suit your time and inclinations; there are a huge number of other tracks and trails in the area waiting to be discovered.

Start from Kington, a pleasant small town on the border between England and Wales. From the Information Centre head west, turning right by the church and then left uphill towards Hergest Croft Gardens (world famous and open to the public in season) on a narrow, dead-end lane that takes you steadily and quite steeply straight uphill for around ¾ mile (1.2km). When you come to a gate with open country beyond, go through and follow the wide grassy track ahead. This is the Hergest Ridge ride, one of the few bridleway sections of the Offa's Dyke long-distance footpath which divides England from Wales.

The climb from here is easy, and you are soon on level ground, blasting along the grass track on top of the ridge with splendid views on all sides. Ignore all other tracks, and follow the main track as it bears round to the left, passing an incongruous mini plantation of Monkey Puzzle trees and a small pool near the top of the ridge at 1,388ft (423m). From here you pick up occasional Long Distance Footpath markers, forking left and passing another lonely pool to the right. You then start a steep downhill on the grassy track, heading towards a prominent knoll. The track bears left round the side of the knoll, joining a rough stone surface that soon leads downhill to the outskirts of Gladestry.

Bear right on the lane by the Offa's Dyke sign, and then take the first left past the pub. We found this a pleasant, welcoming place with outside seating, but since this stage is fairly early in the ride it may be better to postpone a visit until the return section. Take the right turn past the church, and then turn left again up the side with a barn on the right. Take the next left fork and follow the narrow lane ahead, turning right at a T-junction. Some way on you come to the farmstead at Wain

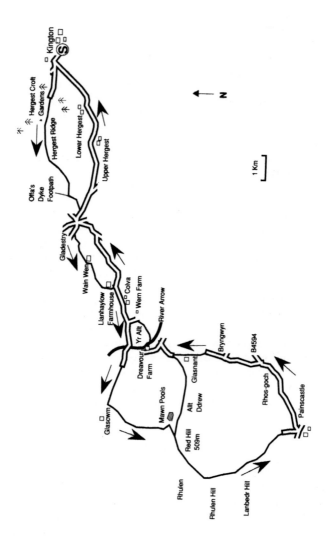

Wen. Here the tarmac lane comes to an end and bridleway takes over, but there's no signposting and the way is none too obvious.

Bear left and right through the farmyard past the back of the house, turning left uphill through a gate and riding on up the side of a field by a fence, following the track round to the right along the side of a forestry plantation at the top of the hill. At the next gate the track ahead becomes less distinct, apparently bearing north to head up into the high hills ahead. This is not the way to go. Bear left onto a less distinct track which takes you to the gate ahead on the far side of the field, leading on down past the old longhouse-style farm and byre at Cywynace. Here it becomes a tarmac track, going through the gate at the bottom of the valley beneath the house before you ride steeply uphill on the other side and follow the track to the road by Llanhaylow farmhouse.

Turn left along this quiet, pleasant road, riding past the church at Colva, ignoring the first left turning, and following the road steeply downhill to cross the River Arrow at the next crossroads. Go straight over here, heading towards Glascwm. At the top of the hill, before you drop down into Glascwm (where there's a YHA, open 1 March to 31 October. Tel: 09824 415) there's a track heading straight up the hillside, where you come to open land by the side of a hedged field. Head up this track which is steep, but not too steep to ride, and navigate your way to the big Mawn Pools to the south, which are found on the highest land on these hills.

Once it has gained some height the track passes through heather and is good riding, though care needs to be taken with direction and a compass is necessary. Take the first turning to follow the track along the hillside and then turn off to the north to continue climbing, gradually coming over the top with the Mawn Pools on your left. As you start to go down the other side, take the left fork, which is a more rocky track, bearing round to the right and gradually dropping downhill to a small pool where the track crosses the bridleway coming up from Rhulen.

Follow the track ahead along the side of Red Hill, with the hillside falling steeply down to the Rhulen valley on the right below. This is a good riding on a fast surface – even when it's raining so hard that you can't see – following the side of a wall and fence. After an easy up and down over a hillock the track hits the road on a bend at the top of Rhulen Hill, where you turn left and follow the road downhill all the way into Painscastle. It's fast going all the way down from Llanbedr Hill and you're unlikely to meet many cars, but watch out for the sheep which wander across the road on the grass and bracken moorland side of the cattle grid.

Painscastle, about 6 miles (10km) north-west of Hay-on-Wye,

is a small hamlet with a friendly pub that is used to catering to horseriders who are hill trekking in the region. It's an optional place to start this ride from, though apart from the pub there is no obvious place to park. Before leaving Painscastle you may also like to check out the small area of hill and moorland to the south, known as the Begwns. There's an excellent track which runs from east to west across them, and you could put together a quick tour of the area in less than an hour.

Painscastle is also about the halfway point in the ride, with all kinds of options for getting back to Kington. The easiest route is totally onroad, following the B4594 direct to Gladestry. A more interesting alternative route turns off the B4594 at Rhos-goch to follow an up and down lane northwards across hill and moorland via Bryngwyn to Glasnant. If you would prefer to ride most of the way offroad to Glasnant, you can retrace your wheel tracks to the top of Rhulen Hill, and ride on beneath Red Hill as far as the crossing track by the Doctor's Pool, where the bridleway comes up from Rhulen. From here you turn right along the bridleway, following it eastwards over level ground to Allt Ddrew. This is good fast going with some minor ups and downs in wild surroundings, and there are fine views over the valley to the right. As the track gets closer to the road it begins to bear left, before dropping down a steep, stony track on a hillside to join a tarmac lane on a hairpin bend. Take the left lane here, going through the gate which tells you it's for Glasnant Farm only – it's a bridleway, so don't worry. The tarmac soon disappears, as the track drops on a gentle downhill, passing the drive to the farmhouse and crossing a stream. From here it heads back uphill, before going steeply down to the road close by a farm, which when I rode by was notable for some ferociously yapping dogs.

Turn left along the road here, and then left again along the side of the valley, following the sign for Glascwm. When you come to the large buildings of Dreavour Farm, there's a bridleway track that snakes round the south side of the hill called Yr Allt. There's no sign for the bridleway but the farmer confirmed its existence; turn right into the farmyard, head towards the farmhouse, and then bear left and right between farm buildings. You have to hop off to cross a stream, and then you join a really nice track which climbs steadily round the side of the hillside, passing a small ruination of abandoned cars and a tiny but very beautiful ancient barn on the way. At the road, turn left steeply uphill, passing Wern Farm and rejoining the outward route on the road to Gladestry by turning right at the next crossroads.

From here it's mainly a fast and very pleasant onroad downhill into Gladestry. To get back to Kington from there you can either head back along the Hergest Ridge, starting with a savage climb, but once on top giving a lovely ride down towards Kington. Alternatively, if you prefer to stay onroad, follow the minor road on past the Offa's Dyke sign, keeping left for the hamlets of Upper and Lower Hergest as you follow the bottom of the ridge above the River Arrow for 5 miles (8km) or so pleasant riding back into Kington.

# Ride 37   RADNOR FOREST

**Area:** Radnorshire. A tour of the Radnor Forest.
**OS Map:** Landranger 148.
**Start & Finish:** New Radnor, just off the A44, at grid ref 213608. Roadside parking.
**Nearest BR station:** Dolau, about 1 mile (1.6km) from Llanfihangel Rhydithon on north-west corner of circuit.
**Approx length:** 21 miles (34km). Allow 4 hours.
**Ride rating:** Moderate.
**Conditions:** A fairly strenuous ride. Some of the tracks can be seriously muddy. Plenty of ups and downs.
**R & R:** Pubs at New Radnor and Bleddfa.

This ride takes you on a tour of the Radnor Forest area of mid-Wales, where a big area of hills and forestry is bounded by the A44 in the south and the A488 in the north. There are some steep climbs, but most of the climbing is on metalled tracks and lanes, and the ride ends with a great crossing of the wild moorland to the west of Radnor Forest, culminating in a magnificent downhill section beneath the peak of Nyth-grug.

Park in New Radnor, just off the A44. There's plenty of onroad parking, and the village has two pubs, two well-stocked general shops, and a greengrocer. The ride starts fairly savagely with a long uphill. From the main street by the pub, turn right into Church Street and then, after a short distance, take a lane going left by a dead-end sign. Follow this uphill, ignoring signs to right and left for bridleways – it's a hard enough climb on tarmac.

Eventually you come to Forestry Commission territory ahead. The lane bears left round the side of the woods with a yellow footpath sign; you fork right onto the hard forestry track, following it as it snakes right, left and right again uphill through the woodland on a good surface that is easy climbing. Eventually you reach the top and ride into open country on the north-east side of the woods by a large, modern barn close to Whinyard Rocks. Go through the gate, and follow the hard track ahead along the hillside with fine views out over the valley below.

Keep on this up and down track along the side of Bache Hill until you reach the next gate, which takes you into a rather depleted area of forestry at the top of Ednol Hill. Unlike those

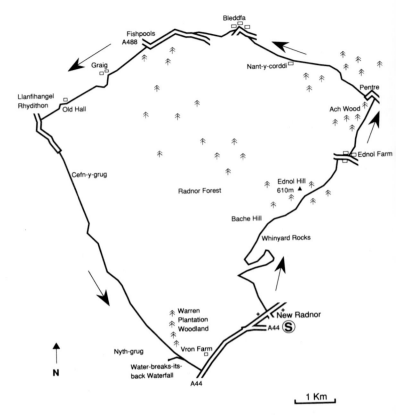

in most forestry areas, the tracks are easy to follow here. Bear right and follow a fast track downhill through the woodland, ignoring a right fork and going straight over a crossing track, and on down a narrower, steeper track with trees close on both sides until you come out at the edge of the forest. Go straight on through a rickety old gate here, and down the right side of the field ahead – this is bridleway, though completely unmarked. Ride on through a gate on the right, following the grass track down to the lane ahead.

Turn right along this lane until you reach Ednol Farm. A bridleway track turns left between the farm buildings, taking you across fields towards Ach Wood. At the edge of the woods go straight over a crossing track, and on down the right side of the woods on a medium-fast grassy descent until you reach the next gate. Go through here, down a well-overgrown track until you emerge by the side of a small, pink house.

You join a lane here, carrying straight on downhill to come to the hamlet of Pentre by the bridge that crosses the stream. Turn left here, taking the next right fork by a dead-end sign before you reach the phone box. This is another steep uphill on tarmac; when the hill begins to level out you take the first right turning, which if my memory serves me correctly – and it may not – was signposted to Wood Farm.

When you reach the farmstead, go straight ahead through a gate into more forestry, bearing left and riding downhill across a wide crossing track. When we rode it this part of the downhill trail was covered by chopped down bits of trees, making the going tricky. Carry on downhill in the same direction, past the next crossing track, which is as flat and wide as a motorway. Further down the track can be extremely muddy as it levels out past the gate that takes you out of the forestry area. When you see the farmhouse at Nant-y-corddi, a modern building on the hillock to the left, go through the gate by the house and ford the stream to join a metalled lane for a short uphill on the other side.

This lane soon brings you to the A488, where you turn left and pedal a short way up the hill to the 100 Years pub. This is at the halfway point of the ride, just under two hours and 10 miles (16km) out from New Radnor. We passed by here too early to try the pub, but it looks a welcoming place with outside seating for muddy bikers, and additional interest is provided by the art gallery opposite.

To continue from Bleddfa you go west, either onroad or offroad. If you've got plenty of energy, the offroad route follows a lane that forks off to the right, marked by a dead-end sign about 50 yards (40m) past the pub. This takes you uphill on a tarmac surface, and then along a grassy track on the hillside with several gates on the way, before rejoining the A488 at Fishpoles after just short of 1 mile (1.6km). Keep straight on along the A44, which as 'A' roads go is reasonably quiet and pleasant enough riding. Ignore the first track which turns off uphill to the left, and after 1 mile (1.6km) or so take the second track which goes straight ahead downhill to the left, as the road bends right by a right-hand fork.

Follow this track straight along – it's fast riding – passing an old black painted railway wagon in an unlikely position. Ride on past the track, going up to the left opposite a couple of houses well hidden by trees, and follow the main track downhill towards Graig, taking the next sharp left turn onto a rough track that leads to a gate some 50 yards (40m) uphill – don't overshoot as far as the track joining a lane that leads back to the A488.

Go through the gate here, following the track on an easy uphill as it bears round to the left with forestry on the hillside ahead. A track bears off to the right well before the woods; follow this downhill to the gate in the corner of a field, and ride on past a large barn opposite more woods. The track is deeply rutted and the going can be very muddy here, as it leads downhill to the picturesque farmstead at Old Hall, passing a stone wall with the main farm buildings over to the right. Ride straight on past the small duck pond on the left, and up through a gate. Follow the track until it bears right through another gate at the top of a field; go through ignoring the turning immediately to the left, and after about 50 yards (40m) turn left uphill through a third gate well before you come to the large house ahead.

Follow this grassy track uphill by the side of a hedge, keeping on past a modern barn and joining a tarmac lane over a cattle grid. This leads to a crossroads above Llanfihangel Rhydithon – the nearest point of the route to a BR station – where you turn left on tarmac for the last serious climb of this ride. Follow the lane on a steady uphill until you come to a barn at Shepherd's Tump by sheep pens on the top of the ridge. Here you carry straight on ahead through a gate, joining a grassy track over good ground heading in a SSE direction.

From here on it's brilliant riding in a fine wilderness area to the west of Radnor Forest, with good tracks leading along the tops of the hills with spectacular views if the weather is clear. Navigation is fairly straightforward, though every now and then you'll need to check the compass and map. Past the ridge of Cefn-y-grug, ignore the track forking steeply left uphill, and follow the track ahead as it bears right round the side of a great natural bowl carved into the landscape – we had time to admire the view as we punctured here – before keeping on ahead by the side of a fence on a great long downhill.

The track dips down into a gulley to cross the Mithil Brook where you head up the other side, taking the left track which soon turns into another downhill. Keep on in the same direction beneath Myth-grug, and you soon come to a hard track which gives a brilliantly fast downhill as it bears left round the hillside. Go through the gate by the modern barn, and speed on down the track through the forestry. Take care as my companion rider came off here and had a hard landing; he was unhurt as he was dressed for winter riding, but in summer it could have been a different story.

From here you can divert to visit the extraordinarily named Water-breaks-its-back waterfall, which is on the east side of the Warren Plantation woodland. To get there you have to double back on a track joining the main track from the left; it's easy to miss as you're tearing down at breakneck speed, and if you find yourself level with Vron Farm over to the left you've overshot it. Both tracks lead on down to the A44, where you turn left for a final five fast minutes of pedalling back to New Radnor.

# Ride 38   ELAN VALLEY

**Area:** Mid-Wales. A tour of the Elan Valley.
**OS Map:** Landranger 147.

**Start & Finish:** Car park just past Elan Village on B4518, 3 miles (4.8km) south-west of Rhayader, at grid ref 923645. Alternative start from Rhayader itself.
**Nearest BR station:** Llandrindod Wells.
**Approx length:** 27 miles (43km). Allow 4-5 hours.
**Ride rating:** Moderate.
**Conditions:** Most of the ride is easy, but parts of the Ancient Road are tricky and you can go off the trail.
**R & R:** Pubs and cafés in Rhayader.

We rode this circuit on a spectacularly cold and clear day in December, when the roads and tracks were completely clear and we met hardly a soul on the way. However, one can imagine lots of cars crawling round these narrow roads in summer! The route really divides into three sections: an enjoyable onroad to start; a long and quite tricky offroad section along an Ancient Road; and another enjoyable and very fast onroad to finish. The Ancient Road crosses open moorland and is exposed to all weather. In winter it is liable to be wet, boggy and comparatively slow going; nor is it too difficult to wander off the trail and get lost. There should be no problems during a fine summer, but it is not a good place to be caught by nightfall at other less forgiving times of the year!

From Rhayader follow the B4518 signposted to Elan Village. After 3 miles (4.8km) or so, you pass the left turning down to Elan Village with its large Information Centre, which appears to be closed throughout the winter. Just after this turning you come to the first big dam on the left, with a free car park beneath the cliffs opposite. If you've got this far by car, leave it here and start the ride.

Follow the road on round to the right, and then turn left over the bridge with its spectacular copper cupolas – one can't imagine the modern privatized water companies going to such splendid excess in these days of profit and austerity. Turn left on the far side of the bridge, and follow the road on round the north side of the Caban Coch reservoir, which is extremely pleasant riding when there are no cars to bother you. Keep on following the road past the solitary, incongruous phone box, heading on a steady uphill past the big farmstead at Ciloerwynt.

A short way past here fork off to the right on a higher road that brings you up to the top of the magnificent Cerrigcwplau dam by a noticeboard where you go offroad. Follow the track ahead round the edge of the Claerwen Reservoir, which is easy riding with the mildest of up and downhills. The track leads all the way to the north-west end of the reservoir. Just past here you come to the solitary farmstead of Claerwen on the hillside to the right, while the track bears left and comes to a bridge with a padlocked gate, though as it happens this is bridleway.

However, this isn't the way to go. You want to turn up the

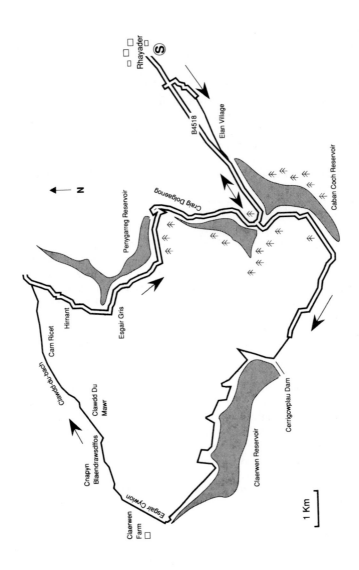

*Following the track round the side of the reservoir on the Elan Valley ride; the going gets tougher ahead!*

hill before reaching the farm, to connect with the 'Ancient Road' that leads north-eastwards across the moors. The vague semblance of a track going up the steep hillside is about 250 yards (229m) east of the Claerwen farmstead. Push up the grassy slope to the top of Esgair Cywion, aiming to head along the top of the highest hill where you'll find a wide grass track that eventually joins the Ancient Road.

At first this is an easily followed track, dropping down and then up round the right side of the crags at Cnapyn Blaendrawsdffos. From here the track carries on in a NNW direction and is easily followed, except at one point where it bears down the left side of a bluff at Clawdd Du Marw, and appears to fork right and left into two tracks. The right track goes uphill, and looks the most obvious way to go since it is worn by four-wheel-drive vehicles; the left track is very indistinct and grassy, but is the correct way to go. It eventually becomes easier to follow along the ridge of Clawdd-du-bach, while the other track simply leads to nowhere.

The other problems when navigating the Ancient Road are water and bogs. Some parts of the track disappear under water; you don't realize how deep it is until you attempt to ride through and end up with soaking feet – no problem in the summer, but bad news in the winter when there's still a long way to go. The track also crosses numerous bogs. Some are firm enough to ride or push through; others are so soft that you can sink down to your thighs in no time, getting very cold and muddy in the process.

At the top of Carn Ricet, one of the highest points of the ride, a weather station comes into view on the right. From here the going becomes much easier, with the clearly defined track swooping down across grassland on a good surface, though watch out for the ruts. The reservoir of Craig Goch comes into sight ahead, as you follow the track downhill to the left towards the road. Unfortunately, this is not a classic descent, as the ruts force you to ride on a narrow strip on the outside of the hill with a mildly vertiginous drop within inches of your wheels.

From here the onroad section back to the start proved very pleasant on a mid-week day in winter, with plenty of fast downhills, great views, and not a single car all the way. Turn right, passing the farmstead at Hirnant and bearing left past Esgair Cris after a good downhill. This brings you to the dam at the head of Penygarreg Reservoir which is a magnificent sight with tons of water cascading down its front. If you want to stop here, there's a beautifully sited picnic table on the other side.

The road continues from the bridge crossing the reservoirs beneath Craig Dolfaenog, with a fair amount of up and downing as you ride back to the car park above Elan Village. The village itself is no more than a few houses with neither pub or shops, though the architecture is attractive if you're interested in that kind of thing. From there you can follow the valley bottom road back towards Rhayadar; alternatively there are a number of offroad options available, such as taking the track which leads up past Carn Gafallt to get a view from the other side.

# The Far North

*Northumberland and County Durham offer some great wilderness riding close to the Scottish border. Conditions can be hard and real care needs to be taken in winter, but the upside is the potential for some wonderful riding. It's not all rated 'hard' and 'severe'; to start check out some of the great railway trails of the County Durham area.*

## Ride 39   DERWENT VALLEY

**Area:** County Durham, Tyneside and Durham area. Swalwell via Rowlands Gill to Blackhill.
**OS Map:** Landranger 88.
**Start:** Swalwell car park, at grid ref 199620.
**Finish:** Blackhill, Consett, at grid ref 100521.
**Nearest BR station:** Gateshead.
**Approx length:** 10 miles (16km). Allow 90 minutes north to south (uphill); 45 minutes south to north (downhill).
**Ride rating:** Easy.
**Conditions:** Easy track.
**R & R:** Shops, pub, restaurant in Rowlands Gill. Great fish and chip shop in Blackhill.

Once a rail route connecting virtually every type of coal-powered industry you could imagine – steamships at the River Tyne, cokeworks, brickworks, and eventually ironworks at Consett – this is now a really interesting ride, even if you're not interested in industrial archaeology. For much of the route trees have overgrown the track, giving it a different character for every season; as a result it is worth two or three visits a year just to make the comparison.

There is a visitor centre at the old Swalwell Station car park, our start point. Ten years ago you would have covered the first ½ mile (0.8km) in the company of the vast Derwenthaugh Cokeworks, but now the site is virtually cleared, although you may still see the odd heap of bricks and recognize the landscaped spoilheaps.

You cross the River Derwent for the first time via a most substantial stone viaduct where you may have to stand on your bike to get a view over the side. The track continues to climb through woodland, although you can hear vehicular traffic on the main road only yards away, until you reach Rowlands Gill.

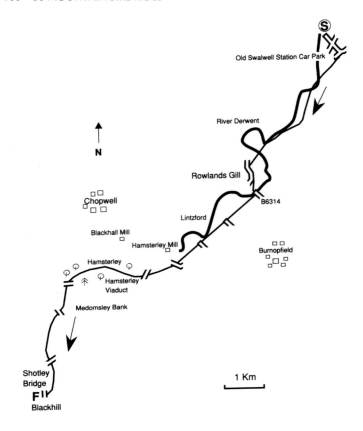

There is a bit of main road to negotiate here because the railway was quickly replaced by the new road soon after it closed. Ride along past the petrol station, turn left onto the B6314 towards Burnopfield, then after 330 yards (300m) turn right into a picnic area before you cross the road bridge over the river, and you'll see the start of the second leg.

## Rowlands Gill to Blackhill

As soon as you start the second leg you recross the River Derwent on a steel viaduct which has been surfaced with concrete, no doubt to protect the deck, but it seems totally out of place. Two impressive viaducts, which afford you real treetop views, come in quick succession near Lintzford. The second, Hamsterley viaduct, is built of the off-white bricks which were produced from local clay at Rowlands Gill.

Soon after you pass Hamsterley Mill you cross Medomsley Bank, so often the scene of a lot of walking on the Great North Bike Ride, but for us it is easy – we simply cross it and continue up through the woods. Across the valley to the north

*Derwent Walk Country Park information board – watch out for walkers along the trail!*

of Chopwell, are Blackhall Mill and on our side Hamsterley, once very important pit villages. These have survived, others vanished completely when the coal was worked out. The final miles are more open, but you still know this is a valley ride as you contour around above Shotley Bridge to Blackhill and those excellent fish and chips. Are they really so much better than the others, or is it just hunger as a result of your exertions?

You can reach the Waskerley Way by riding SSW across the landscaped wasteland of the old Consett Iron Works site, then cross the A692 above The Grove onto a narrow little road to Hown's Farm – this route can be linked to the Waskerley Way and/or the Consett and Sunderland Cycle Path to give an extended tour.

# Ride 40   WASKERLEY WAY

**Area:** County Durham. From Hown's Farm via Burnhill Junction to Fell Haven.
**OS Maps:** Landranger 87 and 88.
**Start:** Hown's Farm, Consett, at grid ref 101494.
**Finish:** Fell Haven, Stanhope Common, at grid ref 000432.
**Nearest BR station:** Gateshead or Durham.
**Approx length:** 9.3 miles (15km). Allow 90 minutes east to west (uphill); 45 minutes west to east (downhill).
**Ride rating:** Easy, unless the wind is against you!
**Conditions:** Easy track.
**R & R:** Nothing exactly *en route*, but ride ½ mile (0.8km) off route to Honey Hill near Smiddy Shaw Reservoir.

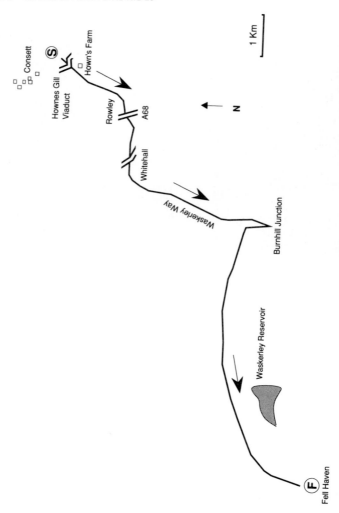

This is one of the most exposed railway rides in the country. Starting at 787ft (240m) on the south-west fringe of Consett it rises to 1,444ft (440m) on Stanhope Common, only 33ft (10m) lower than Drummochter Summit near Dalwhinnie on the Highland Line. Much of the route is set well above the surrounding countryside, not difficult to believe when you see the number of radio and television transmitting masts around you, and as a result is open to everything the weather can throw at you.

When the wind is in the west, which it usually is, the outward journey can be unbelievably difficult, and the return journey incredibly swift. The only comfort I can offer in these circumstances is the fact that despite the difficulties the railway is still the easiest way to access these high places on a bike. Everything else is either very steeply up or very steeply

*One of the most exposed railway rides in the country, though the forestry gives some protection.*

down; just look at the number of gradient arrows on the OS map.

I considered a circular route to complement the railway, but decided against it for two reasons. Firstly, the surrounding seriously hilly terrain; and, secondly, the thought that you will really enjoy the return journey because you've earned it. I hope you agree. Obviously the out and back journey will amount to nearly 19 miles (31km), a fair undertaking for a novice, but quite possible. A friend announced that there was no way she was going to attempt that sort of mileage 'up there'; but did, managed very well, then boasted about it for a month.

## Hown's Farm to Burnhill Junction

The huge Consett Iron Works slag hopper marks the start of the Waskerley Way, as it does the Consett and Sunderland Cycle Path. On this occasion we set off west straight onto the incredible Howns Gill Viaduct. Horseriders are advised to dismount! Prior to the bridge being built in 1858, there were funicular railways up and down either side of the valley at this point which hauled the trucks three at a time. They must have been going night and day.

About a mile (1.6km) further west you cross the A68 at Rowley Station. At least you would if it was there. The entire establishment was removed and rebuilt at Beamish Museum, and all that remains is a picnic area. Beyond Whitehall the track swings south through deep cuttings, and you can be forgiven for imagining you have missed something when you see another track across the fields to the north-west. This was the old incline that was superceded by the line we now travel. A final damp cutting takes you to Burnhill Junction where we turn hairpin right and head northwest on the second leg.

## Burnhill Junction to Fell Haven

This is the bleak bit. Initially you are protected by trees, but by the time you reach Waskerley you're on your own. Nowadays there are only about three buildings to mark the village. At one time there were wagon repair shops, a goods station, a shed for six engines, a school, church and chapel, shops and, of course, houses for the railway workers. The line eventually closed in 1969 and now little remains.

The final 3½ miles (5.6km) cut across the high commons above Waskerley Reservoir, treeless and terrific. It is wild with a capital W up here, and in winter it is something else to crunch through the ice pools all the way to Fell Haven, a quick bite and warm drink from your flask, then a flee back down to civilization before darkness engulfs you.

# Ride 41   CONSETT AND SUNDERLAND

**Area:** County Durham. Leadgate via Chester Le Street to Fatfield.
**OS Map:** Landranger 88.
**Start:** Jolly Drovers, Leadgate, at grid ref 132519.
**Finish:** Fatfield School, Washington, at grid ref 309547.
**Nearest BR station:** Durham.
**Approx length:** 13 miles (21km). Allow 1 hour west to east (downhill); 2 hours east to west (uphill).
**Ride rating:** Very easy, and very enjoyable.
**Conditions:** Easy track.
**R & R:** Several towns and villages *en route*.

The extreme western end of this route is still in the course of construction, linked to the redevelopment of the Templetown area of Consett. The official start point is marked by one of the huge Consett Iron Works slag hoppers, but then there is a confusing gap across to Leadgate. This part of the route should soon be completed, but for the time being we'll start at the Jolly Drovers, Leadgate, and then there's no confusion.

There are several unusual features on this trail that relate to the novel *Celestial Railroad*, which can be obtained from the Sustran's address on the information  boards. The only problem is that the tale starts at the Sunderland end, the opposite way from our ride, but the features are excellent nevertheless.

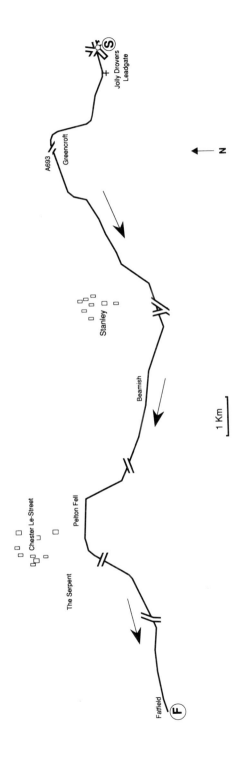

## Leadgate to Chester Le Street

The first test comes as soon as you leave the Drover's roundabout. See if you can ride through the maze without using your brakes. Then it's along to the church, where great judgement will be required to weave your bike through the anti-motorcycle barriers without dismounting!

An open, elevated section follows affording great views down to Lanchester where another route lies, then you are presented with the Old Transformers – enormous metal structures inspirationally created from old electrical transformers, one still dribbling its vegetable-based cooling oil from the cable box. They are very impressive. Soon after there's a lovers' seat decorated with appropriate graffiti! And nearby, at the right time of year, the biggest patch of cowslips I have ever seen. If you are dawdling, the old limekilns are also worth a look at this point.

An element of care is required as you cross the main road at Greencroft; you pass the last of the heather and then pick your way over a bed of ironworks cinders. (This short section will make you appreciate your mountain bike, otherwise an ordinary bike would have sufficed.) Then follow the signposts along past the chapel and down towards Stanley. In railway terms this was a steep section, and it was not unknown for laden steam trains to pause at Beamish to build up a head of steam or enlist diesel assistance to make the grade. It must have been a great sight to see a steam engine giving its all at the front and a diesel straining away at the rear of a line of ore trucks.

As you approach the tunnel in the cutting at Beamish you see cows have strayed onto the track, but it's not until you get very close you find they're metal sculptures. They are really convincing as Sally Matthews has captured the natural stance of the animals beautifully. In what were the sidings at Pelton Fell there is a small collection of trees where the signal box stood – lilac, laburnum and apple. No doubt some old railwayman's pride and joy. Soon after, the hardest test arrives. You can ride sedately by on the official path, but the adventurous should try and ride the ridge of The Serpent. We are riding in the right direction to start easily at the tail, but can you reach the head? Very few do.

## Chester Le Street to Fatfield

The recommended Start/Finish point for this section of the path comes at the Wheatsheaf Pub, Chester Le Street, just after you cross the main London–Edinburgh line; but there's still another couple of miles to go to Fatfield, so you may as well do them too. Then, for the super determined, east of the school there's an unfinished stretch which is wet, lumpy and quite

*Bertie was here – it's easy and very pleasant riding on these old railway lines.*

technical in places, but don't take the inexperienced because it is strewn with rubble and you need to climb up the embankment onto the new road at the far end.

# Ride 42   SALTER'S ROAD

**Area:** North Northumberland. Alnham via Bleakhope and Hexpethgate to Cocklawfoot.
**OS Maps:** Landranger 80 and 81.
**Start:** Alnham, at grid ref 995109.
**Finish:** Cocklawfoot, at grid ref 852186.
**Nearest BR station:** None within easy reach; Alnmouth Station is 18 miles (29km) from Alnham.
**Approx length:** 12 miles (19km). Allow 4 hours, less in very dry weather.
**Ride rating:** Moderate/mild severe.
**Conditions:** Variable riding under your wheels.
**R & R:** None whatsoever.

The Salter's Road was a commercial route through the Cheviot Hills as far back as the thirteenth century. As its name suggests it was used for the carrying and indeed the smuggling of salt into Scotland from the Northumbrian coast. Most of the eastern section has been adopted as normal tarred thoroughfare, but the highest parts remain unsurfaced, although well defined, and are now probably in better condition than at any other time as a result of being used by pneumatic tyres as opposed to hooves.

In terms of the larger mountain ranges the Cheviot Hills are

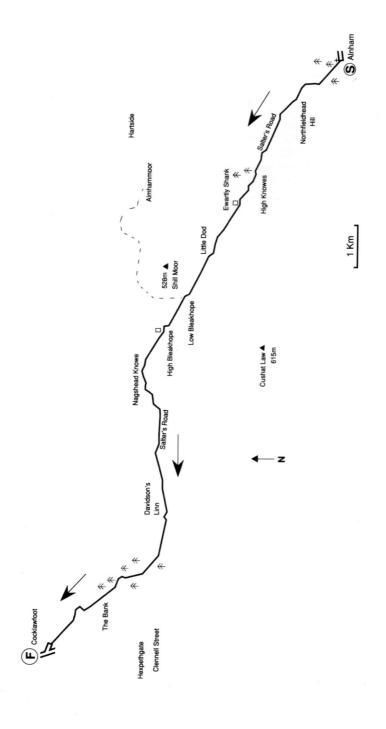

mere pimples, but they can still produce their own weather system and their rounded shapes can confuse the best. It is essential that you carry the OS maps, principally for route confirmation, but also in case escape is dictated. The route rises to 1,762ft (537m) at Hexpethgate on the Border Ridge.

## Alnham to Bleakhope

Depart west along past the church, then turn right across a minute ford and through the trees beside the vicarage garden wall. A short but very steep walk will take you up to a gate alongside a wood where things improve. The next test is the soft ground past the deciduous wood on the left, and the climb up to the gate on Northfieldhead Hill. Make for the red farm road that crests the hill, but as soon as you get over the top quit the road and use the grass track that makes its way north-west across the pasture towards the fence, and eventually through a gate at a spot called White Gate. (I'm sure the actual metal device was painted blue last time I passed, but I could be wrong!)

Beyond the gate there's an enjoyable technical track towards a stell where you must keep left and high to cross High Knowes col through the ancient gate. The views from here are terrific. You are really getting into the Cheviots and on a clear day can even pick out the course of the Salter's Road climbing up onto Little Dod and beyond. In the meantime, keep right of the wood on a good track and aim for Ewartly Shank.

At Ewartly Shank follow the bridleway arrows through the farm and beyond to the shelter of a belt of trees. When you exit the wood you will see the climb up Little Dod before you. It can be ridden but most folk settle for a walk at some point! From the summit the track drops initially, then up again with the arrows before dropping down the side of Shill Moor. To the west is Cushat Law, at 2,018ft (615m) the fourth highest hill in the Cheviots, but virtually unridable even on a horse due to huge soft peat hags – it's a bleak place.

A tarmac road runs east from Low Bleakhope to Almhammoor, and thence to the public road at Hartside. It's the last escape route before the real hills.

## Bleakhope to Hexpethgate

Low Bleakhope leads you to High Bleakhope, then a couple of stony fords and a tractor track take you to Nagshead Knowe as the route swings west. Follow the tractor tracks again as they climb to a gate in the fence above a shed. This is now the hardest part of the route!

The next gate you need to look for is only 656ft (200m) south of the fence you have just crossed through, but the sheep tracks

*Clennell Street, at the start of the final ridable push to Hexpethgate with half of Scotland in sight ahead.*

tend to wander well away from it. Try to keep high and choose the best route through the sphagnum bogs. It's not easy to stay clean! Beyond the gate the track through the infant forest is easier to follow. Then when you reach the forest road turn right for 85 yards (80m) until you see a signpost announcing 'Salter's Road'. Turn left into the trees again, and it's easy after that.

Well, it's easy to follow because it's signposted, but the riding is still demanding. The 1:25000 Pathfinder map shows a couple of fords on the route; at most times of the year these are simply deeper troughs of water, but the wettest test comes at Davidson's Linn. (Northumbrian waterfalls are frequently called linns, and this is one of the best.) Alas, the spectacle is accompanied by a substantial stream which is often safer to wade than leap. Take care.

The final hard bit commences with the slog up the valley side away from the linn, but it is such a good hill it is not unknown for people to have a go at riding down again just to see if they can do it! The bridleway now weaves its way up through the trees, across the forest road, through more trees, then across the moor to join Clennell Street and the final ridable push to Hexpethgate. On a clear day you have half of Scotland spread out before you, but have a good look because you'll see very little on the way down to Cocklawfoot.

## Hexpethgate to Cocklawfoot

Two miles (3.2km) of descent on ancient grass road. In places there are deep ruts bedded with small stones which call for either great nerve and skill or brains in the back pocket. Chippy the Gippy always leaves me behind here and, being a friend, I credit him with the former, but at times I have my doubts!

Unfortunately, there's a gate in the saddle before The Bank which means you've got to pedal uphill for 180 yards (200m), but then it's down again, smoother and faster and faster. Brilliant! Last stop before Cocklawfoot comes in the little wood above the farm. The gate is usually closed so look for it, just in case speed has blurred your vision. Then it's the final drop to the farm. Don't fall off at the five-bar gate!

## Ride 43    EAST ALLEN DALE

**Area:** South-West Northumberland. A tour of the East Allen Dale Moors.
**OS Map:** Landranger 87.
**Start & Finish:** Allendale Town, at grid ref 838558.
**Nearest BR station:** Haydon Bridge.
**Approx length:** 27 miles (43km). Allow 5 hours, slightly less in good firm dry conditions.
**Ride rating:** Severe.
**Conditions:** Enjoyable in a warped sort of way!
**R & R:** Café, pubs, hotels in Allendale Town. Pub just off route at Whitley Chapel, the Click 'em In, GR930577.

This extreme south-west corner of Northumberland was a major industrial area in the mid-1800s. Lead mining was at its peak and a network of carriers' ways led to the furnaces at Allendale

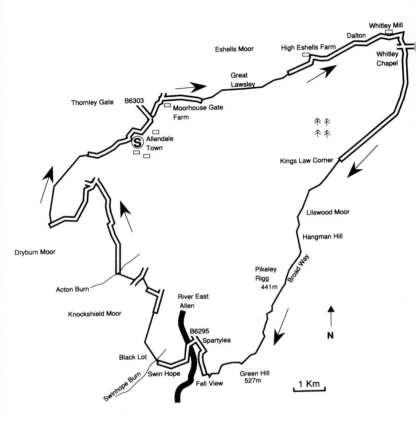

Town. Today grouse will probably be your only company on most of this tour which could just as easily be started at Allenheads, Whitley Chapel, or our chosen focus, Allendale Town.

## Allendale Town to Whitley Chapel

The first moor to cross is Eshells Moor. Leave Allendale Town by the B6303, the main road towards Hexham, and turn right up a narrow steep road as soon as you complete the hairpin left bend which crosses the Philip Burn 600 yards (549m) from the Market Place. This lane climbs 230ft (70m) in just over ½ mile (0.8km) to Moorhouse Gate Farm where you turn right along past the grey shed, so you should be quite warm when you get there.

The offroad starts here. An undulating stony farm road takes you ¾ mile (1.2km) to the edge of the moor where the signpost announces 'Bridleway Hexhamshire', and also points roughly east. Check the OS map and you will see that the bridleway leaves the end of our lane at an angle of about 30 degrees to the north, in other words keep high. Going straight ahead will just take you into a monster reed bed. This end of the moor has the fewest tracks, so take your time and look carefully for what starts as a sheeptrack, gradually grows in stature to a good ridable path as it climbs gently across the side of Great Lawsley, and then becomes a Landrover twintrack where at times the best route is down the middle. Keep heading east between the burn in the valley on your right and the rounded top of Great Lawsley on your left, and you are sure to pick up the track.

A tempting grouse road crosses the burn 1.4 miles (2.25km) into the moor; disregard it, in fact turn your back on it, veering north for 100 yards (90m) to the line of shooting butts with the main eastbound track. When wet this stretch is hard work but you'll soon reach the top of the knoll, then it's down all the way to the edge of the moor. Even after you leave the moor it's down again, initially on a wide stony byway to High Eshells Farm, then on narrow tarmac all the way to Dalton where you cross the main road to continue on to Whitley Mill. Beyond the farm the road turns hairpin right up a hill to Whitley Chapel, where it is straight on at the crossroads and straight on all the way to the edge of Lilswood Moor nearly 3 miles (4.8km) distant.

## Whitley Chapel to Fell View

This is the cruncher. The first 3 miles (4.8km) to Lilswood Moor are nearly all uphill followed by over 6 miles (10km) of testing terrain. The first 2 miles (3.2km) offroad from Kings Law Corner to Hangman Hill are a real challenge.

Fifty yards (40m) after crossing the cattle grid at the wood at Kings Law Corner go straight on to a Landrover track that follows the wall. After 100 yards (90m) the four-wheel-drive track veers left onto the lower moor and we are left to follow the line of the Broad Way. You shouldn't have any trouble. The old carriers' route has left an eroded trough in many places and on a clear day you can see the triangulation pillar on the top of the moor to aim for. The route is single track, technical in places, and forever up, up, and a bit more up.

As you near the top of the hill you will find that the track doesn't actually go right up to the pillar, it skirts the western flank then drops down to a 'crossroads' on Hangman Hill. We cross a grouse road and drop down a rough four-wheel-drive track into the col, then fight our way up the obvious path to a gate in the fence on the ridge. Fight is usually the operative word for this section. It always attracts a lot of water, the thin peat has been eroded to a large degree, exposing slippery mud in places, and unless it is bone dry the effort required to gain the gate at the top seems totally unreasonable.

Broad Way part 2 now begins. It is easier, just as technical, and as a result even more fun. Turn right as soon as you go through the gate on the ridge and follow the obvious track south-south-west over Pikeley Rigg 1,447ft (441m), across onto Tedham Moss where sadly they are 'improving' the track, past the black shooting cabins and on to Green Hill, 1,729ft (527m). It looks as if the days of this route being a classic are numbered. The drivable road from the south used to finish at the shooting cabins and from there on it became a challenge. Last year it was extended another ½ mile (0.8km) north. Now you meet it as soon as you start to climb onto the Moss; eventually we'll have a motorway all the way. Ride it before it's too late.

The grouse road turns left 620 yards (567m) beyond the summit of Green Hill, but our bridleway goes straight on steeply down the fell side. There are little posts to show you the way down to Fell View, but take care. The track has a good grassy sheep-nibbled top, don't carve it up, and by the same token exercise caution in winter. It is an exposed hillside susceptible to icing and can be quite lethal as a result.

## Fell View to Allendale Town

We join the B6295 dale road and turn right towards Allendale Town. If the weather has turned against you or a weaker member of the party is showing signs of fatigue it might be sensible to use this escape option and follow the main road back to Allendale. This last leg has some fierce climbs, and coming as they do late in the day it is as well to be aware of what lies ahead.

Follow the main road north to Spartylea where we turn left down a steep hill past the Post Office, across the bridge over the River East Allen and left with the 'main' road up to the old Board School where we turn right towards Swin Hope and Black Lot, beautiful places! A hundred yards (90m) after crossing the little bridge over the Swinhope Burn, bear right up to Swin Hope. It is unbelievable. There must be too much detail on the OS map for them to indicate the steepness of the hill, or perhaps the double arrows indicating 1 in 5 or steeper aren't enough! The only consolation is the fact that it's not too far to walk up to the stone-roofed cottage where we turn right through the gate and follow the tractor tracks up onto the fell.

The challenge continues as you follow this road up onto Knockshield Moor, but it eases a little after the 1,378ft (420m) contour, tops out just over 1,637ft (430m) then descends through a little ford just before we turn right onto a lesser path down to Knockshield. Look for it. You shouldn't miss it, an old packhorse route called the Black Way, perhaps from the colour of the cargo the horses carried, or perhaps from the colour of the little Galloway horses themselves.

Enjoy the descent to Knockshield, even this is a bit of a test in wet weather, then turn left, left again, then right to the hills at Acton Burn. This time there are OS arrows, but the test is easy compared to the last. Slightly less than 2 miles (3.2km) of undulating tarmac carry you to the last major ascent of the day. Then climb onto Dryburn Moor. Turn left onto the main moorland road and weave your way nearly to the top. Twenty yards (18m) before the second left-hand bend there is a wicket gate on the right in the fence which gives access to a little track to the chimneys. You can't go wrong – this is the biggest and best landmark for miles around. Aim for the nearest chimney.

The course of the old mill flues are marked on the map. They start near Thornley Gate, ½ mile (0.8km) downstream from Allendale Town, and culminate in these huge smoke stacks over 2 miles (3.2km) away on the moor. There are a couple of places where you can look inside the flue, and you'll probably be astonished how clean it is. The reason is simple, they used to sweep them. During the lead smelting process, silver was also refined, but most of it was carried away in the smoke from the furnaces, deposited in the soot in the flues, then collected periodically when the furnaces were standing idle.

The bridleway follows the main track after the first chimney, well over a mile (1.6km) of wacky enjoyment. Don't kill yourself! When you reach the tarmac it is down again. If in doubt at any junction just go down, try not to miss the slot near the cemetery, then weave around to the bridge and back up into Allendale Town. You are even allowed to walk the last hill if you wish, but after all you've done it should be easy!

# Ride 44    BORDER RIDGE

**Area:** Northumberland. The Border Ridge and The Street.
**OS Map:** Landranger 80.
**Start & Finish:** Slymefoot, Upper Coquetdale, at grid ref 860115. Park on hard standing near the bridge.
**Nearest BR station:** None within easy reach.
**Approx length:** 15.4 miles (25km). Allow about 3 hours, but weather and conditions underfoot can make a considerable difference.
**Ride rating:** Mild/Severe.
**Conditions:** The weather can greatly affect the degree of difficulty. Once committed to the route along the Border Ridge there is no easy escape.
**R & R:** Pub in Alwinton 6 miles (10km) back down the valley. Mountain Refuge Hut at Yearning Saddle about halfway along the Ridge. Shelter only – go prepared.

Upper Coquetdale is one of the most remote parts of

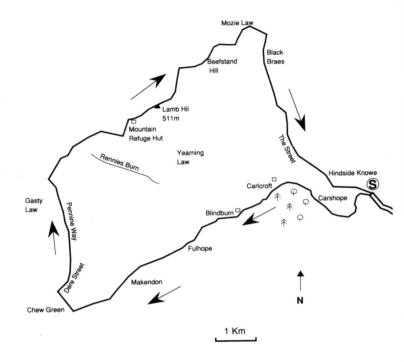

Northumberland, due mainly to the fact that access through the military ranges at the head of the valley is only allowed at lambing time when there is no shooting, although it is possible to force a way through the extreme north-western corner using the Pennine Way. Our route follows the valley to Chew Green, then strikes north onto the Border Ridge which it follows to Plea Knowe, then returns to Slymefoot using The Street.

There used to be an inn of ill repute called The Slymefoot at the junction of the Rowhope Burn and the River Coquet, perched on a large rock that serves as the base of one end of the bridge where we start. It was the haunt of sheep stealers and smugglers plying their trade over the Border, and the winter haunt of the sheep farmers of the area. Nothing now remains.

Depart west up the unclassified road that hugs the river and keep your eyes peeled. The whole of the area to the south of our route lies within the Otterburn Military Ranges and you may unwittingly become part of a military exercise. It is not unknown for cyclists to ride obliviously past a platoon of soldiers secreted in a ditch – it is when they leap out it becomes alarming.

You will notice that all the farms sit in the valley bottom, it is simply too bleak on the hills. Carshope is now a military establishment; Carlcroft boasts carpets of snowdrops in early spring; then Blindburn provides a blind corner you can't see around, so take care. The hill behind Fulhope is the first examination of your fitness; you are allowed to stand up in the granny gears because it's tarmac, but if it's muddy you may need to dismount!

The hill at Makendon, the last farm in the valley, doesn't rate special designation on the OS map but seems just as steep as its mate at Fulhope, and there is an excuse to stop at the top. The little cattle shed is the last protection until you reach Yearning Saddle, well along The Ridge, so make use of it – if it is windy, take longer. Unbelievably the final part of this leg is downhill, past the barrier where the tarmac turns south-east into the ranges. We go straight onto a rough track then turn right 220 yards (200m) later at the signpost for the Border Ridge. This is Chew Green, the ancient Roman Camp of Ad Fines, the end of the world! It's not like that at all, except perhaps when a rain-laden westerly whistles over the hill from Coquet Head and batters you into submission. Most days it's just a trifle bleak.

## Chew Green to Plea Knowle

This is the Ridge leg. When it is bone dry it is possible to ride up the uneven moorland track that follows the line of the bridleway beyond the earth banks that mark the camp, then bear right to follow the line of Dere Street up onto the Border Ridge to meet the Border Fence. The Fence is one of the finest navigational aids in the world. It faithfully follows the national boundary and coincides exactly with the bridleway for much of the Ridge. Even in the densest cloud you can ride along it, the only problem being when to turn off and head for the valley.

This stretch also doubles as the Pennine Way and from time to time you will encounter weatherbeaten posts bearing a plate which used to say 'PW'. See if you can spot one still sporting a hint of the painted letters. The main benefit of sharing the route with the long-distance footpath is that boardwalks are being established across the worst of the peat hags, a tremendous boon in wet weather. Inevitably these wooden crossings have focussed all the traffic onto one route, and where originally the bridges were level with the peat there is now a step up onto them, great entertainment when it is dry, but difficult and quite lethal when wet.

The shepherds' track meets the Border Fence on the northwestern slopes of Brownhard Law, 1,663ft (507m), then for the next 6 miles (10km) you will have incredible unrestricted views into Scotland on a fine day. In good conditions the next 2 miles (3.2km) are excellent, ridable but sufficiently testing to make it worthwhile. Occasional peaty holes will draw the best from your technique, there are little bridges to hop on and off, and the very technical descent to the head of the Rennies Burn. It is ridable when dry and at high season when the passage of many feet disperse the loose stones, but dismounting is the sensible option at other times. The far side is a push/carry in any case, which eases to a rewarding ride to the corner of the fence. Then it's down all the way to the hut in Yearning Saddle at GR804129.

The refuge is a simple affair, a large wooden box with a concrete base, but draughtproof and the only place you can sit in comfort, without getting wet for most of the year. Often we have sat outside and enjoyed the scenery of the steep sided hopes and laws to the north, but just as frequently have we postponed our departure into the elements for as long as possible. The climb onto Lamb Hill, 1,676ft (511m), starts 40 yards (50m) from the door of the hut. You drop down over the floor of the Saddle and immediately attack the hill. If it is wet forget it, but dry and compacted the 230ft (70m) of ascent is just about ridable.

Winter can be a different tale. On 14 January 1989 a friend and I traversed this route, and encountered two walkers who refused to speak to us near Chew Green. I'll let my diary account tell the tale:

Just as we passed the Mountain Refuge Hut the jolly walkers emerged, and we were forced to carry again. They seemed determined to overtake us, and we were equally determined to prevent it. Nothing was said but it was obvious. We didn't know how good they were, but were about to find out.

All I needed at this time was a race. This was the worst stretch for bikes by far, Lamb Hill 1,841ft (561m), to Mozie Law 1,811ft (552m). Two-and-a-quarter miles (3.6km) of hell. Prolonged carries. Unridable descents. This was the reason I hadn't been back for two years, and it had been a nice day last time. Of course, Willie didn't know what lay ahead, had the head down, and was going for it.

The amount of swearing was probably the best indicator of the amount of effort being made. I was over the 'bars again. Willie came off. It was awful. Much more swearing. More duckboards were gratefully accepted in the most dire bits. Not much was said. We tried to get a rhythm. Dire, oh, so dire. 'Some of these walkers do all the Pennine Way. They must be crackers!' 'I wonder what they think of us carrying bikes?' 'It's good training.' (Silent reflection, 'What the hell for?'.) 'Any day out is a good day.' A bit profound for me under the circumstances. 'We're not gaining much on them' . . .

The wind reached monumental proportions as we climbed Beefstand Hill. I managed to use the bike as a spinnaker which went some way to alleviating the pain in my shoulder. Hardly any of the 2 miles (3.2km) was ridable but we kept trying. It was so hard, every time I came off I teetered towards cramp in my legs, and occasionally I just fell off to avoid the cramp. I was aware that I was expending far too much energy, but wasn't about to back off!

I thought Mozie Law was never going to come and resorted to counting steps on the final assault. I recall on the third hundred getting 59, 60 or 59, 70 mixed up but dug deeper and decided it didn't matter, just keep counting and keep going. At the top we cleared the brakes and set off down, only to flip over the 'bars again. I was sick of it, but as I pulled myself together I saw the walkers a whole hill back. We had broken them. Yippeee!

At most times of the year it is much easier!

## Plea Knowe to Slymefoot

Plea Knowe is one of the ancient crossroads on the Ridge. Situated at GR835150 it is the point where The Street now crosses into Scotland, an old trade route for commodities both legal and otherwise for hundreds of years. It is now little more than a moorland track on the heights north of the Border, but our route back down to Coquetdale is brilliant. Compressed by military vehicles from time to time it provides a magic mix of speed and unpredictability, more than enough reward for the earlier labours of the day.

The initial section across to Black Braes requires a little effort, then the grassy descent needs instant decision. The best route varies from week to week, but they are all good. Let's face it, a drop of over 328ft (100m) in less than 0.6 miles (1km) has got to be good. Follow the obvious track up and around Swineside Law, then it's down again and around to Hindside Knowe at 1,407ft (429m). Keep quite close to, but right of the fence, and you can't go wrong.

The final downhill drops 570ft (174m) in just less than 1 mile (1.6km), finishing with the steepest section. Again, keep right of the fence and fairly high with the main route initially, look out for the softer depressions, and good luck on the terminal twintrack. You could finish up in the river!

# Scotland

*Once north of the border the potential is immense, but care needs to be taken to ensure that routes are viable. Four of these routes are within easy reach of Edinburgh, visiting the three major hill ranges in the south-east and checking out a disused railway line; there's also one of many on offer in the Highlands, plus a visit to the Mull of Kintyre.*

## Ride 45   MULL OF KINTYRE

**Area:** West coast of Scotland. South Kintyre.
**OS Map:** Landranger 68.
**Start & Finish:** The harbour car park at Campbeltown, at grid ref 721208.
**Nearest BR station:** None within easy reach.
**Approx length:** 50 miles (80km). An all-day ride – allow 8 hours.
**Ride rating:** Moderate.
**Conditions:** Mostly easy riding, but it's a good distance and there is a tricky section east of Tangy Loch.
**R & R:** Cafés, pubs, shops in Campbeltown; pub at Peninver grid ref 758250.

The Mull of Kintyre is a long spit of land on the west coast of Scotland. Despite the fact that it's a long drive from anywhere, the Mull is not as remote as you might imagine. The main town of Campbeltown operates a large fishing fleet and the area as a whole is popular for holidays, and while it doesn't compare with the rugged grandeur of the Highlands for riding, it's a highly enjoyable place to get out on your bike to enjoy the tracks and trails.

Campbeltown is not a bad place, although from experience it can look pretty grim in the rain which frequently visits the area. There's not much to do there, but it's worth watching the fishing fleet come in during the late afternoon with their catches of fish and prawns – most of it goes straight to London, Paris and other big cities, though you can sometimes buy the odd fish for your tea. Otherwise there are various cafés and pubs in the town, none of which seem very inspiring; while if you're into malt whiskey Campbeltown has its own brew, with an amazing selection of malts in the distillery shop, many of which sell at even more amazing prices.

This route is a good day's riding, making use of tracks and quiet roads within easy reach of Campbeltown. Head out of the town on the A83 going west, and on the outskirts of the town take a lane going due east. This heads steeply up the hillside, passing a few houses with the radio mast on the hillside above Campbeltown Loch ahead. Just past the walls of the last house bear left, still heading uphill on a track which levels out, passes through a gate, and follows a much narrower track round the side of the old fort at Knock Scalbert. Leave this track to drop down to the side of Aucha Lochy here, walking your bike across the top of the loch to join a track which passes through Whitehill Farm and then joins the road at Ballywilline.

Turn north here. The road is little used apart from farm traffic, with easy ups and downs leading through open countryside. A mile and a half (2.4km) on at A'Chruach a track goes off to the left. Leaving out this western circuit cuts the route by approximately 10 miles (16km) and also cuts out the most difficult riding, but if you feel adventurous this is the most interesting offroading and well worth the extra effort; if not, keep northwards along the road towards Skeroblin Cruach.

A little care with navigation is needed on this western circuit. Follow the hard track down to the farmhouse at Skerobinraid, from where a grass track follows the hillside above Skeroblin Loch. From here the route goes uphill into forestry along a gravel track that is easy to follow, going west and then south along a further band of forestry. This track heads downhill to the south-east corner of the forestry, where the route joins a rough, broken and unridable section of track heading southwards steeply up Ranachan Hill. A much better forestry track goes straight on down the side of the woods which brings you out to Kilchenzie, but this descent is soon over and isn't half as much fun to ride as the Ranachan part of the circuit.

The track leading up Ranachan Hill is in fact an old road that becomes ridable nearer the top, from where there's a fine view from the Trig Point at 696ft (212m). It's also rough but ridable as it winds its way downhill, bearing right to join a track past the farmstead at Lower Ranachan, and from there going down to the main A83. Turn north-west along this road for 2 miles (3.2km), taking the first right fork which leads up and down hill to the tiny hamlet of Tangy. Just past the phone box turn right, heading eastwards on a rough track, passing the old water mill at Tangy over to the right, and heading uphill into wilder country towards the imposing principal farm at Tangy.

This is good riding through fine countryside, and although the track to Tangy Loch is not marked on the OS map it continues through the farmyard and on to the east towards the loch which is hidden from view. Take a left fork and a right turn along the bottom of the valley, and you'll eventually come to the western end of this remote and unspoilt inland water. There's a faint track round the southern side of the loch, though it's tricky riding. At the far end there's a kind of beach, which on a fine day is a good spot to stop and rest awhile.

From the loch you have to get through the woods to join the track at the top of Skeroblin Hill. There's no obvious route, but if you pull and push your bike southwards uphill between the trees the short struggle will be rewarded by reaching a plateau where this forestry track starts and finishes. From here on it's forestry tracks across the Mull, and they are fast, enjoyable riding all the way. From Skeroblin Hill follow the track down to the road, turning north past Skeroblin Cruach. The next track to the right that crosses Glen Lussa Water is one that heads east, but if you want to explore the waters of Lussa Loch take time out to head further north. The OS map shows the track heading way on into the heart of the forestry beyond Braid Hill; I have not ridden it, and whether it comes to a dead-end as shown I don't know.

The eastwards track passes the big pipes of a complex irrigation system and then winds its way along the hillsides towards Kildonan. The riding is good, but as with so many forestry areas the views that might be are severely restricted by uniform rows of conifers. One gets an occasional glimpse over Ardnacross Bay, but this wonderful view is now largely obliterated. The track eventually winds downhill to the B842 coast road at Kildonan. If you've had enough turn right for an easy 8-mile (13km) pedal southwards to Campbeltown; if you want some more, turn left towards Saddell.

The main reason for going to Saddell is that it has a very nice beach with a few houses and castle, which looks good although it's not open to visitors; this makes a great place for a picnic, with no cars allowed unless they are residential. Saddell also has the remains of an old abbey inland, and another optional offroad circuit that leads along Saddell Glen by the side of Saddell Water, winding through the forestry below A'Chruach to rejoin the road just south of Saddell, ready for the ride back along the quiet road to the start point at Campbeltown.

# Ride 46   GLEN SHIELDAIG

**Area:** Highlands. From Shieldaig via Tornapress, Applecross and Inverbain to Shieldaig.
**OS Map:** Landranger 24.
**Start & Finish:** Shieldaig, at grid ref 815539.
**Approx length:** 32 miles (52km), 24 (39) of which are tarmac but include the 5-mile (8km) ascent of the infamous Bealach na Ba, climbing from sea level to 2,054ft (626m). Allow 6 hours, slightly less on a calm day, but these are a rare occurrence up here. A very early start might help.
**Ride rating:** Mild/Severe.
**Conditions:** The weather could turn it into an epic.
**R & R:** Hotel (Easter-October) in Shieldaig. Inn with good wholesome menu (all year) in Applecross.

An extraordinary amount of tarmac for a mountain-bike route. Fair comment, but see if you complain after you've ridden it. This route has three main elements, and is set in some of the most impressive countryside on the mainland. Shieldaig is gorgeous, and has a Hebridean atmosphere. Set at the foot of its own glen and at the head of its own sea loch, it is an ideal place to start, and an even better place to finish on a summer evening. On the other hand the inn at Applecross is open all year round, is cosy, and a great place to stay.

The first part of the route follows the A896 through Glen Shieldaig to Tornapress; the second section crosses the Bealach na Ba to Applecross; then the third segment is the tough offroad

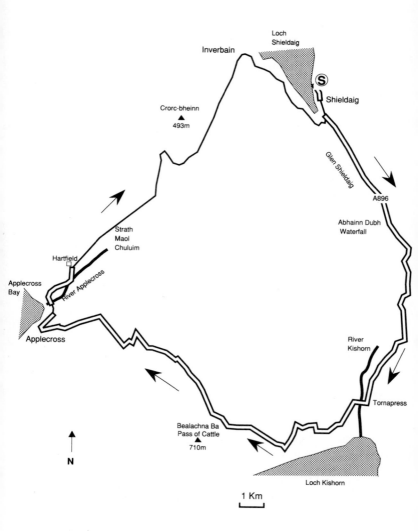

crossing to Inverbain on the western shore of Loch Shieldaig. The sting in the tail, the ride around the head of the Loch, has yet another character and is best completed in daylight!

## Shieldaig to Tornapress

The easiest part of the route, true, but not without considerable interest. Don't be deterred by the road classification. In common with many of the 'A'-class roads in Wester Ross this is a narrow road with passing places, the sort of byway that would provide an English Sunday motorist with conversation for a week, but there are hundreds of miles of them up here. This is some of the wildest country in Britain. It is not unusual to see red deer in the Glen. They will probably just look at you if you keep moving. Stopping usually provokes them into bounding away up the hillside in that majestic manner of theirs, and if it's a large stag you'll get the message that he is not pleased.

The col is 427ft (130m) above sea level, which isn't a bad climb when you've started at the lochside, and now you get it all back on the 4-mile (6.4km) descent to Tornapress, which comprises one house, a caravan and a signpost to Applecross.

## Tornapress to Applecross

The sign discouraging caravans and coaches from using this road will give some indication of what lies ahead. From the sea level bridge over the River Kishorn at Tornapress to the summit of the Bealach na Ba, the Pass of Cattle, is 4.99 miles (8km), and you will climb 2,054ft (626m). It starts gently as you skirt Loch Kishorn then becomes steeper and steeper as you climb, the stiffest section arriving after 4 miles (6.5km) where the rock walls of Sgurr a' Chaorachain rear up alongside you, and the drop down to the Allt a' Chumhaing doesn't bear thinking about. The side of the road is now protected by Armco barriers in the exposed places, which means *all* of the top section, but it's not many years ago that there were only posts and a dry stone wall boasting many gaps to protect you.

It is worth pausing at any stage of the climb to admire the view (any excuse!), but make sure you do so before you commit yourself to the great cleft of the final assault. There is an obvious wide corner after 2.6 miles (4.2km) where the vista south and west is incredible. You can see across Loch Kishorn to Plockton and the hills of Lochalsh, and perhaps spot a tiny train weaving its way around to the Kyle. If the weather permits you can see across the Inner Sound to the misty Isle of Skye, so even if you don't *need* a rest, stop and drink in the atmosphere.

The crunch is the straight below the walls up to the hairpin bends. There is barely enough room for the road; it feels as if it is nailed to the side of the mountain, sustained and oh, so steep! On one occasion two of my companions took to racing the whole thing, the leader actually vomiting on this stretch, but refusing to capitulate; while I, so slow in comparison, was entertained by a ptarmigan still half adorned in his white winter plumage wandering slowly across the road in front of me and cackling from a gravel mound. Of course, if you come down in the opposite direction the speeds are incredible. We even made a 7.15 start one summer morning to get a traffic-free run. I wouldn't dare tell you how fast PDE went, but you've got 57 mph (92kph) to beat!

The place is worth making extraordinary efforts for. The sunset scenes from the top, with Skye just across the Sound

and the Outer Hebrides way out on the horizon, are worth the
freezing on the descent. Applecross is 6 miles (10km) down the
far side, bleak and beautiful. As with all descents, take care,
especially if it is windy. Some of the corners, particularly near
Creag Ghorm, are very exposed and it's not unknown to have a
front wheel lift in extreme conditions when gales whistle
across the peninsula. I don't think that the pub at Applecross
closes during the day. It has an extensive, wholesome menu,
and if you have suffered a freezing coming down from the Pass
the 'soup of the day' is highly recommended.

## Applecross to Inverbain

Until 1973 the tarmac road ended at Applecross, and there was
no way around the north-western tip of the peninsula.
Motorized transport was forced to retrace over the Bealach, but
a mountain track led across to Inverbain. This is the route of
the third leg.

After the ups and downs of the preceding miles the toddle
around the head of Applecross Bay is nothing short of idyllic. It
only lasts about four minutes, but is a splendid start after a
break. As soon as you cross the bridge over the River
Applecross, turn right onto a coarse metalled road up the
valley, the Strath Maol Chuluim. The first 3 miles (4.8km) are
good estate road, becoming more interesting beyond Hartfield,
but eminently ridable just the same. The first navigational
decision is required at Spot Height 88, where you cross a
sleeper bridge onto the land between the rivers. The next
decision is the hard one. The more obvious track lures you up
out of the complications among the streams at the bottom of the
steep part of the fells too far to the right (SE); check the map
and try to ensure that you stick to the north-west bank of the
stream, climbing steeply towards the cairn on the col at Spot
Height 371. There is a more ridable, but longer, option from
SH88 at GR748491, which is to follow the more northerly path
to GR756512, then turn south-east to join the direct route at
GR764507.

The col beneath the Crorc-bheinn should herald a terrific run
down to Inverbain, but it doesn't. What once was a well-paved
track is now a collection of awkwardly spaced boulders,
impossible to ride, and difficult to walk. There are prolonged
carries, and temptations to try to ride across the moor, but the
whole mountainside is a boulderfield and you are well down
the track before ridable stretches appear and even then they
will demand all your trails technique. This is extreme
mountain biking.

Consolation for all this endeavour comes in the shape of the
vast waterfall of the Abhainn Dubh on the opposite side of the
valley – 100ft (30m) wide and 100ft (30m) high – it is a

*Tarmac can be welcome when it comes to a long uphill on the Glen Shieldaig ride.*

formidable spectacle. Thereafter the track is quite good all the way to the tarmac at Inverbain.

## Inverbain to Shieldaig

This final 4-mile (6.4km) stint was supposed to be a nice run around the head of Loch Shieldaig. Instead it is monumental. The Ordnance Survey have awarded eight steep-hill arrows in the first 3 miles (4.8km), three up but five down. Needless to say the downs are great, but the ups are awful.

We arrived at Inverbain as the last semblance of daylight vanished, and set off to ride around to Shieldaig without lights. Exciting wasn't the word. The little lights of the village were obscured by the trees most of the way, the road twists and turns, dives and rises in the most alarming way, and it started to rain. It was crazy. There was no traffic whatsoever, only the swish of tyres or the squeal of brakes. At one point two deer decided to race us down the road – I don't know who got the biggest fright. This loop is totally different. Extreme, but totally different.

# Ride 47    PENCAITLAND RAILWAY

**Area:** South-East of Edinburgh. From Dalkeith along the Pencaitland Railway and beyond.
**OS Map:** Landranger 66.
**Start & Finish:** Dalkeith House on the outskirts of Dalkeith, at grid ref 335677. Parking by main entrance.
**Nearest BR station:** Stoneybank.
**Approx length:** 22 miles (35km). Allow around 3 hours.
**Ride rating:** Easy.
**Conditions:** Good on railway; could be muddy offroad.
**R & R:** Plenty of pubs and cafés in Dalkeith; otherwise try Pathhead.

The area around Edinburgh used to have a huge network of railways, mostly built to serve scores of small coal mines in the area. The mines have gone and with them the railways, but a few have been preserved as 'trails' open to riders and walkers. This ride follows the remains of the Pencaitland railway, and then heads offroad through some pleasant, easygoing countryside before heading back to Dalkeith.

Dalkeith is a big, bustling kind of town, which once existed to serve Dalkeith House (now an educational centre) and its enormous park on the north side. The park is now a popular place for walkers, with a superb adventure playground for those with young kids, which must rate among the best in the UK. There's car parking by the entrance to the park – turn left out of here, follow the road to the roundabout, and then turn left onto the A6094 towards Musselburgh. A short way on, take the first turning on the right, which is signposted as a dead end. Look out for the railway bridge, and find your way down onto the disused track below.

Follow this track northwards for 2 miles (3.2km). Where the track widens take care not to stray off to the left, and past the overhead power lines find your way back up onto the road by

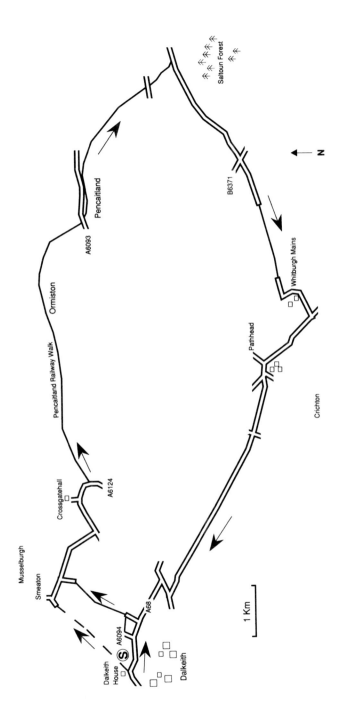

*Signals on the old Pencaitland Railway line, now sadly forgotten and abandoned.*

the bridge at Smeaton. Turn right along this quiet lane, passing old spoil heaps. At the T-junction take a left towards Crossgatehall, turning right on the A6124 and following the signs to join the start of the Pencaitland Railway Walk.

Despite being a 'walk' it's open to both bike and horseriders, so be prepared to slow down and pull over if required. It must have been a single-track, narrow-gauge railway in its time, and much of the way is comparatively narrow with nature closing in on both sides; in wet weather it's also quite muddy, and be prepared for dirty black pools of coal dust all the way along. The other reminders of its past are the 'tombstones' which line the route, in memory of the pits which may be long closed but still remain to haunt the line.

The riding is pleasant and easy, as you clock up the miles past Ormiston and Pencaitland, both of which have car parks and information boards. Beyond there towards the end of the line the condition of the track deteriorates and really becomes quite interesting, until a lonely railway signal shows you've reached the end of the track as it remains today, just north-west of Saltoun Forest. From here on you're in pleasant, open Scottish countryside with farmland all around. Turn right along the very quiet road – cars are the exception – and follow it for a couple of miles, crossing the B6371 and going straight ahead. After another ½ mile (0.8km), keep straight on along an overgrown track which is lumpy, bumpy riding but nevertheless OK. Ride on beneath the power lines, following the edge of a huge field with trees on the left, and joining a hard track which leads out onto the road by the prosperous-looking farmstead at Whitburgh Mains.

Turn left here, and follow the lane round to the busy A68. Turn right towards Pathhead; it's a wide road and it's all downhill, so you'll reach the village in double quick time – the fish and chip shop may be of interest. As the road heads steeply down through the village, look out for the left fork immediately after the left turn to Crichton Castle. This is the old road to Dalkeith, and much more pleasant than its modern replacement which it meets again some 4 miles (6.4km) on. Turn right uphill on the A68, and then after a few hundred yards take the first left turn which will lead you straight back towards Dalkeith House.

# Ride 48   PENTLAND HILLS

**Area:** Pentland Hills, near Edinburgh (south-west). From Flotterstone Visitor Centre across the Pentlands to Threipmuir Reservoir, returning across the Pentlands from Listonshiels to Carlops.
**OS Maps:** Landranger 66 and 65.
**Start & Finish:** Flotterstone Visitor Centre, just off the A702, at grid ref 235630. Car parking available.
**Nearest BR station:** Currie.
**Approx length:** 18 miles (29km). Allow 3 hours.
**Ride rating:** Moderate.
**Conditions:** Mainly easy riding; some of the track going south from Listonshiels is tricky to ride.
**R & R:** Pubs at Flotterstone, Carlops and Nine Mile Burn.

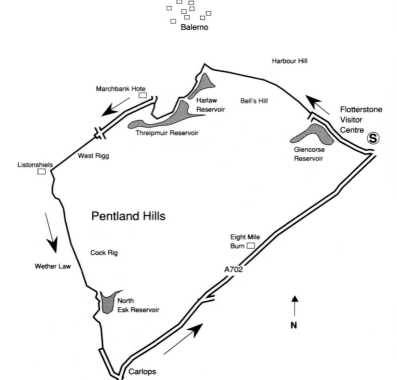

The Pentlands are a beautiful range of hills within a few miles of the centre of Edinburgh. This closeness brings its own problems, and the Pentland Hills Ranger Service (Tel: 031 445 3383) has issued an advisory leaflet on biking in the area. This shows recommended routes, pointing out that if biking is to be accepted bikers must act responsibly or face up to the possibility of the sport being banned.

This ride follows recommended tracks, giving an enjoyable tour of the north-east Pentlands. Past the Visitor Centre at Flotterstone a metalled lane (no cars) leads uphill into pleasant hilly country, running along the side of Glencorse Reservoir. At the top of the reservoir go through the gate and offroad, following the track that leads ahead towards Balerno; the alternative right-hand track signposted to Bonaly becomes seriously steep!

The track – which is not the easiest of riding – leads up to the 'pass' between Bell's and Harbour Hill, followed by an easy descent across flattish country towards Balerno. The track here

*Finding the way across the Pentland Hills. Stick to the
routes recommended by the Rangers.*

had been well used by mountain bikes and had clearly suffered
under the onslaught of knobbly tyres. Using a track like this
makes it all the more important to stick by the Pentland
Rangers' Code:

    1. Keep to Rights of Way;

    2. Carry Over Mud – Ploughing through damages the path,
and eats chains, bearings and all moving parts;

    3. Give Way to Walkers;

4. Avoid Erosion – Don't lock your back wheel.

The track improves by the side of Harlaw Reservoir, where the route turns left to follow the side of Threipmuir Reservoir – this part of the route would make easy and enjoyable family biking. Past a small car park the track bears left to join a metalled lane; the left turn here is the start of one recommended route back over the Pentlands, but I opted to go further, turning right and then left by the entrance to the Marchbank Hotel, and following the long, straight and very quiet road towards Listonshiels. Where the road bends 90 degrees right, carry straight on along the track ahead by the side of woods at West Rigg. The riding here is across flat country, but with plenty of bumps and lumps some carrying is necessary. Beyond the woods head for the clump of trees with Listonshiels beyond, joining a hard track which bears left to a gate and the start of the route back over the Pentlands.

This is a much more dramatic crossing of the hills than on the way out, with the track deteriorating as it leads uphill between Wether Law and Cock Rig, where some carrying may be necessary. Once over the top the scenery changes and becomes more mellow as the track leads down to the North Esk reservoir; here a little care is needed with navigation, as the route has been diverted away from the reservoir, crossing an open field to join a hard track leading to the solitary building at North Esk.

From here it's all fast, enjoyable riding downhill through the foothills of the Pentlands to the roadside at Carlops. Then it's 7 miles (11.3km) or so onroad along the fairly busy A702 (an old Roman road) back to the start point, with the option of extending the ride offroad and back into the Pentlands by turning off at Eight Mile Burn halfway along the road.

# Ride 49    MOORFOOT HILLS

**Area:** Moorfoot Hills, south-east of Edinburgh. From Fala via Fala Moor, Heriot, Broad Law and Middleton Moor to Fala.
**OS Map:** Landranger 66.
**Start & Finish:** Fala, on the A68, at grid ref 437609. Limited car parking.
**Nearest BR station:** None within easy reach.
**Approx length:** 22 miles (35km). Allow 3–4 hours.
**Ride rating:** Easy/Moderate.
**Conditions:** Mainly easy riding on fast tracks.
**R & R:** Pubs at Fala and North Middleton.

The Moorfoot Hills on the southern boundary of Midlothian are much less visited than the Pentlands and offer some good riding. This circuit on the north-eastern end of the range starts

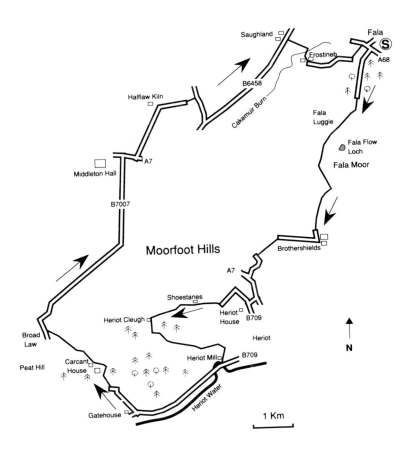

by crossing Fala Moor, a flat area of high ground with good views to the north and west.

From the roadside hamlet of Fala a straight, hard track leads up through forestry onto the moor which is very exposed in poor weather. However, the track which crosses it is excellent, passing the ruined tower house of Fala Luggie and Fala Flow Loch (which according to local folklore has no bottom), and with a few easy ups and downs leading to the farmstead at Brothershields. From here a tarmac lane leads quickly downhill to the A7 in the valley.

Turn left along the main road here for a short distance, taking the first right turn-off, signposted to Heriot. Where the road bends left, turn right up a lane (there are two small shops on the corner) for a small offroad tour of the immediate area; if you want to give this a miss you can just carry on along the B709. Follow the lane to the left towards the farm at Shoestanes, going through a gate by the side of the farm buildings and joining a track which heads steadily uphill on

*Heading downhill to join the road by Heriot Mill, before heading back up the Moorfoots.*

the edge of the Moorfoots. From the top of the rise it leads down to a solitary house at Heriot Cleugh, turning back towards the east to cross a field and head back between woods in the direction of Heriot; you need a little care with the navigation here to ensure you're on the right track.

Once past the woodland on the right, the track begins to head downhill, bending hard right and going steeply down to rejoin the B709 by the side of Heriot Mill. Turn right along the road here, following the valley by the side of Heriot Water – it's very pleasant riding even with a steady uphill. A couple of miles (3.2km) or so on the road bears right and heads downhill; on the bend, turn off by the gatehouse, joining the long driveway that leads to Carvant House. A track leads fairly steeply uphill past the back of the fine looking house; follow this up through the trees, breaking out onto the top of the Moorfoots and heading on across open country by the side of Peat Hill. The track is easy riding and easy to follow, joining the B7007 at Broad Law.

Turn right along the road for a long and very satisfying downhill with great views to the north. Keep on past Middleton Hall until you join the A7; turn right here and then almost immediately left at the end of the cutting, following a track that leads through farmland to the farmstead at Halflaw Kiln. Go through a gate and turn right between woodland here, crossing the old railway (sadly unridable) and then turning right at the next road for the start of the final section.

At the next T-junction turn left along the B6458 for some easy pedalling. After 2 miles (3.2km) look out for the first sign of habitation at Saughland on the left, and directly opposite turn right onto a track that runs along the side of the fields, dropping downhill to cross Cakemuir Burn and passing a few houses hidden away at Frostineb. Here the track joins a metalled lane, with just over 1 mile (1.6km) of easy pedalling uphill to rejoin the A7 at Fala.

# Ride 50    LAMMERMUIR HILLS

**Area:** Lammermuir Hills, south-east of Edinburgh. From Carfraemill Hotel along the A697 past Laude to Cambridge; via Wedderlie across the Lammermuirs to Wrunk Law; north-west onroad to Danskine and Longyester; back across the Lammermuirs via Lammer Law and Crib Law.
**OS Maps:** Landranger 66, 67, 73.
**Start & Finish:** Carfraemill Hotel, at the junction of the A697 and A68, at grid ref 508533. Car park opposite hotel.
**Nearest BR station:** None within easy reach.
**Approx length:** 44 miles (70km). Allow 8+ hours – it's a full day's riding.
**Ride rating:** Moderate/Hard.
**Conditions:** It's a long ride, but conditions are very good. The route crosses high ground, so be prepared.
**R & R:** Pubs at Carfraemill Hotel and Westruther.

This is a magnificent circuit of the Lammermuir Hills which cover a large, unspoilt area in the south-east of Scotland. There's a good deal of onroading including a long stint on the main A697, but it's still a classic ride. The Carfraemill Hotel is a convenient place to start, but you may prefer to choose somewhere else along the route. The ride can also be done in either direction, but I preferred to finish on a high point, getting the road work out of the way and saving the final descent from the Lammermuirs until last.

From the Carfraemill Hotel it's about 8 miles (13km) pedalling, going south-east along the A697 until you reach the turn-off at Cambridge, just past the bridge over Boondreigh Water. Despite its 'A' rating this is a relatively bike-friendly road, and once you reach the turn-off you're on a very quiet road that winds its way past Bruntaburn Mill and on to Westruther. Here it joins the B6456 for about 1 mile (1.6km), before turning off towards Wedderlie and the start of the south-to-north crossing of the Lammermuirs.

A tarmac lane leads northwards past the entrance to Wedderlie House, joining a track and climbing easily across the hills with great views all around. At about the halfway point the route crosses the Southern Upland Way (a long-distance path across the south of Scotland), heading down and up past the Watch Water reservoir. The track skirts Scar Law, passing a

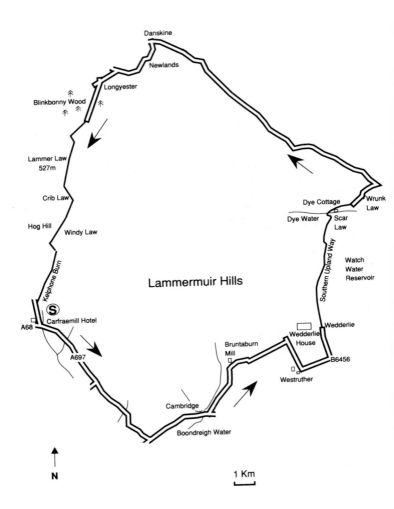

mass of grouse butts before diving down into the valley of Dye Water by Dye Cottage.

Here you're back onroad, but it's very, very quiet and the scenery is very fine. Follow the road eastwards uphill towards Wrunk Law, turning left at the top and following the road across the top of the hills, heading north-west towards Danskine some 10 miles (16km) distant – there's a fair amount of up and downing, and in poor weather it could be very exposed along here. At Danskine turn off left past Newlands, and ride on to Longyester, where a metalled track leads past the side of the farm buildings, heading south past Blinkbonny Wood to recross the Lammermuirs. Joining a rough track it's a steady climb up to Lammer Law but ridable all the way if you're fit and keen, heading on to Crib Law and then starting

*Sir Walter Scott rode here! It's fine riding, but the Lammermuir circuit is best attempted on a fine, sunny day.*

the long descent past Hog Hill and Windy Law. A short way on the track joins a tarmac lane, dropping down to the side of Kelphone Burn at great speed with 3 miles (4.8km) or so of very pleasant riding back to the start point at the Carfraemill Hotel.

## THE OFFROAD CYCLING ACCESS AND RIGHTS OF WAY CHARTER

Offroad cyclists, as individuals, and with the support of the British Mountain Bike Federation, should have the following aims:

1. To enhance the rights of way network, by minimizing wear and tear on trails, and by assisting in the maintenance of bridlepaths and byways.
2. To understand the laws regulating the use of rights of way, and to help educate other offroad cyclists in their knowledge of the law.
3. To foster a climate of courtesy and tolerance with other trail users.
4. To develop good relations with other user organizations, such as the British Horse Society, the Ramblers Association, Trailriders and LARA.
5. To promote and adhere to the Offroad Cycling Code.
6. To campaign for a more comprehensive network of bridleways and byways, by addressing mistakes in the definitive map, through footpath upgrades, and the provision of long distance bridleways.
7. To campaign for unclassified, unsurfaced 'White' roads to be classed as BOATS (Byways Open to All Traffic), and appear on definitive and Ordnance Survey maps.
8. To campaign for the provision of definitive and permissive routes for family cycling, recreational trail biking, and for the demands of the skilled mountain biker.
9. To liaise with local authority officers in rights of way, highways and countryside departments to influence the provision of offroad cycling routes.
10. To liaise with landowning organizations, including the National Farmers Union, the Country Landowners Association, Forest Enterprise and the National Trust to assist in the harmonious integration of offroad cycling.
11. To encourage awareness and responsible copy in television, radio and general press, together with cycling and mountain bike magazines.
12. To liaise and co-operate with the cycle industry and trade to promote the benefits and responsibilities of offroad biking.
13. To foster a 'Responsibility Blueprint' for cycle hire outlets, to ensure that casual bikers are sufficiently briefed on their responsibilities.
14. To promote a positive attitude for offroad cyclists by liaison with the Sports Council, Countryside Commission, Central Council for Physical Recreation, Central Rights of Way Committee, and elected Councillors and Members of Parliament.
15. To assist in the promotion of access responsibilities, by liaising with cycle clubs and encouraging growth in club membership.